Faces of the Church

Faces of the Church
Meditations on a Mystery and Its Images

Geoffrey Preston, O.P.

Texts prepared by
Aidan Nichols, O.P.

With a Foreword by
Bishop Walter Kasper

T&T CLARK
EDINBURGH

T&T CLARK
59 GEORGE STREET
EDINBURGH EH2 2LQ
SCOTLAND

First published 1997

ISBN 0 567 08530 9

British Library Cataloguing-in-Publication Data
A catalogue record for this book is available
from the British Library

Typeset by Fakenham Photosetting Ltd, Fakenham, Norfolk
Printed and bound in Great Britain by Page Bros, Norwich

Contents

Note

The desire is sometimes expressed for a 'post-critical' theology which would integrate the gains of modern biblical scholarship within a contemplative, ecclesial reading of the Bible of the kind that the Church Fathers, and, after them, the spiritual masters and mistresses of the Catholic tradition, practised apparently so effortlessly. If Scripture be the 'soul' of theology then it is after this fashion that it animates the meditations on the Church found in this book.[1]

The peculiar timeliness of Geoffrey Preston's study of ecclesiology is underscored by Bishop Walter Kasper in his foreword. I am grateful to him for his words, and to the editor of *New Blackfriars* for permitting the reproduction of the three closing chapters which, in slightly abbreviated form, appeared in that journal in 1987, for the tenth anniversary of Geoffrey's death.

For those who would know a little of him and his spirit, I may mention the 'Memoir' which prefaces his meditations on following Christ 'through Scripture and Sacrament'.[2] Some reference will be made to these in what follows as to his liturgical sermons, which in my judgment can stand comparison with those of Rahner, Balthasar and Newman.[3]

AIDAN NICHOLS, O.P.
Blackfriars, Cambridge
Solemnity of the Immaculate Conception, 1995

---

[1] For an account of how Geoffrey produced his work, see his 'Wrestling with the Word', *New Blackfriars* 51. 598 (1970), pp. 117–224. His approach to the literal sense of Scripture is outlined in 'Fiction and Poetry in the Bible', *ibid.*, 53. 626 (1972), pp. 300–307.
[2] G. Preston, O.P., *God's Way to be Man: Meditations on Following Christ through Scripture and Sacrament* (London 1978).
[3] G. Preston, O.P., *Hallowing the Time: Meditations on the Cycle of the Christian Liturgy* (London 1980).

Foreword

At the present time in *Mitteleuropa* when people talk of the Church, the lion's share of the discussion falls to 'ecclesial structures'. Considering the state of upheaval in which the European Church now finds itself, that is perfectly comprehensible. There is, however, the danger that these pullulating questions of structure will block people's view of the Church's very essence. Where that happens, the debate rapidly becomes abortive.

The Church is not just a human community. By its very nature, it is more than that. It is the making present – at once symbolic and efficacious – of the mystery of God's salvation, a mystery which reached full realisation in Jesus Christ. In order to keep us alert to this, the Church's dimension of depth, the Second Vatican Council, with deliberate reference to the understanding of the Church in Christian antiquity, described the Church as, first and foremost, a 'mystery' itself. That word is simultaneously the interpretative key for all the other ecclesiological expressions used by the Council. The closing document of the Extraordinary Synod of Bishops, meeting in 1985 at Rome, drew attention to this fact in a very pointed way.

It is also true, however, that the Second *Vaticanum* found itself unable to speak of the mystery of the Church save by a plenitude of images. In that way the Council could draw on a rich treasury of metaphors transmitted from the past, their roots stretching back in some cases as far as the Elder Testament itself.

I acclaim the achievement of Father Geoffrey Preston, O.P., in laying out before the reader these same treasures, and unfolding their riches in historical and systematic perspective. In the mirror of the manifold dimensions of the Church there appears, in impressive fashion, something of what the Church as mystery means. Father Aidan Nichols, O.P., is to be thanked, then, for bringing before a wider public this precious spiritual legacy of his late *confrère* through the editing and publication of this book. I wish the book a wide hearing, and its readers a stimulus, through its pages, to meditation on the mystery of the Church.

Bishop Walter Kasper

PART ONE

Imaging the Church: The Primal Metaphors

I

Ekklēsia

THE New Testament boasts a wealth of imagery where the Church is concerned. There is the salt of the earth, a letter from Christ, fish and fish net, the boat and the ark; unleavened bread, one loaf, the table of the Lord, the altar, the cup of the Lord, wine, branches of the vine, vineyard, the fig-tree, the olive-tree, God's planting; God's building, the building on the rock, the pillar and buttress. Again, there is the mother of the Messiah, the elect lady, the bride of Christ, virgins; the wedding feast; wearers of white robes or a choice of clothing. To this we can add: citizens, exiles, the dispersion, ambassadors, the poor, hosts and guests, the people of God, Israel, a chosen race, a holy nation, twelve tribes, the patriarchs, circumcision, Abraham's sons, the Exodus, the house of David, the remnant, the elect; a flock, lambs who rule; the holy city, the holy temple, priesthood. One can continue with: sacrifice, aroma, festivals; the new creation, first-fruits, the new humanity, the last Adam, Son of Man, the king-dom of God, those who fight against Satan. Nor does the list stop here. It would include also: the sabbath rest, the age to come, God's glory, light, life and the tree of life; communion in the Holy Spirit, the bond of love, the sanctified, the faithful, the justified, followers, disciples; the road, coming and going; confessors, slaves, friends, servants, the witnessing community. Finally, we may add: the household of God, sons of God, the brotherhood, the body of life, members of Christ, the body and the blood, the diversities of ministries, spiritual body, head of cosmic spirits, the body of which Christ is head, the unity of Jews and Gentiles, the growth of the body and the fulness of God. Not all of these are strictly or exclusively images of the Church; but all are in some way ecclesial images, ways of speaking about the life of the Church, before God, in this world.

It is sometimes forgotten that all language has a metaphorical character. We are perpetually using images, and this indeed is

3

language's own highest gift. Language is able to draw into an ordered and significant whole units of what would otherwise be disconnected experience. It can set elements of the world in relation to each other, by making them part of a human world. In a sense, the very possibility of calling an extraordinary variety of objects by the same name ('chair', for instance) is as metaphorical as the language of the most intense of poets. We are rarely far removed from using metaphor, least of all when we come to church. After all, the word 'Church' is itself as metaphorical as any of the terms in the bewildering list I have offered above. Why should one call the phenomenon which is the subject of this book 'the Church'? And what phenomenon are we talking about when we refer to the Church? It is impossible to answer this question by dealing solely in non-metaphorical expressions. Equally, it would be impossible to draw together in one place everyone who belongs to the Church, point to them and say, 'That is what I am talking about'. Not simply physically impossible – because some members of the Church are glorified, some being dead and others alive – but logically impossible. I can point to a chair and say 'chair', but how does the man who doesn't know the language know that I am pointing to the physical object and not, say, the colour? Supposing I stroke the surface when I say 'red', how does he know that I am referring to the colour and not to the material out of which the chair is made? As Ludwig Wittgenstein has taught us, the meaning of a word lies in its use. We learn how to use words from the culture in which we live by some sort of more or less instinctive sorting out of our experience of the situation in which the word is used. To find out the meaning of the word 'Church' we must look to our environment; yet within this environment is an absolutely privileged reference point, and that is the Scriptures. Not that we always have to be talking in the language of the New Testament, still less in the English of the Authorised Version. Nevertheless for Christians the New Testament does form a privileged use of language such that any serious reflection on the realities of the gospel (another metaphorical word!) must take seriously the usage of Scripture. As St Gregory Thaumaturgus remarks in his Farewell Address to Origen, the theologian must observe 'the study of words and their constant practice'.[1]

---

[1] Gregory Thaumaturgus, *Address to Origen*, 1.

When we turn to the Bible we find that the word 'Church' is not a New Testament invention, yet is clothed there with new meaning, drawn from the new ways in which it is used. First of all, it is a good secular Greek word, a noun formed from the verb *kalein*, to call. The Church in the New Testament is *ekklēsia*, a word taken over directly into Latin and the root of the word for 'church' in Romance tongues: the French *église*, for example. (Our English word 'church', like the Scots 'kirk', comes from a quite different root, *kuriakos*, 'belonging to the Lord', even though it is the normal translation of *ekklēsia*.) In ordinary secular Greek, the *ekklēsia* was the convened assembly of the people of a city-state, the supreme legislative and judicial body in the classical days of the democracy of the city-states of Greece. This usage occurs in the New Testament itself, in the story of the fuss at Ephesus over Paul's preaching against the gods:

The city was filled with the confusion, and they rushed with one accord into the theatre ... Some cried one thing and some another, for the *ekklēsia* was in confusion and the greater part knew not why they were come together. (Acts 19.29, 32)

This was evidently more of a mob than an *ekklēsia*, and so Paul said to them:

If Demetrius and the craftsmen who are with him have a matter against any man, the courts are open, and there are proconsuls; let them accuse one another. But if you seek anything about other matters it shall be settled in the regular [*ennomos*, lawful] *ekklēsia*. (Acts 19.38–39)

To the *ekklēsia* all citizens who had not been deprived of their rights for some offence against the State had a permanent right to be summoned: as such they were the *ekklētoi*, the people whom the herald called together. The rights of the *ekklēsia* in these ancient Greek city-states were unlimited. It was the *ekklēsia* that chose magistrates, and dismissed them when it thought fit. It was the *ekklēsia* that made major political decisions about treaties, the declaration of war, the making of peace. But interestingly enough, the *ekklēsia* did not meet to worship the gods, even though all its meetings began with sacrifice. So it seems unlikely that when the early Christians spoke of a Christian reality as *ekklēsia* what they had in mind in the first place was something to

5

do with worship: although when the *ekklēsia* was gathered in one place it *did* worship. Paul will use the term in the context of worship, but worship will not be uppermost in his mind.

> When you come together in *ekklēsia*, I hear that schisms exist among you; and I partly believe it. When therefore you assemble yourselves together, it is not possible to eat the Lord's Supper; for in your eating, each one takes his own supper before another; and one is hungry and another is drunk. What! Have you not houses to eat and drink in? or do you despise the *ekklēsia* of God and put those who have not to shame? (1 Cor. 11.18–22)

But although a non-Christian Greek would not immediately have thought about worship when he thought about the *ekklēsia* of his city, the word would have strong emotive overtones for him nonetheless. The two words most frequently met with in documents about the *ekklēsia* are *isonomia*, 'equality', and *eleutheria*, 'freedom'. In the *ekklēsia* everyone had equal rights, including the right to make their voice heard. The nearest modern equivalent on the same scale would be the assemblies of certain small Swiss cantons. All that the Greeks held most dear in the concept of citizenship was expressed for them in the word *ekklēsia*. This will be very much *ad rem* when we come to look at the General Council as one of the ways in which the Church is focussed.

But these considerations are not enough to explain why the early Christians took over this term and transmuted it in using it for themselves. The word had a pre-Christian usage outside secular Greek politics, in the Greek version of the Old Testament, the Septuagint. There *ekklēsia* occurs as the normal, though not the only, translation of two Hebrew words, *qahal* and *edhah*. *Edhah*, when used of the people of Israel, refers to the whole society, or those who represent it, whether they happen to be assembled or not. *Qahal*, on the other hand, always refers to the actual meeting together of the people. One of the main reasons why *qahal* was normally translated *ekklēsia* is etymological: *qahal* comes from a Hebrew root which means 'to call' to 'summon' and, as we have seen, this is also the Greek root of *ekklēsia*. It would therefore be tempting to lay stress on the precise meaning of *ekklēsia* as 'called out of': after all, the Christians of the New Testament were very conscious that they were called out from this world. But there is no evidence to suggest that they paid any attention at all to this meaning of the word. Nor is there in Greek any use of the verb *ekkalein* in this sort of connection. The original 'calling-out' in the Greek city-states, citizens being summoned from their homes by the herald's trumpet, is reflected in the way the summons was made to the Jewish *qahal* in the Book of Numbers.

> Yahweh said to Moses, Make two trumpets of silver; of turned work you shall make them; and you shall use them for the calling of the congregation. And when they shall blow with them, all the congregation of Israel shall gather themselves unto you at the door of the tent of meeting. When the assembly is to be gathered together, you shall blow. (Num. 10.1–3)

For those Christians who were Jews (and for a while the great majority of Christians, even outside Palestine, *were* Jews), the *ekklēsia* of the city was a foreign reality: they would not normally have the full citizen rights which would allow them to take part. What they *were* familiar with was the term *ekklēsia* as they had heard it read out in their synagogues. The body to which they now belonged by baptism in Jesus' name was the *ekklēsia* of God. Like the people of Israel they were assembled not because they had simply taken it into their heads to do so. They assembled because God summoned them: they were God's *ekklēsia*.

Part of what was involved here was a polemical claim. The *ekklēsia* of God set itself up in deliberate contradistinction to other sorts of *ekklēsia*. These other sorts of *ekklēsia* were not, as we have seen, primarily cultic bodies. The Christians did not claim to be one cult among many. Had they thought of themselves as a mystery religion, for example, they would surely have selected some other word as their primary self-designation. Pagan authors do speak of Christians in just such terms, calling them, for instance, a *thiasos*, the company of a god, but the Christians themselves do not pick up this notion. They thought of themselves as standing over against all the cults of the ancient world, just as for Israel Yahweh was not *a* god.

The word *ekklēsia* is much in evidence in the New Testament, but very rare in the Gospels. Paul begins by using the word to refer to a particular local congregation: 'the church of the Thessalonians in God the Father and the Lord Jesus Christ', 'the churches of Galatia', 'the church that is at Cenchreae', 'all the churches of the Gentiles', 'the church that is in the house of Prisca and Aquila', 'the churches of Asia', 'the church that is in the house of Nymphas', 'the church in the house of Philemon'. Here the Church is being described from the angle of the people who compose it. But much more commonly, it is talked about in terms of its special relationship with God or Jesus Christ: 'the church of God which is in Corinth, those who are sanctified in Christ Jesus, called [*klētoi*: 'summoned'] to be saints'; 'the churches of God which are in Judaea in Christ Jesus'; 'the Church of the living God, the pillar and buttress of the truth'. Here it is not so much a question of a local *ekklēsia*, but of the *ekklēsia* which is in a particular place, so that the emphasis has shifted to the community of Christians throughout the world. This shift was possible because, as we have noted, the word *ekklēsia* in the Septuagint can translate *edhah* as well as *qahal*: it can mean the people whom God has made into a people by his summons even when they are not actually at that moment together in one place. So Paul can talk quite simply about 'the Church of God', the Church which he persecuted. There are many churches and one Church. There is one universal Church absolutely, and the one universal Church is represented in a particular local church.

It is interesting that the word occurs so little in the Gospels: only three times, and two of those occur within the same verse. In Matthew 18, we read about how disputes are to be settled among the followers of Jesus:

> If thy brother sin [against thee], go, show him his fault between thee and him alone; if he hear thee, thou hast gained thy brother. But if he hear not, take with thee one or two more, that at the mouth of two witnesses or three every word may be established. And if he refuse to hear them, tell it to the *ekklēsia*; and if he refuses to hear the *ekklēsia* also, let him be to thee as the Gentile and the tax-collector. (Matt. 18.15–17)

And then there is the famous passage in Matthew 16:

> I say to thee that thou art Peter, and upon this rock I will build my *ekklēsia*, and the gates of hell shall not prevail against it. (Matt. 16.18)

There are clearly two distinct points of reference in these texts. In the first passage, it must be the local *ekklēsia* that is in question: it would not be possible to tell one's brother's fault to the universal Church. Equally clearly, the second passage is speaking of the Church in the absolute and universal sense. The passage about the erring brother does not present many difficulties of an exegetical kind. It can refer quite straightforwardly to any local congregation, even at a period when Christians and Jews had not separated from one another: it would even be possible, perhaps, to take an erring brother before the synagogue. The sense of *ekklēsia* in Matthew 16, however, is much disputed, not least because of polemical considerations deriving from later Christian history. The subject of this text appears to be the messianic community which Jesus was already beginning to assemble around himself and which, after his death, will go and make disciples of all nations, baptising them and teaching them to observe all the things that he had taught. For the Old Testament, and for Judaism in the time of Jesus, it would have been unthinkable to have a Messiah without a messianic community. It is clear from the Dead Sea Scrolls that this saying of Jesus is not so isolated as might once have been thought. It may be isolated in the Gospels, but it does not stand alone in the Jewish world of Jesus' time. (Even in the Gospels there are sayings which bear some relationship to it, the words of Jesus about rebuilding the shattered temple, for instance.) So potent are the Messiah's people that the gates of hell, that is, the place where the dead await the final resurrection, must give way before them. In the mind of Matthew, and the Jewish Christians for whom he wrote, the *ekklēsia* of Jesus was the *ekklēsia* which had the greatest, or the only, claim to be the remnant of Israel, the remnant on which the continuing life of all Israel as the *ekklēsia* of God depended. We know, in fact, of other Jewish communities which saw themselves in this way, such as the community of the New Covenant at Damascus. For Matthew and his audience, the Church or *qahal* of God was embodied and concentrated, from the time of Jesus' death and resurrection, in the *qahal* Jesus had begun to found during his lifetime: the community of the true Messiah. Jesus, then, separates out his *ekklēsia*, founds it on the man who is first to confess that Jesus is indeed the Messiah, and through it looks for the continuance of the *ekklēsia* of God – Israel.

So much for the linguistic usage of the church words in the

New Testament. But one may fairly ask whether their interest is more than antiquarian. These church words have suffered a sea change over two thousand years such that we have lost any sense of their being metaphorical. We are not conscious of using the word 'church' as a metaphor any more than we would be of using 'chair' as a metaphor. Our need is to recover a sense of the metaphorical force of *ekklēsia*, to let the world of the Greek city-states with its concern for freedom and equality in the *ekklēsia* have freer play in our minds, and to allow the Old Testament sense of the *ekklēsia* of God to re-emerge into our consciousness. The image of the *ekklēsia* might also have something to say to us about the place of office-bearers in the community, about the ultimate purpose of all functions within the people of God.

2

The People of God

*L*UMEN *Gentium*, the Constitution on the Church of the Second Vatican Council, remarks:

> It has not been God's resolve to sanctify and save men individually, with no regard for their mutual connection, but to establish them as a people who would give him recognition in truth and service in holiness.[1]

In other words, the history which is made up of the dialogue between God and man aims at the creation of a people, a common society. Here, as in so many other ideas developed in the Bible, the story of the Tower of Babel sets the scene. According to the tale, the whole earth had one language and few words, and as men migrated from the East they found a plain in the land of Shinar and settled there. The story assumes that it is talking about all mankind. There in the land of Shinar they started to build a city and a tower with its top in the heavens, in order to make a name for themselves, lest they be scattered abroad upon the face of the whole earth. And the story goes on to say that the Lord, Yahweh, came down to look at the city and the tower which the sons of men had built. When he saw it Yahweh said:

> Behold, they are one people and they have all one language, and this is only the beginning of what they will do. (Gen. 11.6)

Before saving history begins, mankind is already one people. And yet:

> Yahweh scattered them abroad from there over the face of the earth, and they left off building the city. (Gen. 11.8)

And before he scattered them all over the world he confused their language so that they would not be able to understand each

---

[1] *Lumen Gentium*, 9.

other. The point of the story is that all mankind had made itself one people by its own efforts, and intended to remain one people by the same token. That effort was frustrated by the Lord himself, by the God who was going to create a new people of his own. The expression 'people of God' immediately involves these two elements – newness and the work of God rather than the work of man. The people of God are such primarily because they are God's creation, his handiwork, his building. The genitive 'of God' is a genitive of authorship (cf. 'Pugin's church at Birmingham'), not of possession (cf. 'my pen'). Although when we think of the people of God as a new people we tend to think primarily of that newness in terms of the Church over against Israel, we ought to remember also that Israel is *part* of the newness of God's people. The coming into existence of Israel is a new beginning: God's answer to the wrongheadedness of the first attempt of men to keep themselves one people by their own striving.

In this history of the creation by God of a new people for himself there are a number of turning-points. In the first place, there is the call of Abraham which begins the process:

> Go from your country and your kindred and your father's house to the land that I will show you. And I will make of you a great nation, and I will bless you and make your name great, so that you will be a blessing. And by you all the families of the earth shall be blessed. (Gen. 12.1–3)

Then there is the coming out from Egypt:

> I am Yahweh, and I will bring you out from under the burdens of the Egyptians and I will deliver you from their bondage, and I will redeem you with an outstretched arm and with great acts of judgment, and I will take you for my people, and I will be your God. (Exod. 6.6)

Next there comes the apostasy of the people, their falling away from the vocation to be the people of God, the long slow process of decline and rebellion. The story has its negative dimension:

> You are not my people and I am not your God. (Hos. 1.9)

But in the exile, the second captivity, hope is reborn for the restoration of Israel to its land. This hope too is expressed in terms of the people of God:

Behold the days are coming, says Yahweh, when I will make a new covenant with the house of Israel and the house of Judah, not like the covenant which I made with their fathers when I took them by the hand to bring them out of the land of Egypt, my covenant which they broke, though I was their husband, says Yahweh. But this is the covenant which I will make with the house of Israel after those days, says Yahweh: I will put my law within them and I will write it upon their hearts; and I will be their God and they shall be my people. (Jer. 31.31–33)

This new covenant-making was first enacted in those covenanting ceremonies of which we read in the Books of Ezra and Nehemiah; perhaps also in somewhat earlier ceremonies before and during the return from exile of which we have now no record. In the next crucial stage of the creation of the people of God, however, texts such as this from Jeremiah are taken as referring to the new covenant made in the death of Jesus and to the new people which is the Church. Paul says:

We are the temple of the living God; as God said, 'I will live in them and move among them and they shall be my people'. (2 Cor. 6.16)

At the Council of Jerusalem James, for his part, remarks that

God visited the Gentiles to take out of them a people for his name. (Acts 15.14)

And finally, there is the vision of the end of time, of the coming of God and the establishment of his kingdom, of the new heaven and the new earth. In the new Jerusalem, the voice from the throne declares:

Behold, the dwelling of God is with men; he will dwell with them and they shall be his people, and God himself will be with them and be their God. (Apoc. 21.3)

So the creation of the people of God finds its goal in the consummation of all human history at the end of time.

It seems fair to say that this notion of the people of God is the oldest and most fundamental concept underlying the self-interpretation of Israel and of the Christian Church. In comparison with this, the various images used of Israel and the Church are secondary. The people of God is the reality underlying the images.

Bearing in mind these various stages not only in the history of the concept of the people of God but of the people of God themselves, we can turn now to look at what we mean by peoplehood. What does it mean to be a people, a nation? Because of the pernicious doctrines on this subject which have gained currency in the twentieth century, it is important to be careful in one's thinking and speaking; yet the subject is too vital to be left in abeyance.

An obvious contender for the prime ingredient of peoplehood would clearly be that of *race*. To be a people, one and all must belong to the self-same race. This is a temptation to which Israel was, and to a large extent still is, prone. It is against this idea that the people of God is racially based that Paul is arguing in those long polemical passages of his about the true sons of Abraham, especially in the Letter to the Galatians. There are hints of such a quarrel in the Gospels, too, especially in John, but also in the Synoptics, particularly in connection with the preaching of John the Baptist: 'God is able to raise up children to Abraham from these very stones' (Matt. 3.9). This controversy mattered very much indeed in New Testament times, since the Jews had come to stress the racial basis of their peoplehood far too strongly. The process is seen most clearly in the Books of Ezra and Nehemiah: the attempt to re-establish (perhaps 'establish' would be more accurate) the purity of the race. And so the offers of the Samaritans to help with the rebuilding of the temple were roughly rejected; people who had married foreign wives were required to put them away. This concern for racial purity became increasingly obsessive, though it is doubtful if it ever achieved the full success which seems to be attributed to it in the Books of Ezra and Nehemiah. Their motives were not what we would call racialist – at least, not in the beginning. It was thought that much of the trouble in the religious practice of pre-exilic Israel could be traced to those who were not of the original stock – the foreign wives of some of the kings, for example, who brought with them their own foreign gods and set up shrines for them, even in Jerusalem itself. We should note, too, that while there is a genuine universalism in the great teachers who prophesied the return from exile – notably Second Isaiah – this universalism does not

14

envisage any adulteration of racial purity. Yahweh may be the only God there is, and all nations may be going to worship him in Jerusalem, but their position *vis-à-vis* Israel is not that of equals freely mixing but of servants worshipping the God of Israel. They are going to look after Israel's flocks and cultivate its fields; they will send their wealth to the temple at Jerusalem. But they will not actually *become* Israel.

In the light of this concern for purity of race to safeguard purity of worship there was some touching up of older traditions which remembered that Israel was *not* one in origin, that its unity was not that of an ethnic group. To read the Bible carelessly is to take away the impression that Abraham was the physical father of all those who in later centuries made up the people of Israel. His physical descendants, on this view, went down into Egypt and they alone came out of Egypt at the exodus. They alone stood under Sinai and they alone entered the promised land, driving out the original inhabitants. But here and there we find hints that this was not so. There was always some objection in Israel itself to the increasing 'racialism' of the years after the return from Babylon: the Book of Ruth is an important witness to that with its unlikely insistence that David himself did not come of pure Jewish stock. Then there is the reference to the 'mixed multitude' which came out of Egypt; the numbers given for the exodus cannot possibly be squared with the numbers of the descendants of Abraham; there are allusions too to the people already in the land who stayed there and entered into alliance with those who had come out from Egypt and eventually became one people with them. The touching up of tradition was a dangerous affair, unless what you take from it is the theological point that of the whole of Israel at any future time you may say of any past time: 'They were there!' They may not necessarily have been 'there' in the way hardliners envisaged – in the loins of Abraham, for instance – but certainly they were in prospect. All of future Israel will be able to say 'I came out of Egypt' even if in purely physical terms they were not the direct descendants of the groups of the Exodus.

When we reach the New Testament there is a complete bursting of the bonds of racial unity. The gospel call is addressed, we hear, to all nations. True, there is some uncertainty as to what Jesus himself had done during his lifetime – had he preached to non-Jews or not? Luke in particular writes up the life of Jesus so as to suggest that he had, and he tells various stories to make the point clear that the gospel is for all. But whatever may have been the situation in the lifetime of Jesus, the primitive Church evidently regarded its mission as worldwide. 'Go into all the world, and preach the gospel to all nations, making disciples of them' (Matt. 28.19–20). This catholicity or universalism is unaffected by disputes of the sort resolved, in large measure, at the Council of Jerusalem. There the question was not whether the gospel is for all human beings, but whether, in entering into the promise of the gospel, non-Jews had to become Jews, observing the law and being circumcised. Alternatively, might they enter immediately into the inheritance of Christ? Because of the numbers involved, and the very early decision on this point, it seems a mistake to draw too close a parallel between the entry of non-Jews into the Church and the custom of admitting proselytes into Judaism. There was something radically new in the Christian thing: a new people, a 'third people' as it was often said, composed of Jews and Greeks, a people in which one of the most fixed divisions in the ancient world was overcome. The New Testament stresses, therefore, that the call of Abraham from amongst the nations, and the special relationship between God and Israel, was only a temporary thing. It was ordered to the call of all mankind into the one people of God. But equally, just as Israel was called and set apart for service, for the sake of all, so the Church too is called for the sake of all. As the Second Vatican Council remarks, it is the visible 'sacrament' of the saving unity of all men.[2] The final people of God, as the Book of Revelation shows, will be the whole of mankind.

What other ingredients, then, are there for peoplehood? What about the *land*? Can there be a people without a land? In the early centuries of Israel's history a people without its land would have been hard to imagine. The promise given to Abraham was the promise of what a nomad of that sort – a so-called 'ass nomad' – most hoped for and wanted: offspring and a land to call his own. A partial fulfilment of the promise of land comes about when Abraham purchases a cave, so that at the very least he and Sarah can be buried there. When the people come out of Egypt they carry with them the bones of Joseph so that they too can enter into

---

[2] *Lumen Gentium*, 1.

the promise of land. Throughout history there has been a special relationship between the Jewish people and the land of promise – even in the Book of Daniel the exiles are spoken of as praying in the direction of Jerusalem. There is the longstanding custom of dead Jews being taken back to the land of Israel or being buried with some of the soil of Israel under their heads. And yet, long before the time of Christ there was a considerable diaspora of people who regarded themselves as Jews and were so regarded by other Jews. True, they sometimes went askew, like the Jews of Elephantine – a garrison community, syncretistic in outlook, on an island in the Nile, but on the whole they preserved the tradition of their race and religion intact, even outside the land. This seems to have been due to the way in which, during the Captivity, Israel took into itself some elements of what one might call a Church, and did not simply remain a nation. So there began that long uncertainty among Jews as to whether Israel was a Church or a nation, an uncertainty which still persists and which has been settled in practice in different ways at different times. It is not only the Jews who have managed to survive as a distinct entity by this blending of Church and nation: the Armenians, for example, have done the same. But whereas for Jews the land has always remained a place of special significance, a part of the hope set before them, this has not been the case with Christians. Perhaps we might say that whereas for Jews there is both saving history and saving geography, for Christians there is now only saving history – geography has lost its significance. Strictly speaking, for Christians there are no holy places or holy land: that is, there is now no land of promise in any material sense, no especially holy bit of the earth's surface *in et per se*. The land theme figures rarely in the New Testament, being replaced (by and large) by the theme of the Jerusalem above, our mother, the goal of our pilgrimage. In the Christian notion of peoplehood, if the land theme remains at all it is the *whole* of the earth which is to be transformed. It is not really land, but people, that matters.

Again, we might suggest that for a people to be a people it must have certain elements of a common culture: language perhaps, institutions of certain sorts, offices and customs. There is not much evidence in Scripture for any importance being attached to a common *language*, though at the time of the return from exile quite a fuss was made about some children not having Hebrew.

Nevertheless, a common language is presupposed by the fact that most of the Scriptures are actually in Hebrew, despite certain sections of the proto-canonical books being in Aramaic while the deutero-canonical books are entirely in Greek. (Only recently have Hebrew versions of any of these latter been found.) Even when Jews no longer spoke Hebrew as a matter of course, Hebrew remained the holy language, the language in which prayers were recited and the Scriptures read. In modern times, Hebrew has acted as the focal means for the creation of a national unity in the state of Israel – much to the annoyance of some Orthodox Jews who regard it as the language of Scripture and the age of the Messiah, but improper for secular transactions in the meantime. The question of language is not a trivial one. As has been said, a language is a way of life. The revelation of God is not independent of the particular language in which it is written, or, better, of the language of the people whose life-experience *is* the revelation. For this reason the original tongue, the language of Scripture, retains a normative value.

But again, in the Christian dispensation, this question of language ceases to be important. The existence of the Christian people as a unity does not depend on its having a common language. It is interesting that when St Luke writes up the events of the day of Pentecost, what happens is not that everyone present receives the gift of understanding the one language which the apostles speak, but rather that the apostles speak in the vernaculars of everyone present. Babel is not reversed in any one-to-one sense. The world is not given back a single language; but in all the languages of the world the gospel is proclaimed. For Christians, peoplehood does not depend on a common language in the ordinary sense of that word, though it is not entirely independent of that. For the unity of the Christian people does depend to a degree on the common possession of the Scriptures in their original languages. While it is obviously not necessary that everyone should be able to read them in this form, it is important that they are there, over against the later Church, as the source and norm of its teaching.

What, then, of *institutions*? Is the fact that people are a people dependent to any great extent on the offices within the nation, for example, on kingship? In the earlier Old Testament period, not at all. When people are slaves or nomads, their existence as a people, if such it may be called, has nothing like kingship on which to rely. There must be judging in disputes, there must be some sort of direction; but this does not mean that there must be an institutional office of judge or leader. The functions can be filled by whoever appears at the time best qualified to exercise them. Only later in a sedentary culture, especially when people live together in cities, does it become necessary to have offices, even in the modern bricks-and-mortar sense of somewhere, as well as somebody, to which disputes can be taken. It is well known that this kind of institutionalisation of office was resisted by strong elements in Israel: there was always the lingering sense that things had been better in nomadic days, that settling down like the nations round about had its dangers. Thus it is that there are two traditions in the Books of Samuel about the merits of the monarchy: one sees it as a gift and a blessing, the other as a punishment and a curse. This tension was never really resolved in Israel until the Davidic line ceased. The covenant with David never achieved the importance of the covenant with the whole people, nor anything like it.

In the New Testament, however, the Davidic theme comes to the fore again: Matthew and Luke both arrange things so that Jesus is born in Bethlehem, the royal city of David. In all the Synoptics there is some play with the idea of Jesus as the Son of David. And although Paul does not appear to regard the traditions about the birth and infancy of Jesus as part of the gospel, he does so regard Jesus' Davidic descent.

On the other hand there is a manifest decline in the significance attached to institutional offices among the Christian people. By transferring to Jesus the titles attached to many of the Old Testament offices, the latter were effectively withdrawn from being the outright possession of anyone else in the community. In the Christian community there is only one 'king', only one 'priest', only one 'judge', and apart from Jesus there are neither kings nor masters, neither priests nor judges, neither teachers nor fathers. The Christian people, nevertheless, includes within it functions of all these kinds. Because the primary thing is the transcendental reference to Jesus these functions are not, however, institutionalised in a way that renders them immune to change and adaptation. There is a function of *episkopē* – supervision, watching over, caring for, in the Church. Whether this is exercised by one individual for a given area or not is quite secondary, and not essential to the peoplehood of the Christian people. There is a function of being Petrine, rock-like, witnessing to the faith, in the Church: precisely how that function is exercised at different epochs in Church history is, again, secondary, not essential to the peoplehood of the people of God.

Fifthly, and penultimately, a good contender for the status of what makes a people a people might well be *law*. I am thinking here both of law in the narrower sense of the word which we normally employ, and law in the wider Old Testament sense, still found in Judaism, of law as *torah*, a body of teaching, a way of life. Adherence to a common law has a remarkable power to cement a people together, even if it is objectively quite minor matters which are at stake. The Catholic rule of fish on Fridays had an extraordinary power to shape a common solidarity. On a larger scale, the codification of canon law in the Catholic Church of the West at the time of the Great War did a great deal to give that Church a uniform appearance. In Israel it was the observance of the law, with all its details, and including the 'hedge' around the law to ensure that all those details were kept, which as much as anything else made Israel a nation. The law gave to Israel the sense of being one people, even at times when the Hebrews were widely separated geographically and, later on, in the languages they spoke. At least they all had the same dietary laws, you could feel at home with one another by what you ate; and above all, there was the sabbath. An old Jewish saying still heard nowadays is that it was not so much Israel that kept the sabbath as the sabbath that kept Israel. Interestingly, however, in the books which occupy the space between Deuteronomy and Ezra in our Bibles and in the prophetic books, there is remarkably little concern for the keeping of the law in the Pentateuchal (and modern Jewish) sense. In these two sets of writings we find a great concern for what the law itself is concerned for: the social justice at which the law aimed, the purity of the faith of Israel which it was meant to ensure. But there is surprisingly little attention paid to the law *qua* legal system in all its detailed and manifold requirements. Similarly in the deutero-canonical books, there is little of law in the talmudic sense. Concern for the niceties of law is a preoccupation of the period following on the return from Babylon where, doubtless, observance of the law had been a potent factor in preserving Jewish identity. We all know how in the New Testament some at least of the contemporaries of Jesus showed a quite obsessive concern with legal minutiae. This is clear even when we remember that the Pharisees are types, rather than individuals. In the New Testament there is a strong feeling, on the other hand, that the law has been abolished as a decisive religious factor. We are called as Christians to live beyond law; Paul is the obvious example of this. As St Thomas Aquinas would put it later, the law of the New Testament is principally the Holy Spirit. Yet equally, the dangers of such an attitude are realised. While there is little law-making in the New Testament, there is some. Matthew is the best example: at times he even appears to be writing a new law on the model of the old. In the Pauline Letters, particularly the Corinthian correspondence, there is some primitive casuistry and what some would regard as early canon law (on the dress of women at the Liturgy and so forth). The central thrust of the gospel, however, is surely against the idea that the peoplehood of Christians depends on common laws. The regulations in the New Testament are not presented as the immutable will of God, in the style of the prescriptions of the Pentateuch. In this sense the new law is indeed the grace of the Spirit, who may from time to time lead men to make laws, yet not laws fixed forever.

What, finally, of the theme of common *worship*? The Old Testament experience was increasingly that common worship is necessary if there is to be a people of God at all. One feature of the attempt to recover or preserve the purity of Israel's faith was the concentration of all sacrificial worship on Jerusalem, a movement which eventually produced the custom of praying by facing in the direction of that city – one God, one temple, one place for sacrifice. But this too broke down under the stress of the Babylonian exile. People saw that the attempt to focus everything in Jerusalem was fundamentally misguided despite its element of truth and the practical necessity of it, perhaps, at one period in order to suppress the outright paganism of the countryside. The crisis of the exile in this respect was that, on such a centralist view of worship, if there could not be sacrifices in the temple then there could be no sacrifices at all. The Jews in Babylon discovered that it was perfectly possible to survive without sacrifice. When they returned and rebuilt the temple they continued to insist that only in Jerusalem might sacrifice be offered – but they had realised that sacrifices were not all that important. After the destruction of the second temple there was no crisis of faith comparable to that which afflicted Israel during the exile. The one problem Jews faced was the lack of a centre for the three great annual pilgrimages of the devout. The very real danger that Jews would drift apart was met with that vast labour of love which is the Talmud, and it sufficed. Christians too had no difficulty with this. They knew from the beginning that where two or three were gathered together, there was Christ. No need for buildings of any particular sort, no need for a common liturgy, for the use of identical formulae in prayer. No more holy times or holy places, only holy people.

But if none of these elements was what made the people a people, and still makes us a people, what is it that makes Christians the people of God? Ultimately, only a common history and a common destiny. We are a people because we have been called to make our own a particular history. This history, as yet uncompleted, is rooted in creation (for even of creation it is said that there too God's steadfast covenant love was at work) but recognises that our common humanity without God is not enough (as in the Tower of Babel story). The history begins with Abraham, and runs through the descent into Egypt and the exodus, the entry into the land, the apostasy, the return, the life, death and resurrection of Jesus and the coming of the Holy Spirit. It will issue in the coming of the kingdom of God, of that time when all men will be united as the one people of God. It is this unique history in its entirety which must always be kept present to our minds and hearts. Just as for Israel there is the Passover which recalls not only the exodus but also all the sufferings of the Jewish people in subsequent generations and looks forward to the return of Elijah to usher in the age of the Messiah, so for Christians there is the Eucharist which proclaims the death of the Lord until he comes. Similarly, for Israel there is an entry into that history by circumcision and for Christians there is the mystery of baptism. In that sacrament the nature of the Church is most profoundly displayed, for there the common history and destiny of the initiate with the whole people is proclaimed and effected. That is what makes us the people we are, the people of God.

3

Brotherhood

THE human result of the activity of God as it has been and is experienced in the Judaeo-Christian tradition is the coming into being of a people. This people, being gathered together out of many peoples, can be called 'Church', a gathering, a people that both is gathered and gathers: *ecclesia congregata* and *ecclesia congregans*. The people of God is an ordered people, an ordained people, a people, that is, with a structure of internal relationships which mirror and express the relationship of one and all to Christ and to his Father. So important is this ordering of the people that for generations the word 'Church' could be thought of in practice as synonymous with a particular section of the Church, with one particular group ordered, over against the rest, to sacramentalise the Lord of the Church vis-à-vis the Church. But there is a more important and enduring way of talking about the Church than this.

When we come to think about the sacraments we shall see that ministry is an aspect of the Church which will eventually wither away, like the State in Marxist eschatology. The time will come when there will be no point in having a ministry, for the ministry makes sense only in terms of the time of building, the time between resurrection and parousia. On the other hand, when we come to discuss the sacramentality of marriage, we shall find that the relationship of love in marriage will endure when the service of husband and wife to one another comes to an end. In the same way, the relationship of love in the macro-Church, the *Catholica*, will abide when the service and ministry of the members of the Church for one another has come to its conclusion, when the time for 'edification' is over. Already now, at a time when ministry, ordering, ordination in the Church is essential, the deeper and more permanent reality of the love between the members of the Church, and between them and Christ, ought to be, can be, and is a matter of experience. The

Church is not only set in order with its members over against one another to represent to each other the Lord of the Church. The Church is also together in love, all the members of the Church standing together before the Father. It is the Church as seen from this aspect that we speak of as a 'brotherhood', appealing there to a fundamental human reality and aspiration. We all have some experience of brotherhood and some of us have a longing too for a time when 'men will brothers be the wide world o'er'. (For 'brother' here, and throughout this section, read, of course, 'brother and sister'.)

At the most basic level, of course, brothers are those who have the same father and mother, though in many languages everyone who belongs to the same extended family or tribe is called a brother of all the rest. In a harsh world men could look to their brothers in this biological sense for help and protection against those who were not brothers, the outsiders, the 'others'. But in almost all cultures, as in the Bible, the word 'brother' was used in early times of those who had the same function in the world – and so perhaps needed to stick together for mutual self-help – as, in an earlier period, in trade unions. It was applied as well to those who made themselves brothers by some sort of treaty or agreement – again, usually an agreement for mutual protection. And so brotherhood, both biological and covenantal, tends always to set up some sort of opposition as well as fellowship, an opposition to those who do not belong with the brothers. But the biblical tradition is also conscious of an opposition between brothers themselves: the ideal of brotherhood is always at risk. Sibling rivalry is not an invention of the twentieth century but one of those all-pervasive features of the human condition which the Bible describes in the opening chapters of Genesis in the figures of Cain and Abel. This story plays out in advance many of the central themes of the Scriptures as a whole – dissension between men who all belong to one stock, to a common gene pool; the election of God; the preferring of the younger over the older, of the apparently less significant over the apparently more. It is rivalry, jealousy, which lies at the root of this archetypal quarrel between men who are brothers. Cain is the founder of the human race as we know it, post-lapsarian man: Cain who hates his brother and is a murderer. (The First Letter of John will go on to universalise this: 'Anyone who hates his brother is a murderer'

[1 John 3.15].) Cain stands for that kind of egalitarian mentality which is the destruction of all true brotherhood because it is not prepared to enter into the reality of differences between brothers and refuses to tolerate any disparity in the ways in which different people are treated.

Abel, on the other hand, has no descendants according to the flesh: he dies without offspring. He stands at the head of another way of being human: he is the first martyr, the first man who is prepared to be a victim rather than a persecutor, ready to suffer injustice rather than to perpetrate it. He is the first of those who are prepared to lay down their lives for their brethren, and for this reason his blood cries to God from the ground. But not, despite the well-known hymn, 'for vengeance';[1] not, at least, for the sort of vengeance that would redress the balance by further murder, by the taking of another life. Cain is in fact protected by God from dying a violent death: 'Yahweh put a mark on Cain, lest any who came upon him should kill him' (Gen. 4.15). Abel's blood brings grace to Cain, even though Cain has to wander through the earth bearing the curse of one who has slain his own brother. Abel's blood brings the grace of a continuing humanity still haunted by the ideal of brotherhood, still striving for a brotherhood which in the end it will only be able to receive as a divine gift. The rest of the Book of Genesis shows people striving after a realisation of this brotherhood, trying to see in actual practice 'how good and how pleasant it is when brothers dwell in unity' (Ps. 133.1). It is something that can only be realised by the abandonment of rivalry, by one brother refusing for the sake of the other to insist on all his rights, on fair shares all round. So Abraham says to Lot,

> Let there be no strife between you and me, and between your herdsmen and my herdsmen, for we are brothers. Is not the whole land before you? Separate yourself from me. If you take the left hand, I will take the right; if you take the right hand, then I will go to the left. (Gen. 13.8–9)

So Esau forgives Jacob and does not insist on the reversion of his birthright.

---

[1] From the anonymous Italian hymn translated by Edward Caswall as 'Glory be to Jesus': its fourth stanza contrasts Jesus' death with that of Abel.

> Esau said, 'What do you mean by all this company which I met?'
> Jacob said, 'To find favour in the sight of my *lord*'. But Esau said,
> 'I have enough, my *brother*; keep what you have for yourself.'
> (Gen. 33.8–10)

And so too after the death of Jacob, the brothers of Joseph expect
him to take revenge on them, and ask him to forgive them the
wrong they did to him.

> His brothers came and fell down before him and said, 'Behold, we
> are your servants.' But Joseph said to them, 'Fear not, for am I in
> the place of God? As for you, you meant evil against me; but God
> meant it for good, to bring it about that many people should be
> kept alive, as they are today. So do not fear: I will provide for you
> and for your little ones.' (Gen. 50.18–20)

The mystery of brotherhood is founded on letting God be God,
on men refusing to stand in the place of God but insisting on
being where they are put by God, in a relationship of brotherhood under a single Father.

The covenant community of the exodus, Israel *qua* brotherhood, again depends on God being God. Since this community is
given its existence by God's hand, men can remain true to the
givenness of the situation only by being brothers together.

> You shall not hate your brother in your heart, but you shall
> reason with your neighbour, lest you bear sin because of him.
> You shall not take vengeance or bear any grudge against the sons
> of your own people, but you shall love your neighbour as your-
> self; I am the Lord. (Lev. 19.16–18)

'You shall love your neighbour as yourself': this is the text which
Rabbi Hillel said was the whole law, the fundamental commandment compared with which the rest of the law was merely commentary. Once again, it is founded on the fact that Yahweh is
Yahweh. The commandment to love one's neighbour (and the
rules of Hebrew parallelism make it clear that here 'neighbour' is
synonymous with 'brother') is a gift of God, a gift which creates
brotherhood in community. Even those of the Ten Commandments which deal with the relationships between man and
man are simply concerned to spell out the implications of this
brotherhood.

The scriptural laws about personal relationships are properly understood only by a sympathetic entry into the position of the other person – as Jesus' parable of the Good Samaritan points up. The commandments make full sense only when grasped from the standpoint of the man who has suffered wrong. The commandment against adultery matters most to the man whose wife is taken from him, and so forth. Faithfulness to the covenant meant faithfulness to the dynamics of brotherhood; to break the bonds of brotherhood is to sunder the covenant. The polemic of the prophets of Israel is a polemic against the people's failure to live as brothers, which means a failure to let God be God. The Lord 'has a controversy with the inhabitants of the land', according to Hosea, because

> There is nothing but swearing and breaking faith, and killing and stealing, and committing adultery; they break out, and blood touches blood. (Hos. 4.1–2)

Or as Micah says:

> The godly man is perished out of the earth, and there is none upright among men; they all lie in wait for blood; they hunt every man his brother with a net. Their hands are upon that which is evil, to do it diligently. A man's enemies are the men of his own house. (Mic. 7.2–3)

Here again, to be godly is to be a brother. Jeremiah complains of the people in much the same terms:

> Take heed every one of his neighbour, and trust not in any brother, for every brother will utterly supplant and every neighbour will go about with slanders. And they will deceive every one his neighbour and will not speak the truth; they have taught their tongue to speak lies; they weary themselves to commit iniquity. . . . Even your brothers and the house of your father have dealt(14) treacherously with you. (Jer. 9.4–5)

If a practical rejection of the exigencies of brotherhood is equivalent to a denial of the covenant then, evidently, return to the covenant must be expressed by true fraternity. This is exactly what we find in, for instance, Zechariah:

> Thus has the Lord of hosts spoken, saying, 'Execute true judgment and show mercy and compassion every man to his brother,

27

and oppress not the widow nor the fatherless nor the stranger nor the poor; and let none of you imagine evil against his brother in his heart'. (Zech. 7.9–10)

All this, as Malachi repeats, is based on acknowledging God as the one Father, and not attempting to take his place.

Have we not all one father? Has not one God created us? Why do we deal treacherously every man against his brother, profaning the covenant of our fathers? (Mal. 1.10)

Against this background it was to be expected that when Christians thought of themselves as the people of God they would be conscious of being brothers too. The ground had also been well prepared in the Greek world. Plato could say that he and his fellow-citizens were all brothers born of one another, although here there was an implication (inevitably) that people outside the state were not brothers in the same sense as fellow-citizens were. The notion of brotherhood, as we have seen, entails a separation of those who are brothers from those who are not. The first question, therefore, is where these bounds of brotherhood are to be drawn. For the old Israel, they were the bounds of the Israelite people itself. Samaritans, for example, were not brothers of Israel, even though from time to time other nations in treaty with Israel could be thought of as brothers so long as the treaty lasted. For the infant Church the question of who should be addressed and treated as brothers was the same question as that of who belonged to the Church. Naturally enough, at a time when most Christians were Jews, and synagogue and Church were not yet clearly divided, Christian Jews were quite prepared to go on treating non-Christian Jews as brothers. The Acts of the Apostles are full of this. Stephen addresses the members of the Sanhedrin as 'fathers and brothers'. Peter speaks to the crowd on the day of Pentecost as 'brothers', and does the same at the healing of the man who sat at the Beautiful Gate. Paul calls the people in the synagogue at Antioch 'brothers', as he does the Jewish mob at Ephesus, the Sanhedrin in Jerusalem and the leaders of the Jewish community in Rome. So too in his Letter to the Romans he writes: 'I could wish that I myself were accursed and cut off from Christ for the sake of my brothers, my kinsmen by race' (Rom. 9. 3), although here there is beginning to be, perhaps, a distinction between levels of brotherhood – brothers by race and brothers by grace, brothers according to the flesh and brothers according to the Spirit.

This distinction of levels of brotherhood, and the preferring of brotherhood according to the Spirit over brotherhood according to the flesh was prepared for in the ministry of Jesus himself. As a good Jew, Jesus continued the ordinary Jewish linguistic usage. In the Sermon on the Mount, Jesus says that anyone who is angry with his brother will be liable to judgment, and in the rule for the new community (in Matthew 18) he describes how disputes between brothers are to be adjudicated. Everyone is to forgive his brother from his heart. All his followers are to be brothers; none is to attempt to take over the role of father or of teacher.

> You are not to be called Rabbi, for one is your teacher, and you are all brothers. And call no man your father on earth; for one is your Father who is in heaven. Neither be called masters; for one is your Master, the Christ. (Matt. 23.8–10)

The followers of Jesus, in being his followers, are *ipso facto* brothers. But it is a new brotherhood that they enter; and they do so at the cost of leaving an old one.

> There is no man who has left house or brothers or sisters or mother or father or children or lands for my sake and for the sake of the gospel, who will not receive a hundredfold now in this time, houses and brothers and sisters and mothers and children and lands, with persecutions, and in the age to come eternal life. (Mark 10.29–30)

They leave an old family and enter a new, as Jesus himself left an old family and created a new one around him.

> His mother and his brothers come to him; and standing without they speak to him, calling him. And a multitude was sitting about him; and they say to him, 'Behold your mother and your brothers outside seek for you.' And he answers them and says, 'Who is my mother and my brothers?' And looking around on those who sat round about him, he says, 'Behold, my mother and my brothers! For whoever shall do the will of God, the same is my brother and sister and mother' (Matt. 12.46–50)

Here we are with the Synoptics. But in the perspective that the Fourth Gospel offers, this brotherhood of Christians with Jesus is based on his resurrection. It is only after the resurrection that Jesus speaks of his followers as his brothers. This is in keeping with St John's conviction that it is the resurrection that brings Jesus close to us in bringing him to the Father:

> I go to the Father; I go to prepare a place for you; I will come again and will receive you to myself; if a man love me, my Father will love him, and we will come to him and make our abode with him. (John 14.12, 2, 3, 23)

And so it is the risen Jesus who gives Mary Magdalene the Easter message with the words:

> Go to my brothers and say to them, I am ascending to my Father and your Father, to my God and your God. (John 20.17)

In the final chapter of the Gospel, Christians are referred to, apparently quite casually, as 'the brothers'. Once again, then, it is a brotherhood of choice, of the Spirit, dependent on there being a single Father for all. Only when Jesus speaks to God as not just his own Father (*the* Father) but Father too of all his followers ('my Father and your Father') does he call his disciples his brothers.

If John places the entry into common brotherhood at the resurrection and the Synoptics see it as in creation during the ministry of Jesus, the writer to the Hebrews puts the decisive initiation of this new fraternity even earlier. For him, the new brotherhood is indeed based on choice, but the choice lies at its deepest level in the choice of God and God's Son, the mystery of our election.

> For it became him for whom are all things and through whom are all things, in bringing many sons unto glory, to make the Author of their salvation perfect through sufferings. For both he who sanctifies and those who are sanctified are all of one; for which cause he is not ashamed to call them brothers, saying, 'I will declare your name to my brothers; in the midst of the Church will I sing your praise'. Since then the children are sharers in blood and flesh, he also himself in like manner partook of the same, that through death he may bring to nought him who has the power of

death, that is, the devil, and may deliver those who through fear of death were subject to bondage all their lifetime. (Heb. 2.10–14)

The plan of salvation in the mind of God is that the eternal Son should be what the Letter to the Romans calls 'the firstborn among many brothers':

> Those whom God foreknew, he also fore-ordained [predestined] to be conformed to the image of his Son, that he might be the firstborn among many brethren; and whom he predestined those also he called; and whom he called, those also he justified; and whom he justified, those also he glorified. (Rom. 8.29–30)

As the patristic tradition puts it, we are sons in the Son, and therefore brothers both of the Son, Jesus, and of one another. So brotherhood for Christians depends not only on having a common Father but also on having a common brother, Jesus of Nazareth.

Jesus of Nazareth, then, is more importantly the firstborn of many brethren than he is the Lord of the Church. He stands indeed with the Church before the Father, so that his attitude to the Father becomes the attitude of his brethren to the Father. Standing with him they can pray as he prays, pray that shattering prayer which addresses the Ground of Being and the Granite of it as *Abba*, 'dear Father'. 'When *you* pray, say *Abba*.' This comes prior to any sort of polarisation – I use the word non-pejoratively – within the Church. Whatever need there may be within the brotherhood for representation of Jesus as Lord, or high priest or Teacher, the primary Christian experience is that of brotherhood itself. The Letter to the Hebrews, for instance, makes the brotherhood of Jesus the necessary ground for his being high priest:

> It behoved him to be made like his brothers in all things, that he might be a merciful and faithful high priest in things pertaining to God, to make propitiation for the sins of the people. For in that he himself has suffered being tempted, he is able to help those who are tempted. (Heb. 2.17–18)

People are initiated into the Church of Christ as into a brotherhood. Ananias says to Paul after his blinding on the road to Damascus: '*Brother* Saul'. Paul calls Timothy his brother, and likewise Onesimus and Philemon and Tychicus; he speaks of the Christians in Corinth as 'the brothers and sisters'. And while *agapē* is owed to everyone without exception, within the Church there is another sort of love, subsumed under *agapē* yet not owed to those outside the Church: this is the love of the brethren, *philadelphia*. The New Testament letters are filled with this love:

> In love of the brethren be tenderly affectioned to one another, in honour preferring one another. (Rom. 12.10)

> But concerning love of the brothers, you have no need that one write to you, for you yourselves are taught of God to love one another, for indeed you do it towards all the brothers who are in all Macedonia. But we exhort you, brothers, that you abound more and more. (1 Thess. 4.9)

> Let love of the brothers continue. Do not forget to show love to strangers. (Heb. 13.1)

> Honour all men. Love the brotherhood. Fear God. Honour the king. (1 Pet. 2.17)

> Add on your part all diligence. In your faith supply virtue, and in virtue knowledge, and in knowledge temperance, and in temperance patience, and in patience godliness, and in godliness love of the brothers [*philadelphia*], and in *philadelphia agapē*. (2 Pet. 1.5–7)

This love of the brothers comes from sharing the same birth with them:

> Seeing that you have purified your souls in your obedience to the truth unto unfeigned *philadelphia*, love one another from the heart fervently, having been begotten again, not of corruptible semen, but of incorruptible, through the word of God which lives and abides. (1 Pet. 1.22–23)

In this Christian love of the brethren the mystery of brotherhood adumbrated in the pair of brothers Cain and Abel and extended through those pairs of brothers which crop up at crucial points in the history of salvation (Ishmael and Isaac, Esau and Jacob, David and Jonathan, perhaps the two robbers on the cross, perhaps Judas Iscariot and Saul who became Paul) finds its fulfilment in the final overcoming of sibling rivalry.

> We know that we have passed out of death into life because we love the brothers. He who does not love abides in death. Whoever hates his brother is a murderer; and you know that no murderer has eternal life abiding in him. By this we know love, because he laid down his life for us, and we ought to lay down our lives for the brothers. But anyone who has the world's goods and sees his brother in need and shuts up his compassion from him, how does the love of God abide in him? (1 John 3.14–17)

Not that brotherly love in the Church is perfect. There are 'false brothers' like those who put Paul in peril and who are 'privately brought in, who come in privately to spy out our liberty which we have in Christ Jesus, that they might bring us into bondage' (Gal. 2.4). There remains always the task and duty of fraternal correction.

The implications for the life of the Church of all this are simply enormous. Perhaps the first in importance is for the size of Christian communities. As Joseph Ratzinger writes in his study *The Meaning of Christian Brotherhood*:

> Brotherhood can first be realised only within the local community. . . . The size of the parish community ought to be governed by this. It should be possible for everyone to know everyone else, for you cannot live in brotherhood with someone that you do not know. Christian brotherhood demands concretely the brotherhood of the individual parish community. This brotherhood has its source and centre in the celebration of the eucharistic mysteries. In fact in the classical theology of the Church, the Eucharist has been seen . . . as the *concorporatio cum Christo*, as the Christians' becoming one in the one body of the Lord. A celebration of the Eucharist that is to be the source of brotherhood must both be inwardly recognised and performed as a sacrament of brotherhood and also externally appear to be such. The recognition that *ekklēsia* and *adelphotēs* (Church and brotherhood) are the same thing, that the Church which fulfils itself in the celebration of the Eucharist is essentially a community of brothers, compels us to celebrate the Eucharist as a rite of brotherhood in responsory dialogue – and not to have a lonely hierarchy facing a group of

laymen each one of whom is shut off in his own missal. The Eucharist must become visibly again the sacrament of brotherhood in order to be able to achieve its full community-creating power.[2]

This surely implies that the local Church must develop a brotherly style of life outside the time of the eucharistic celebration as well as within it. As Ratzinger goes on:

> The individual organisation is justified only insofar as it serves the brotherhood of the whole community. Today a trade union or a party can exist as a live and fraternal community, and so the actual experience of brotherhood for all the Christian members of a parish community can, and therefore should, become a primary goal. It would be a universal experience which transcends all barriers, for in every parish there are men of different professions and often of different languages and nationalities. It is this universality which gives the parish a superior position to an organisation based on any other community of interests.[3]

It is as a realised brotherhood, or a brotherhood in process of realisation, that the Church (the local church, which is as much the Church as the Church throughout the world) is a sign for the unity of all mankind.

But it is also to be an instrument for the achievement of such unity. The necessary boundaries created by brotherhood have always to be extended. The object of the brotherhood that already exists is the extension of brotherhood throughout the whole of mankind. This means a positive attempt to recognise our brotherhood with others outside the Christian community, to recognise it or to create it. The extension of the brotherhood in the spirit of the gospel will first of all be directed towards those in need, for those, though outside the Church, we were given as brothers by Jesus himself. 'Insofar as you did it to one of the least of these my brothers, you did it to me' (Matt. 25.40) are his own words about the underprivileged, the poor of the earth. In making himself the least of men in his passion, death and descent into Hell, Christ has made himself the brother of all those who count

---

[2] J. Ratzinger, *The Meaning of Christian Brotherhood* (ET London 1966; San Francisco 1993), pp. 67–68.
[3] *Ibid.*, pp. 69–70.

for nothing. The Church of the brothers thus becomes the Church of the poor, the Church of those who, in the eyes of the various secular messianisms of the last century, are the germ of a new and more human future for mankind.

4

Temple

WHEN the Church meets together in order to be made
Church, at the Eucharist, one of the commonest greetings
that pass between individual Christians is *Dominus vobiscum*:
'The Lord be with you', or 'The Lord is with you'. It is either a
wish or a statement, and so the reply comes back in the same vein:
et cum spiritu tuo: 'May he be with your spirit too', or 'He is also
with you'. God is not only a God who acts, he is also a God who
is present, present in particular to his people and with his people.
For this the Bible uses the language of being-with, being-
amongst, being in the midst (literally 'in the womb'), of seeing the
face of God, of God's dwelling among men. There is, however, a
basic difficulty in coming to terms with the total biblical idea of
the presence of God, a difficulty peculiar to the Jewish-Christian
tradition and not encountered to the same extent in other religious traditions. In any theistic religion, any religion which has a
God and is concerned with the God-question (as Buddhism, for
example, is not), people will always ask 'Where is your God?' or
'Where are your various gods?'. God or a god may be in his
shrine; his presence may be imaged there in a cult-object or an
'idol'; his presence may be in a fetish. Or, on the other hand, God
may be said to be in the heavens, utterly transcendent, not
imaged in any way, his presence not more in one place than
another, and certainly not confined to any one place or number
of places. This is the answer of classical Islam to the question,
'Where is your God?'. By and large, religious traditions focus
directly on God in one way or the other. The peculiarity of the
Jewish-Christian tradition in this respect lies in its being what we
may call 'bifocal'. It lays tremendous emphasis on the transcendence of God, conceiving him as altogether unaffected by the
world, sovereignly free. And yet there is also a strong insistence
on the presence of God in particular areas of the world, whether
those areas be spatial or temporal. God is the God of Israel, the

God who dwells in Zion, the God who acts in such a way that some events in the world's history may be called 'acts of God', 'mighty works of God', in a sense that other events may not be.

The Old Testament can offer us examples of both approaches. For instance, on the one hand we hear:

> Why should the nations say, Where is their God? Our God is in the heavens, he does whatever he pleases. (Ps. 115.2–3)

Or again, in Solomon's prayer at the dedication of the temple:

> But will God indeed dwell on the earth? Behold, heaven and the highest heaven cannot contain thee; how much less this house I have built. (2 Chron. 2.5–6)

Yet on the other hand we read in the psalms that God 'is near' (Ps. 119.151). In Deuteronomy, Moses says to the people of Israel:

> What great nation is there that has a god so near to it as Yahweh our God is to us whenever we call upon him? (Deut. 4.7)

Then there is the Isaianic prophecy about Immanuel, 'God with us', taken up in the New Testament to refer to Jesus.

> Behold, a young woman shall conceive and bear a son and shall call his name Immanuel. (Isa. 7.14)

From one point of view, the whole biblical history can be regarded as the history of Immanuel, the story of the intensifying movement of God's dwelling with men.

Nevertheless, both sides of the problem remain, in the New Testament as in the Church. Even now God does not cease to be altogether other, transcendent, 'in the heavens', despite the confession of Jesus as Immanuel. (One might note in passing the importance of this for eucharistic theology, for example: in the Eucharist God does not become simply available – the body of Christ is present, but Christ is not present bodily in the sense of 'locally'.) Some biblical texts manage to hold both foci together. Perhaps Isaiah 57.15 is of all these the most apt:

> For thus says the high and lofty One who inhabits eternity, whose name is holy: I dwell in the high and holy place, with him also that is of a contrite and humble spirit, to revive the spirit of the humble, to revive the heart of the contrite.

There is a further distinction to be drawn. This lies between God's presence by action, and his presence by 'tabernacling' in this world. God's presence may be his activity, a militant presence, a presence to help his people or to punish them, the presence in his actions of the God who acts. Such a presence is of its nature transient, though nonetheless real for that: 'That's God, that was', we may sum it up. Any reference to the saving works of God involves this sort of presence. But then there is his abiding presence, his tabernacling presence, his available presence. God is present in the midst of his people so that they can seek him, can worship him. He dwells amongst his people, or walks amongst them, or goes to and fro amongst them. This is, if you like, the 'substantial' presence of God, of the God who is close at hand. (This distinction is also of value in sacramental theology. God is present by action in most of his sacraments, but in the Eucharist – and in some way in marriage too – his presence is a tabernacling presence, like his presence in the lives of Christians as a whole.)

These various modes of the presence of God are reflected in the different literary strata of the Bible. In the 'mythological' features of the narratives of Genesis 1–12, it is generally assumed that God lives somewhere else, coming and going as he pleases, but never in more than one place at a time. This is part of a primitive (perhaps deliberately pseudo-primitive) way of writing up ancient folk-tales. God walks around the Garden of Eden in the cool of the day, and Adam and Eve hear the rustle of his footsteps. Cain is able to 'go out from the presence of the Lord' (cf. Gen. 4.16), and though the reference to the presence of Yahweh is not here specifically localised, it is localised in some fashion. Again, Yahweh shuts up Noah in the ark and closes the door; he comes down to see the city and tower which the children of men build at Babel. The patriarchal narratives of the later chapters of Genesis show us Yahweh as a God who appears at various places, normally by speaking there. So it comes about that there are diverse places where he may be invoked, altars at sanctuaries where there had been an epiphany. Nevertheless, he is primarily a God of people, of people on the move, and so a wandering God. At Beersheba he says to Jacob:

> I will go down with thee into Egypt, and I will also surely bring thee up again. (Gen. 46.4)

38

He has not yet established a permanent dwelling-place for himself on earth. He epiphanises, sometimes in human form as when Abraham can talk with him as a man with his friend.

The exodus marks the beginning of a new relationship between God and his people. Here for the first time we meet with the sense that God may have, in the proper meaning of the word, a *dwelling*-place on earth, somewhere he will *remain*. Obviously enough, the idea is fraught with all kinds of dangerous possibilities (though so too is the idea of a purely transcendent God). Most of the religious history of Israel will be concerned with coming to a correct understanding of what is, and is not, implied by the tabernacling presence of God with his people. In the *lingua franca* of the Ancient Near East at the time of the exodus, Aramaic, we find the root *shakan* from which comes the later Hebrew word *shekinah*. This word referred first to the place where God dwells, and then to the indwelling presence of God itself. In the exodus narratives, and later stories whose authors have situated themselves in the milieu of the exodus, that indwelling presence is often manifested by a cloud. When Moses encounters God in the tent of meeting a cloud hovers over it; the pillar of cloud (and of fire) leads Israel on its journey through the desert, a permanent manifestation of Yahweh guiding Israel. Clouds belong in the sky, in the heavens, yet they can come down; and this ambivalence gives them their significance as symbols in Jewish and Christian tradition. Heaven can come to earth, or earth be taken up into heaven. The cloud speaks of God as both 'up' and 'down', as both transcendent and immanent. So it is that a cloud fills the tent in the desert when it is consecrated and a cloud fills the Jerusalem temple at its consecration by Solomon. Ezekiel too prophesies that a cloud will come down on the temple that will be, when the exiles return from Babylon to Zion. Significantly, when we read of the building and dedication of the second temple there is no mention of the cloud, even though the prophecies of the rebuilt temple have a very definite expectation of the visible glory of Yahweh filling the house. St Luke's account of the presentation of Jesus in the temple depends on this. It is only when the infant Jesus enters this temple that the glory of God enters it. Because of this, Simeon can call Jesus 'the glory of God's people Israel' (Luke 2.32).

'Glory' is another word which holds together the transcendence and the immanence of Yahweh. The glory of Yahweh both is and is not Yahweh, in something of the way in which in the Fourth Gospel, the Gospel of glory, Jesus says, 'I and the Father are one' (John 10.30) even though, evidently, the Father is himself and not Jesus, just as Jesus is himself and not the Father.

The sign *par excellence* of the tabernacling presence of God in Israel, however, at least in pre-exilic times, is the ark of the covenant, the box covered with the solid gold slab of the mercy-seat. The ark was meant for carrying, even though it was insisted that Yahweh carried Israel rather than Israel Yahweh. Even in the permanence of Solomon's temple, the ark remained potentially mobile. The poles with which it was carried were left in position so that they could be seen, and the front of the Holy of Holies was built like a tent. The ark was the supreme focal manifestation of the presence of Yahweh. Indeed, it was a vehicle of that presence, although insofar as it was a mobile vehicle the freedom of the Lord was not impaired in this concrete manifestation. The ark, speaking of Yahweh, led the people towards the promised land, Yahweh's land, the land which Yahweh made his own as the people of Yahweh made it their own.

For the land too is a sign of the immanence of God in Israel. The land was not naturally Yahweh's land as Creator: it became it by adoption. As the psalm of the exodus puts it, 'Tremble, O land, before the presence of the Lord' (Ps. 114.7): *the Lord*, not Yahweh, the personal name of God, but the title which means 'master'. The land has a new lord, a new *adon*, a new master. Appropriately, as Jericho is the first-fruits of the land in the Conquest, it is specially 'devoted' to Yahweh. All the yearly first-fruits of the land belong to him. The soil of the land is the only place where sacrifice may be made to him. To be away from this land is, as David found, to be away from Yahweh himself. Just as Israel is Yahweh's portion so the land is Israel's portion, and the various tribes have an inheritance in the land which is the inheritance of all the tribes. The presence of Yahweh, focussed as it is in signs like the cloud and the tent of meeting and the ark of the covenant, has reference to a particular portion of the earth's surface as well. There is not only saving history: there is also saving geography.

In the early centuries after the Conquest, although all the land was Yahweh's, there was no one place in the land which in its own right was a focus of his tabernacling presence. There were numerous places where people could call upon him and seek his face, his presence. Insofar as there could be said to be any special place among these it was the place where the ark happened to be. The importance of the ark could be overestimated here: the story of the capture of the ark by the Philistines serves as a warning to those who would mistake the focus of the Lord's presence for the Lord himself. After the Philistines gave back the ark the lesson seems to have been well learned – perhaps too well learned, for the ark underwent a period of real neglect. Its prestige was not enhanced again until the time of David. David, it will be recalled, had first made himself king of the two southern tribes; only after a considerable time was he accepted as king of the northern tribes as well. When that happened, Hebron ceased to be a suitable site for his capital. The capture of Jerusalem, on the boundary between north and south and with sacred associations from the past (compare the Melchizedek story in Genesis) offered a good choice as capital for the united kingdom. But there had to be some way of making Jerusalem a cult centre as well as a political capital: anything else was unthinkable to a theocratic people. There had to be some way of identifying Jerusalem with the tabernacling presence of Yahweh, and the way that David found was that of bringing the ark of the covenant into the city. Although this enormously enhanced the prestige of Jerusalem, it also enhanced the prestige of the ark by recalling people's attention after a time of eclipse. Under Solomon (and the influence of his wives with their foreign ideas) a temple in the Phoenician style was built in Jerusalem, a temple with a *hieron* (the whole sacred enclosure) and a *naos* (the 'house' of the god, the shrine proper). A pagan *hieron*, like the Acropolis at Athens, might possess more than one *naos*, for more than one god; and at times in the later history of Israel we read of the foreign wives of the kings setting up shrines for their own deities within the Jerusalem *hieron*. To the Jerusalem temple Solomon transferred the ark of the covenant, and, again under the influence of religious ideas from Israel's pagan neighbours, the temple soon came to be thought of as, not just a focus for the presence of Yahweh in the land or in the whole earth, but as the very locus of that presence. It came to be assumed that Yahweh was committed to his

41

temple, although independently of the dispositions of his people. This is what Jeremiah was attacking when he cried

> 'The temple of Yahweh, the temple of Yahweh, the temple of Yahweh' – but I will do to this house what I did to Shiloh. (Jer. 7.14)

So in Ezekiel's prophecy there is a vision of the *shekinah* taking wing from Jerusalem before the destruction of the city and going off to the exiles who sat by the rivers of Babylon. The presence of Yahweh is asserted once more to be a presence *to* people rather than a presence *in* a place.

> This says the Lord Yahweh: 'Though I removed them far off among the nations, and though I scattered them among the countries, yet I have been a sanctuary to them for a while in the countries where they have gone.' (Ezek. 11.16)

For Ezekiel, indeed, the essential aspect of the new covenant is to be Yahweh's dwelling among his people. At the return the ark had disappeared without trace: it is Jerusalem itself which is to be called the throne of Yahweh. But only disappointment attended the return: the subsequent history of the Jews was that of a people subject to a long succession of foreign overlords. So there could be no satisfaction with the way the presence of Yahweh was experienced; instead, the longing for a new experience of the Lord's presence among his people could only be more and more intensified. It is in this light that the New Testament's account of the body of Christ as the temple of the Lord must be understood.

The New Testament texts on the new temple fall into three main categories. First of all, there are those where the human body of Jesus, the body that passed through death and was raised by the Father through the Holy Spirit, is set in continuity, and in contrast, with the Jerusalem temple. Next there are texts which speak of the body of each Christian or of the whole Church in terms of the temple of God. Finally, there are a number of passages which speak of a temple in heaven, whether that is conceived of as an already existing temple or as a temple still to be built.

It is the Fourth Gospel that has most to say about the personal body of Jesus. Almost at the beginning we are told that 'the Word was made flesh and tabernacled among us' (John 1.14), and again and again throughout the Gospel we hear of how persons dwell in and with one another. The Father dwells in Christ and Christ in the Father; the Christian in Christ and Christ in the Christian. The Father and the Son 'come to him and make their abode with him' (John 14.23). The Holy Spirit too dwells in those who belong to Christ. In the Johannine Letters there are many references to our dwelling in God and God in us, or again to our dwelling in love (for 'God is love' [1 John 4.8]). Almost at the very beginning of the public work of Jesus the Fourth Gospel sets the story of the cleansing of the Jerusalem temple with the words of Jesus, 'Destroy this temple, and in three days I will build it up' (John 2.19). The author glosses:

> He spoke of the temple of his body; when therefore he was raised from the dead, his disciples remembered that he had said this; and they believed the scripture and the word which Jesus had spoken. (John 2.21–22)

In this temple, according to the Letter to the Ephesians, 'all the fulness of God dwells bodily' (Eph. 1.23).

But long before the Fourth Gospel was written, Paul had told the Christians in Corinth that they were *themselves* the temple of God.

> Do you not know that you are God's temple and that God's Spirit dwells in you? If anyone destroys God's temple, God will destroy him. For God's temple is holy and that temple you are. (1 Cor. 3.16)

And again:

> We are the temple of the living God; as God said, 'I will live in them and move among them and I will be their God, and they shall be my people.' (2 Cor. 6.16)

It is in the Letter to the Ephesians, however, that the image is most developed:

> You are no longer strangers and sojourners, but you are fellow-citizens with the saints and members of the household of God, built upon the foundation of the apostles and prophets, Christ Jesus himself being the cornerstone, in whom the whole structure

43

is joined together and grows into a holy temple in the Lord; in whom you also are built into a spiritual house. (Eph. 2.19–22)

Interestingly, in all these references to the Christian community as a temple, the word used is not *hieron* (the sacred area), but *naos* (the innermost shrine) – the Holy of Holies, the very place of the very presence of God. The Christian community, in other words, is the place where God and man meet and are reconciled, atoned, at-oned: it is the temple not made by the work of man but rather God's workmanship; it is the sign of the presence of God on earth, the translation into tangible and visible terms of the body of Jesus which was destroyed and built up again by God in the resurrection. The language of temple building can be used of individual Christians as well. At times it is unclear whether Paul is referring to the body of the whole Church as God's temple or to the body of the individual believer and this ambiguity is itself an interesting comment on the relation of Church and churchman. To the Corinthian Christians, at the end of an exhortation against sexual offences, he says

> The fornicator sins against his own body. Do you not know that your body is a temple of the Holy Spirit within you, which you have from God? You are not your own; you were bought with a price. So glorify God in your body. (1 Cor. 6.18–20)

Alongside quite clear and definite statements that the Christian community is (already) the temple of God we find, however, considerable use of the metaphor of building in the active sense of that word: not a fully constructed building but the *process* of building. The language of temple does not entail a 'triumphalist' approach to the mystery of the Church. At the moment, the Church is in the act of being built up of living stones, as St Peter puts it. There is still something to be hoped for, something to be expected. The Church is the fulfilment of the hope of Israel – and behind Israel, of the human hope – inasmuch as God indwells it here and now. It falls short of that fulfilment, however, inasmuch as his indwelling in this age of the world is both concealed and incomplete. The tremendous claim the Church makes for itself in appropriating the title 'temple of God' is tempered by the recognition that it possesses its destiny only in part.

44

And so we come to the New Testament witness to a heavenly temple, about which the Letter to the Hebrews in particular has so much to say. The author describes the Jerusalem temple and the worship in that temple on the feast of Yom Kippur, the 'day of Atonement'. He goes on to make the point that this is not the real thing. Jesus by his death and resurrection entered into the real Temple, the temple in heaven of which the Jerusalem temple was but a pale adumbration. He is 'a minister in the sanctuary and the true tent which is set up not by man but by the Lord' (Heb. 8.2).

> But now Christ has come, as the high priest of all the blessings which were to come. He has passed through the greater, the more perfect tent, which is better than the one made by men's hands because it is not of this created order; and he has entered the sanctuary once and for all, taking with him not the blood of goats and bull calves, but his own blood, having won an eternal redemption for us. (Heb. 9.11–12)

Yet this temple in heaven is not altogether separate from the Church on earth. Even now the Christian community can

> enter into the sanctuary by the blood of Jesus, by the new and living way which he opened for us through the curtain, that is, through his flesh. (Heb. 10.20)

The Book of Revelation also envisages a communion in worship between the Church heavenly and the Church earthly (both of them militant), but it looks too for a time when heaven and earth will be altogether one. In that day there will be a new heaven and a new earth as the holy city, new Jerusalem, comes down from God out of heaven. The visionary of the Apocalypse says:

> And I saw no temple in the city, for its temple is the Lord God, the Almighty, and the Lamb. (Apoc. 21.22)

This is equivalent to saying that in the age to come the whole city of the redeemed, embracing earth and heaven, is the temple – just as in Old Testament prophecy it was the whole city of Jerusalem that would be called Yahweh's throne, and as the Lord himself was a sanctuary to the exiles in Babylon. The length and breadth and height of this new Jerusalem are equal: it is in fact a perfect cube, like the perfect cube of the Holy of Holies in the temple in

45

Jerusalem of old. That is, the whole redeemed creation is the innermost shrine of God; there is to be no longer any difference between the holy and the profane. (The 'profane', *pro-fanum*, is what lies outside the *fanum*, the temple.) And so:

> The dwelling of God is with men; he will dwell with them; God himself will be with them. (Apoc. 21.3)

We come to the term of the history of Immanuel, the ultimate goal of the fellowship and communion of God and his people, God no longer dwelling with his people but in them.

The image of the Church as temple is, then, one more starting point for a fruitful reflection on the mystery of the Church. We may touch in conclusion on some implications of what we have seen. First, the temple is the temple of *God*, and for the New Testament (with some rare exceptions) that must mean the Father. The Church stands with Christ before God. Christ is the cornerstone of the temple, the one in whom the temple is being built up, but the temple is not *for* Christ: it is for the Father, to whom all glory and honour is to be paid through Christ, with Christ and in Christ, in the unity which the Holy Spirit creates – that unity so well symbolised by the way stones in a building hold each other in position and raise each other high. Christ as the cornerstone determines the lie and shape of the building and makes possible its unity and growth. We might say that he *is* its unity, though it is there for the glory of the Father, to be ultimately a place in which God is glorified. The activity of the Christian community will one day consist solely in the worship of God. Even now, in a time of building, of ethical struggle, the Church is never more itself than when it is anticipating its ultimate destiny, offering to God through Christ a sacrifice of praise. This does not simply mean liturgical worship. The image of the Church as the temple of God points to the priestly activity both of the whole Church – without distinction from this point of view between those who minister and those who are ministered to, and to the priestly activity of the Church the whole of the time – in all the details of the daily lives of its members. Works of charity, for instance, are seen in the New Testament as sacrifice to God. Everything a Christian does that is not incompatible with his being a Christian at all is a part of the worship offered to God on behalf of the whole world. But the Christian body, together and in its members, can carry out this work of glorifying God only because God is really Immanuel, because he is dwelling with it and building it around the centre of unity, the cornerstone, Jesus Christ our Lord.

5

Flock

THE Church, the people of God, the brotherhood, can be talked about, therefore, in ways which we immediately experience as metaphorical, even though it is true, no doubt, that all language has something of the metaphorical about it. In talking about Christians as the temple of God it is patently obvious that we are using language metaphorically: trying to discover points of contact between a group of people and a temple to see how people and building elucidate the significance of each other. Perhaps it is the mutuality of it all that makes for a strict metaphor rather than a simile: in a simile, only the object or person which is 'like' something else is elucidated. In a good metaphor, neither term will be quite the same again. So when the Christian community is described as 'the temple of God' (rather than it being said that the community is 'like' God's temple) the temple too emerges in a new light. This is also true of another metaphor of the Church which we should consider: the Church as *flock*.

This image is rooted in the very ancient consciousness of man. From at least the end of the last Ice Age, men have been shepherds. Shepherding flocks represents man's first step in modifying his environment. When man starts to shepherd animals, non-human nature no longer counts for everything. It is now no longer a matter of people finding their food as it lies to hand or even inventing more or less sophisticated ways of trapping and killing food. Apart from the dog, the sheep was the first animal that man domesticated. Sheep (and goats) have no natural migrations: they simply wander in search of food. When man domesticates sheep, he takes on the role of nature in their regard. He assumes the task of finding food for them, of guarding and protecting them, of substantially modifying their life rather than simply living alongside them, in the way (for instance) that the Lapp does with his reindeer. A flock of sheep represents man's

48

first great humanisation of the natural world, his first discovery that man can lord it over, and be god to, the world of the animals. When he starts to keep flocks, man finds that his life ceases to be a life alongside that of any other animal species. This is also true, of course, of the farmer: yet between the farmer and the herdsman lies a sharp contrast relevant to our interest here.

Agriculture can be defined as the modification of the life of the vegetable world by which people cease to reap what they find growing wild and begin to cultivate plants, staying to look after them and harvest them. A somewhat later development, it depended, it seems, on the chance mutations of some strains of wild wheat in the Fertile Crescent. The life of the farmer remains more symbiotic than that of the herdsman, because the farmer is more dependent on chance than the shepherd is. He is more at the mercy of forces of nature which (for long stretches of human history) he scarcely understands. As a result, he is more likely to try to secure what he needs by appeals beyond himself, appeals to the forces of divinity. Even though agriculture permits the development of civilisation and a higher culture, in itself it does less to distinguish man from the world of nature than does the keeping of flocks and herds. In keeping animals, man is more conscious of his rôle as shepherd and guardian of the world of nature, of participating in the rule of God over the world. By means of flocks and herds, he escapes from the magical world of crops and grain.

The Bible, in the story of Cain and Abel, sees the fundamental dichotomy between the two styles of life and expresses its preference for that of the herdsman.

> Abel was a keeper of sheep, but Cain was a tiller of the ground. And in process of time it came to pass that Cain brought of the fruit of the ground an offering to Yahweh. And Abel, he also brought of the firstlings of his flock and of the fat thereof. And Yahweh had respect to Abel and his offering, but to Cain and his offering he had not respect. (Gen. 4.2–5)

Throughout the Old Testament there is a sense of how dangerous it is for people to be farmers, how farming represents a threat to their integrity before God. For are not farmers constantly tempted to seek help from the gods of nature and not from the only God there is, even though in point of fact it is he who makes the earth fertile and tells man to cultivate the garden and care for it? In the creation accounts of Genesis it is with the animals that man most fundamentally belongs, although he belongs with them as sharing God's dominion over them. The earth is told to

> put forth grass, herb yielding seed, fruit tree bearing fruit after its kind, and every thing that creeps upon the ground after its kind. (Gen. 1.11)

But the animals are given an immediate reference to man:

> And God said, 'Let the earth bring forth the living creature after its kind, and the cattle after their kind, and every thing that creeps upon the ground after its kind.' And God saw that it was good. And God said [on the same day!] 'Let us make man in our image, after our likeness; and let them have dominion over the fish of the sea and over the fowl of the air [created on the previous day] and over the cattle and over all the earth and over every creeping thing that creeps upon the earth.' And God created man in his own image, in the image of God created he him, male and female created he them. And God blessed them and God said to them, 'Be fruitful and multiply and replenish the earth and subdue it; and have dominion over the fish of the sea and over the fowl of the air and over every living thing that moves upon the earth.' (Gen. 1.24–28)

And in this second creation story it is the animals that God brings to man to name and so make part of his world:

> And out of the ground the God Yahweh formed every beast of the earth and every fowl of the air, and brought them to the man to see what he would call them; and whatever the man called every living creature, that was the name of it. And the man gave names to all cattle and to the fowl of the air and to every beast of the field. (Gen. 2.19–20)

In the Middle East the life of a shepherd with his sheep involved a much closer familiarity between man and beast then we are used to in the Western world. There, in the East, sheep are kept more for milk and wool than for meat. They live a longer time, therefore, and a longer time with man. For the Middle Eastern shepherd spends his whole time with his sheep; he is with them day and night from their birth till their death, sleeping in or across the entrance to the fold where they are driven for the night. Travellers' tales are full of accounts of the intimacy between Palestinian shepherds and their sheep. Take, for instance, this passage from H. V. Morton:

> The shepherd never drives his flock as our shepherds drive their sheep. He always walks at their head, leading them along the roads and over the hills to new pasture; and as he goes he sometimes talks to them in a loud sing-song voice, using a weird language unlike anything I have ever heard in my life. The first time I heard this sheep and goat language I was on the hills at the back of Jericho. A goatherd had descended into the valley and was mounting the slope of an opposite hill when, turning round, he saw his goats had remained behind to devour a rich patch of scrub. Lifting his voice, he spoke to the goats in a language that Pan must have spoken on the mountains of Greece. It was uncanny because there was nothing human about it. The words were animal sounds arranged in a kind of order. No sooner had he spoken than an answering bleat shivered over the herd, and one or two of the animals turned their heads in his direction. But they did not obey him. The goatherd then called out one word and gave a laughing sort of whinny. Immediately a goat with a bell round his neck stopped eating and, leaving the herd, trotted down the hill, across the valley and up the opposite slope. The man, accompanied by this animal, walked on and disappeared round a ledge of rock. Very soon a panic spread among the herd. They forgot to eat. They looked up for the shepherd. He was not to be seen. They became conscious that the leader with the bell at his neck was no longer with them. From the distance came the strange laughing call of the shepherd, and at the sound of it the entire herd stampeded into the hollow and leapt up the hill after him.[1]

The Middle Eastern shepherd not only finds for his flock places where there is grass but in dry seasons actually feeds them by cutting down leafy trees.

All of this can become rather sentimental, with that sort of sentimentality which led the lords and ladies of the late-eighteenth-century French court to besport themselves as exqui-

[1] H. V. Morton, *In the Steps of the Master* (London 1934), pp. 154–155.

sitely dressed shepherds and shepherdesses, all the while forgetting the harsh realities of shepherd life. It must be admitted that
the shepherd-and-sheep imagery of the New Testament has often
led to sentimental interpretation in Christian devotion. It is
salutary to remember that in the Judaism of the time of Jesus the
shepherd was a despised person. In a rabbinic list of thieving and
cheating occupations the shepherd appears side by side with the
tax-collector. Like tax-collectors, shepherds were too untrust-
worthy to give evidence in courts of law. Presumably they had
too many temptations to steal in the long summer months,
wandering unsupervised over considerable distances in search of
feeding for their flocks. The rabbis found it hard to understand
how God could be spoken of in the psalms as 'my shepherd' when
shepherds were such despicable people.

Yet to call a king or any leader 'the shepherd of his people' was
not confined to Israel. In Sumerian royal inscriptions the king is
described as the shepherd appointed for them by the gods. In
Babylonian and Assyrian it is common to find the word 'shepherd' as a synonym for 'king', and the verb 'to pasture' in the
place of 'to rule'. (Latin can do the same: in the Vulgate Psalm
22/23, 'The Lord is my shepherd' appears as *Dominus regit me*.)
The ruler has the shepherd's function of gathering together those
who are scattered, of looking after them properly, and of caring
for the weak and the sick. Gods too can be spoken of in shepherd
terms. In Egyptian monuments we find the god or the king with a
shepherd's crook, for all the world like a bishop with his crozier.
The reason for all this is not far to seek: the societies formed by
sheep are like most human societies, stupid, affectionate, gregar-
ious, easily stampeded, wanting a leader and lost when none can
be found. And, as we have seen, to keep a flock is the most
primitive way in which man is in the image of God as the
shepherd of the world, the one who sets the world in order and
cares for it. The shepherd takes on the rôle of nature and providence for his sheep.

There is nothing casual about the way God is called 'shepherd'
in Israel. It is not just because all Middle Eastern gods were called
'shepherds', or because he is Israel's true king and all kings were
known as shepherds. In fact, God is called 'shepherd' surprisingly rarely in the Old Testament, even though many shepherding words are used of his activity towards his people. He is said to

'go before' his flock, to 'guide' it, to 'lead it to pasture', to 'feed' it, to 'carry the young in his bosom', to 'guard it with his staff', to whistle to the dispersed sheep and gather them together, to take them to places where they may rest beside running streams. Normally, these expressions are employed with reference to the exodus from Egypt or to the forthcoming exodus from Babylon – for these are the paradigms of God's activity on behalf of Israel. But in calling God 'shepherd' directly from time to time, the books of the Old Testament seem to be making some sort of polemical statement. It is *God* who is the Shepherd of Israel – *God* and no other. While we often come across political and military leaders being termed 'shepherds', especially in the oracles of Jeremiah, there is no instance of the Israelite king being so termed – in conformity with that characteristic ambiguity in the biblical tradition about the value of kingship as such. People never forgot that the real king of Israel was God. If they did eventually opt for a human king, that king was never divinised.

But there is a second sort of ambiguity here. There *is* a possible shepherd for Israel other than Yahweh, but this shepherd is wholly a future reality: he is the coming Messiah, the Son of David. The *locus classicus* here is Ezekiel 34 with its lament over the unfaithfulness and selfishness of those who have been shepherding Israel, and its promise that God himself would take on his own proper rôle of shepherding the flock.

> I myself, even I, will search for my sheep and will seek them out. As the shepherd seeks out his flock in the day when he is among his sheep that are scattered abroad, so will I seek out my sheep. I myself will feed my sheep and I will cause them to lie down, says the Lord Yahweh. (Ezek. 34.11–12, 15)

The new and greater David is also to enjoy this rôle:

> I will set up one shepherd over them, even my servant David; and he shall feed them, and he shall be their shepherd. And they shall know that I, Yahweh their God, am with them, and that they, the house of Israel, are my people, says the Lord Yahweh. And you my sheep, the sheep of my pasture, are men, and I am your God, says the Lord Yahweh. (Ezek. 34.23, 30–31)

Here we have a different sort of ambiguity about kingship: an unwillingness to speak of the future Messiah in terms of kingship, the preference for him of the title 'shepherd'. This image undergoes further modification in one of the last of the prophetic books, Zechariah, where the shepherd becomes a sufferer, as the servant does in Isaiah. This is the text which according to Mark and Matthew was on the lips of Jesus just before his passion:

> Awake, O sword, against the shepherd and against the man who is my fellow, says Yahweh Sabaoth; smite the shepherd and the sheep will be scattered. (Zech. 13.7)

Thus begins the purification of the people by God, a time of trial through which a remnant pass safely into the time of salvation.

In the New Testament Jesus refers to himself as this Shepherd-Messiah. Usually, there are overtones of the shepherd of Zechariah's prophecy whose death begins a time of salvation for his sheep. So we read of Jesus as 'the shepherd and guardian of our souls', as 'the great shepherd of the sheep;' and as 'the prince of shepherds' (literally, the arch-shepherd). Above all, the shepherd here is one who saves his flock. But from the early second century onwards, Jesus as shepherd is understood much more as one who *guides* his flock, especially by his teaching. (In this way the early Church took up Philo's allegorical interpretation of the shepherd language of the Old Testament.) We find this in an inscription associated with Bishop Abercius of Hieropolis in Phrygia, written during the reign of Marcus Aurelius.

> My name is Abercius. I am a pupil of the holy shepherd who feeds his flocks on the mountains and in the plains. His eyes are large, and everything comes within range of his vision.[2]

From the third century on there are many drawings and paintings in the Catacombs of Christ as the Good Shepherd, with the sheep on his shoulders perhaps, or again, surrounded by his flock, a youthful and beardless Jesus.

But in the New Testament it is not only Jesus who is called shepherd. The shepherd-function of Jesus towards his disciples is shared by certain of his followers. The letter to the Ephesians says that

> When [Jesus] ascended on high, he led captivity captive and gave gifts to men. And he gave apostles and some prophets and some

[2] J. Quasten, 'Abercius, Epitaph of', *New Catholic Encyclopaedia* I (New York 1967), pp. 18–19.

evangelists and some shepherds and teachers, for the perfecting of the saints unto the work of ministering, unto the building up of the body of Christ. (Eph. 4.8, 11–12)

In this text shepherds appear to be equivalent to teachers, in which case it would count as an early example of the shepherding activity of Jesus being thought of primarily in terms of his teaching. *Who* these shepherds were is apparent enough.

The presbyters among you, I exhort, as a fellow-presbyter and witness of the sufferings of Christ and as a partaker of the glory that shall be revealed: Shepherd the flock of God which is among you, exercising the oversight [anachronistically, 'bishoping'] not from constraint but willingly, not as lording it over the charge allotted to you but making yourselves examples to the flock. And when the arch-shepherd shall be manifested, you shall receive the crown of glory that fades not away. (1 Pet. 5.1–4)

Similarly in the Acts of the Apostles, Paul calls to himself the presbyters of the church of Ephesus and says to them:

Take heed to yourselves and to all the flock in which the Holy Spirit has made you overseers [*episkopoi*] to shepherd the church of God which he acquired with his own blood. (Acts 20.28)

In Matthew's Gospel, the parable of the lost sheep refers to the duty of the shepherds of the churches to seek out those of the flock who have strayed, even at the expense of the sheep who have not. It is not until we come to the charge of the risen Jesus to Peter in the Gospel of John ('Feed my lambs, feed my sheep' [John 21.15, 16]) that it is the whole Church which is in question.

The image of the Church as a flock has fallen on hard times. There are too many unacceptable connotations to the concept of being sheep for us to be quite happy with it. And yet there are perhaps aspects of the image which we forget, but which we could well make use of without feeling affronted. In the character of the sheep are virtues which belong to the heart of the gospel: gentleness, for instance, and non-violence. It is because the Church is the flock which has Jesus for its shepherd that it can afford to be non-violent. Wanting to 'be somebody', to assert our own reality, is a basic human need. This need is as fundamental as the need for food and drink and warmth and shelter, and if it goes unsatisfied, we are not really persons at all. The being somebody is called by the Bible *kabod*, 'glory', literally 'weight', the weight a person carries in the world, rather in the sense that we speak of the weight of someone's arguments in a discussion. But if Jesus is the glory of Israel, the way in which the Church matters, its 'weight', then he shows us a way of having glory which does not mean being aggressive and fighting for it. Here we may find a way of being somebody which does not consist in dominating others. Our glory now will consist of being disciples, followers, sheep of the Good Shepherd. We can afford not to take up arms to defend ourselves, whether literally or metaphorically, and depend instead on him.

On the other hand, none of us can simply be a sheep. All have to be shepherds, to carry out the shepherding function of Jesus (who in New Testament imagery is also, let us remember, a lamb as well as the shepherd of the flock). According to the will of the historical Jesus there is a shepherding function in the Church. Some people are so much involved in this ministry that they are known, quite simply, as pastors. Nevertheless, as in all forms of ministry in the Church, they bring to a point and make obvious what must be an aspect of each Christian life within the flock. All Christians have to be involved in the work of caring for others. It should not be assumed that this is a soft and sentimental affair. One of the principal functions of a shepherd is to guard his flock, and this may even mean destroying whatever threatens the flock with destruction. In early Christian art, Christ as Good Shepherd occurs not only in the midst of a gambolling flock or with the lost sheep on his shoulders, but also as the Davidic shepherd who smites the lion and the bear. He is *Christus Victor*, the one who overcomes the enemies of the flock, wins triumphantly through in the battle with the non-human forces that threaten his people, the chaos and disorder described in the Apocalypse as beasts coming up from the sea.

A balanced theology will accept that the flock is faced with demons. The Church's teaching accepts the common report that between God and man lies a realm which is neither man nor God. This is the area the New Testament speaks of as 'the principalities and powers': powers good in principle, in that they exist, but bad in practice, in the way they exist now and ensnare mankind. If

Jesus as the Good Shepherd has won a victory for man over this demonic realm, that victory has to be claimed by us. Claiming it will be one of the principal functions of the shepherd which we all have to exercise. We are told that we are fighting not against flesh and blood (that is to say, not against any of our fellow-men) but against the principalities and powers, the world-rulers of this present darkness, the spiritual hosts of wickedness in the air. These angelic powers express themselves in all those social forms and dogmas that constitute fate, rather than destiny, for so many people. We encounter them in the tyrants of the business world and the home, in inexorable laws of supply and demand, in the worship of the national spirit, in the traditions which become inflexible complacencies. They are those insidious authorities of unreason and passion which speak through propaganda and the mass-media, 'in the air'. To fight against the demons is to fight for a human world where economic and social and psychological laws do not lord it over us: for we have only one shepherd. It means to find new ways of breaking through inevitabilities, ways of 'turning the other cheek': that gesture which is successful because it is so totally unexpected, so sheep-like. To fight the demons as a shepherd is to fight for the reality of forgiveness, liberation from the grip of time past. It is to affirm the gospel message that new beginnings are possible because Christ is victor.[3]

---

[3] On the shepherd theme, see also G. Preston, O.P., *Hallowing the Time*, pp. 127–131.

6

Kingdom

IT is not so very long ago that any Catholic theologian who was engaged in mapping out New Testament ways of thinking about the Church would have turned very early on in his exposition to Jesus' parables in the Synoptic Gospels. These he would have expounded as having direct and immediate reference to the mystery of the Church. Nowadays, however, people tend to be much more cautious in their use of the parables for this purpose in particular. The reason for such caution lies in the fact that the great majority of the parables are introduced in the Gospels themselves as parables of the kingdom of God ('the kingdom of God is like ...'). At the time of writing there may well be too much hesitancy about applying to the Church anything that is said about the kingdom. In this chapter we shall investigate what, if anything, is the mutual connection of Church and kingdom, and so discover whether any of the Synoptic parables can be used to throw light on the Church in the midst of time.

First of all, a word about vocabulary. The Gospel of John carries one reference only to the kingdom of God, in the interview Nicodemus has with Jesus. On this occasion he is told that

> Unless a man is born anew from above he cannot see the kingdom of God ... a man cannot enter into the kingdom of God unless he is born from water and spirit. (John 3.3)

In the trial scene in the same Gospel there is an altercation between Jesus and Pilate about the kingdom, but this time it is the kingship of Jesus rather than that of God which is in question – although even here there may be less difference than is sometimes alleged. The overwhelming prominence of the theme of the kingdom in the Synoptics, on the other hand, is undisputed, and there can be no doubt that it represents an important element in the preaching of Jesus himself. As between Matthew on one side and Mark and Luke on the other we may be struck by a difference of terminology in the way the theme is expressed. It is Mark and

Luke who speak of 'the kingdom of God', whereas Matthew has 'the kingdom of heaven'. In fact these expressions are exactly equivalent, and differ only because of the differing religious backgrounds of the evangelists and the people for whom they are writing. Matthew is strictly Jewish, and writes for Jewish Christians. He prefers therefore to avoid the use of the world 'God' whenever possible, so as to steer clear of any danger of misusing the divine Name. Mark is a less strict Jew writing for Jews and Gentiles alike, while Luke is a Gentile writing for Gentiles. Both can afford to be less scrupulous in their use of language. So it is not the case that Matthew is concerned with, shall we say, what happens after people have died: 'heaven' for him is God, not a place where people go when their time on earth is over.

A second possible misunderstanding derives from the consideration that in English the word 'kingdom' immediately suggests an area of land ruled over by a king. It is in this way that we speak, for instance, of 'the United Kingdom of Great Britain and Northern Ireland'. But the Aramaic word that lies behind the Greek *basileia* (which also tends to suggest a territory) is a word (*malkuth*) which functions as an abstract noun, referring not to an area of land or a group of people over whom a king rules, but to the act of ruling itself. 'Sovereignty' or 'kingly rule' or 'reign' or 'kingship;' would be better translations than 'kingdom'. Very often modern scholars for this reason prefer to speak about the 'reign of God': a privileged mode of God's activity.

In what may be the earliest of the Gospels Jesus begins his preaching after his baptism in these terms:

> The time is fulfilled and the reign of God is at hand. Repent and believe in the Good News. (Mark 1.15)

In Matthew, too, Jesus begins his preaching: 'Repent, for the reign of heaven is at hand' (Matt. 3.2). Luke does not use the expression 'reign of God' here, but when Jesus preaches in the synagogue at Nazareth and claims that the prophecy of Isaiah is now fulfilled he has him spell out a little of what the reign of God involves.

> The Spirit of the Lord is upon me, because he has anointed me. He has sent me to preach good news to the poor, to proclaim release to the captives and recovery of sight to the blind, to set at liberty

those who are oppressed, to proclaim the acceptable year of the Lord. (Luke 4.18–19)

In this moment Jesus establishes his continuity with the Jewish thought of his time. On the one hand, Jews recognised the kingship of God over Israel, a kingship to which they had the duty of submitting by the faithful keeping of the Torah. On the other hand, and more importantly, they saw the reign of God in a futurist way – either as to occur at some datable moment of future time or, apocalyptically, as what would come into being when God brought historical time to an end and inaugurated a new creation. In either case the reign of God was precisely the reign of *God* and not the reign of Satan or of Palestine's imperial overlords. Both usages occur in the Synoptics, but the emphasis is overwhelmingly on the second sense. Something is happening in the life of Jesus, as his contemporaries encounter him, which has not happened before and which until then had only been an object of hope. 'The time is fulfilled. ... Today this scripture is fulfilled in your hearing'. Jesus proclaims that the kingdom of God is 'at hand', 'in your midst'. These Gospels do not show us a Jesus who preaches eternal truths, but a Jesus in whose person and in whose activities (especially his exorcisms and miracles) something new and decisive is occurring. Something has happened to time. John the Baptist stands at the dividing line of two eras, the time of the reign of Satan or of 'this world', and the time of the kingdom of God. What so many generations of people have looked forward to has now happened: it is now, and can now be experienced and entered into. Because something new and decisive has happened, people must change their lifestyle, they must 'repent'. But the something is gospel or 'good news'. Repentance is in virtue of good news, not of any threat which the reign of God raises against them.

This is not to say that nothing further is to be expected. On the contrary, the passion narratives of all the Synoptic Gospels make it quite clear that a further decisive intervention of God will come. At the Last Supper in Mark, Jesus says:

I will not drink again of the fruit of the vine until that day when I drink it new in the kingdom of God. (Mark 14.25)

and during his trial he tells the high priest:

You will see the Son of Man seated at the right hand of power and coming with the clouds of heaven. (Mark 14.62)

Matthew has Jesus say to his disciples at the Last Supper that he will drink the fruit of the vine anew with them 'in my Father's kingdom' (Matt. 26.29). Luke's sense of what is still to come is yet stronger. As the last meal of the Lord with his followers begins, Jesus remarks

I have longed and longed to eat this passover with you before I suffer, for I tell you that I shall never eat it again until it is fulfilled in the kingdom of God. (Luke 22.16)

At the first cup he says:

Take this and divide it among yourselves, for I tell you that from now on I shall not drink of the fruit of the vine until the reign of God comes. (Luke 22.18)

The new wine belongs to the new heaven and the new earth that the apocalyptic writers looked for, to the time beyond time, the time when God would bring time to a close. The kingdom of God, then, has both already come upon the people of Jesus' own generation, and yet is still to come 'with power' as the Gospels put it. This twofold aspect of the reign of God is there throughout the diverse linguistic forms of the rest of the New Testament. Jesus is Lord, Jesus reigns; and yet the Church prays, 'Come, Lord Jesus!'. It is this double character of the reign of God which makes any direct and unqualified identification of the Church with the kingdom impossible.

On the other hand, it is going too far to say that the Church and the reign of God are simply different. In Matthew's Gospel in particular, what came to pass in Jesus is identified with the group of persons whom Jesus formed around himself, his Church. The parable of the net, for instance, can only refer to the Church.

The kingdom of heaven is like a net which was thrown into the sea and gathered fish of every kind; when it was full, men drew it ashore and sat down and sorted the good into vessels but threw away the bad. So it will be at the close of the age. The angels will come out and separate the evil from the righteous, and throw them into the furnace of fire; there men will weep and gnash their teeth. (Matt. 13.47–50)

The parable of the wheat and the tares, again, is interpreted in such a way that

> the good seed means the sons of the kingdom; the weeds are the sons of the evil one; the harvest is the close of the age. (Matt. 13.39)

The scribes and Pharisees are said to 'close the kingdom' (Matt. 23.13) to others, while the scribe who is learned in the kingdom, and the doer and teacher in the kingdom, are officers of the Church. Tax-collectors and prostitutes enter the kingdom of the Church before the Jews.

Elsewhere in the New Testament the reign of God is not much mentioned, though it is certainly there, and not always in a futurist sense. What seems to have happened is that while Jesus preached the kingdom of God, the apostles preached Jesus as the risen and exalted one: Jesus is Lord. The reign of God in its present manifestation, in other words, came to be identified with Jesus himself. As Origen puts it, Jesus is himself the kingdom, *autobasileia*.[1] And so to be 'in Christ' is to be in the kingdom of God even though the reign of God has yet to come in its fullest manifestation, still to come with power.

In later theology there was a tendency to make an immediate identification of the Church with the reign of God. A good example of this comes in Augustine's *City of God*.

> The kingdom where the man keeps the commandments and the man who contemns the commandments is said to be is one, while the kingdom into which the man 'who says but does not do' will not enter is another. Where both sorts are, is the Church as it is now; but where the better sort are is the Church as it shall be hereafter, utterly exempt from evil. And so the Church now on earth is both the kingdom of Christ and the kingdom of heaven.

The thrones of the Book of the Apocalypse and those who sit upon them to whom judgment is given

> may not be understood of the last judgment, but by the thrones are meant the places of the rulers of the Church and the persons themselves by whom the Church is governed; and as for the judgment given them, it cannot be better explained than in these

[1] Origen, *Commentary on Matthew*, XIV. 7.

words, 'Whatsoever you bind on earth shall be bound in heaven, and whatsoever you loose on earth shall be loosed in heaven.'[2]

In the centuries after Augustine, the identification of Church and kingdom was taken much further, in one of two directions. Either the Church in the sense of ecclesiastics was taken as being the kingdom, with the pope as viceregent of God, a view we find in Gregory the Great. Or, alternatively, the Christianised Roman Empire in its recreated form became the kingdom, with the emperor exercising God's kingship on God's behalf. In these milieux it was believed that since the king reigns with Christ, he bestows with Christ and exercises with Christ all the powers which belong to Christ's kingdom. A reliable locus for discovering changing attitudes to the kingdom of God consists in the commentaries on the Lord's Prayer which crop up in every age of the Church. Shifts of emphasis of the clause 'Thy kingdom come' accurately reflect these attitudes. And yet the very fact that Christians have always had to pray, liturgically and personally, for the coming of the kingdom must surely have made it impossible for them to forget altogether that there was anything more to be hoped for.

And this is as it should be. For in other parables of the kingdom it is crystal clear that the kingdom is yet to be, for the reign of God is the goal towards which God is drawing the whole of creation. The parabolic form itself – a story with a beginning, a middle and an end – is a sufficient indication that things both are happening and will happen in the future. The phrase that introduces most of the parables is usually translated 'The kingdom of God is like'. But this is misleading. The kingdom of God is not like a sower who went forth to sow his seed, nor a king who made a great supper for his son. Rather, it is like the *story* of both of these. 'It is with the kingdom of God as it is with a king who made a great supper. . . .' and so forth. The unfolding of the story is the unfolding of the history of the reign of God. The coming of the kingdom in power is signified in all those parables where the story element predominates. It is the *dénouement* of the story, the marriage feast or banquet God has prepared, the seed that grows finally into a great tree. So while the kingdom is already in

[2] Augustine, *City of God*, XX. 9, with internal citations of Matt. 23.3 and 18.18.

existence and God is already asserting his sovereignty, the full unfolding of its power belongs to the future.

Nevertheless, according to the closing words of the First Gospel, all authority has been given to Christ in heaven and on earth. As a result of God's gift to him of this authority, Jesus tells his disciples to

> go, therefore, and make disciples of all nations, baptising them in the name of the Father and of the Son and of the Holy Spirit, teaching them to observe all things that I have commanded you; and lo, I am with you always, to the close of the age. (Matt. 28.19–20)

So too Paul can say that Christians have been

> qualified to share in the inheritance of the saints in light. God has delivered us from the dominion of darkness and transferred us to the kingdom of his beloved Son, in whom we have redemption, the forgiveness of sins. (Col. 1.12–14)

Though the Church as an object of present experience is not the reign of God in Christ, yet even now the Church is the milieu in which that reign is exercised and acknowledged, the community in which the lordship of Christ is confessed and proclaimed, albeit imperfectly and with compromises. Already Christ is king, and

> he must reign until he has put all his enemies under his feet; and the last enemy to be destroyed is death. (1 Cor. 15.25)

The Church is the sphere in which Christ is now militant, the king of those who fight for him and with him against the principalities and powers. But, we must never forget,

> then comes the end, when Christ delivers up the kingdom to God the Father after destroying every rule and every authority and power. When all things are made subject to him then the Son himself will also be made subject to him [God] who put all things under him, that God may be all in all. (1 Cor. 15.24, 28)

The time of the Church is the in-between time, the time when Christ is king and working to overthrow all the enemies of God. God's rule in the full sense is a characteristic of the age to come, the age for which the Church still waits as it waited in the time of

Paul. Yet it is a time that can already be experienced in the life of the Church. The Letter to the Hebrews speaks of Christians as those who 'have tasted the powers of the age to come' (Heb. 6.5). In line with other epistles, this refers, almost certainly, to the present experience of the Holy Spirit who is at work in the Church through the charisms he distributes in the whole body. In this time between the resurrection of Jesus and the great and general resurrection, God's absolute rule is being prepared for *by* the Church (especially in its work of preaching and exorcism) and *in* the Church (with its real, though limited, experience of the joy and peace of the last time, the messianic kingdom). The resurrection of Jesus is itself an irruption of the last day into the present age. The great and general resurrection follows on the resurrection of Jesus as a thunderclap follows a flash of lightning: no one can be sure how long the thunder will take to arrive, though arrive it will. The purpose of the present reign of Christ – confessed, proclaimed, and exercised in and through the Church – is the absolute reign of God, when Christ himself will be subject to God. Then God will be all in all: this is Christian panentheism, the affirmation of the total and visible presence of the reign of God which is to come.

And so the Church, insofar as it lives by the resurrection of Christ, being born a second time from the waters of the font, is already a reality of the age to come. As the body of Christ it has been raised from the dead and glorified: 'You have died and your life is hid with Christ in God' (Col. 3.3)

God who is rich in mercy, out of the great love with which he loved us, even when we were dead through our trespasses, has made us alive together with Christ, and raised us up with him, and made us sit with him in the heavenly places in Christ Jesus. (Eph. 2.4–6)

But the Church is still 'on the way': God has acted thus so that

in the coming ages he might show the immeasurable riches of his grace in kindness towards us in Christ Jesus (Eph. 2.7)

and:

when Christ who is our life appears, then we also will appear with him in glory. (Col. 3.4)

Unless the pilgrim nature of the Church is asserted alongside its eschatological reality, we shall miss out, and disastrously so, on the Church's need for forgiveness, something for which we also pray in the Lord's Prayer.

The Church as we experience it here and now is, despite spots and wrinkles and corruption, not just a negative pointer to the coming kingdom: it is not simply evidence that the reign of God has not yet fully arrived. The Church here and now carries about in the bodies of its members the dying of Jesus: it is a Church of the cross. But it does so in order that the life of Jesus also may be made manifest in our mortal bodies: it is a Church of glory. It already has the keys of the kingdom of heaven and the promise that the gates of hell shall not prevail against it. It will endure until the kingdom of God comes in power and then be not destroyed but transfigured: it will *appear* with Christ in glory. And so we have that earliest of all Christian eucharistic prayers, which we meet with in the *Didache*, a document of the early second century:

> Lord, remember your Church, to deliver it from all evil and make it perfect in your love, to gather it together from the four winds into your kingdom which you have prepared for it, this Church which you have hallowed.[3]

And again:

> As this broken bread was scattered upon the mountains but was brought together from the ends of the earth into your kingdom, for yours is the glory and the power through Jesus Christ for ever.[4]

The destiny of the Church, then, is not to disappear but to be changed, to achieve its perfection in love. This is what we pray for in the second eucharistic prayer of the Roman rite:

> Lord remember your Church scattered throughout the world, to make it perfect in charity.

In the Book of the Apocalypse, when the New Jerusalem has come down out of heaven from God, his servants continue to 'serve him as priests' (20.6), and 'they shall reign with him for

---

[3] *Didache*, X. 5.
[4] *Ibid.*, IX. 4.

ever and ever' (22.5). The reign which they exercise at present in the interim period becomes an eternal reign. It is obvious that much of what is connoted by kingship must fall away here. There is no longer any battling to be done, no one to rule over. But the most important aspect of this kingship – its sovereign freedom – continues. The glorified members of the Church now enjoy the freedom of God himself, no longer being bound by any 'musts' or 'oughts' or 'shoulds'. Although their company is still the Church, the assembly summoned and convoked by God through Christ in the Holy Spirit, it is no longer described in the language of 'Church'. Instead, it is the bride of the Lamb, the holy city, the new Jerusalem. It is now altogether the kingdom of God, the sphere of his reign and sovereignty. Indeed this sphere is now co-terminous with the whole of creation. It is the great banquet, the marriage supper, the full harvest, the mature tree of the Gospel parables, the ending of their story.

The time of the Church is a time of God's mercy and grace, a time when the gospel can be preached and the numbers made up for the definitive reign of God. It is a time when the Church has the duty of preaching the gospel, calling men to repentance in the light of the coming kingdom. In this interim period, the kingdom of God is far from distant. It is ever accessible. The stuff of the parables is the stuff of ordinary everyday events, precisely because the kingdom is to be found in the midst of everyday reality, not only at specially favoured times and places. The Church lives as those for whom the kingdom is truly a present reality, living free as befits those reborn free, reborn to be kings.

7

The Poor of the Lord

IT was not only by parables that Jesus proclaimed God's rule to be at hand. His miracles and exorcisms did so as well, being enacted parables, instantiations of the kingdom. But then there is also the preaching of Jesus in non-parabolic form, and more especially that epitome of the kingdom and the qualities necessary for those belonging thereto which we call 'the Beatitudes'. The Beatitudes have come down to us in two versions, of which the more familiar is Matthew's, set rather solemnly as this is at the beginning of the Sermon on the Mount.

> And seeing the multitudes, Jesus went up into a mountain; and when he had sat down, his disciples came to him and he opened his mouth and taught them. (Matt. 5.1)

All of these expressions are designed to emphasise the solemnity of the occasion. It is *ex cathedra* teaching, not the sort of teaching a rabbi would give as he walked down country roads or strolled along in city squares. The teaching of the Sermon on the Mount is not chance teaching: it is given with forethought and deliberation; it is official. To say that Jesus 'opened his mouth', for instance, is to say a good deal more than that he began to speak. It suggests that what is to come is of the greatest importance. The very tense of the verb 'taught' in the Greek shows that the Beatitudes are a summary of what Jesus continually and consistently gave to his disciples. The Sermon on the Mount is the essence of his teaching throughout his ministry; and the Beatitudes are the essence of that. The other version of the Beatitudes comes to us in Luke's Gospel, once again at the beginning of a sermon by Jesus, the so-called 'Sermon on the Plain'. While there is obviously a common original, the two forms are different. Matthew's is very much a character sketch of the citizens of the kingdom, a description of what people would be like if they really lived as those who believe the kingdom to be at hand. In Luke, however, Jesus addresses a particular group of people, the disciples, the nucleus of the Church.

> And he lifted up his eyes on his disciples and said, 'Blessed are you'. (Luke 6.20)

The Sermon on the Plain is a description of life in the new Israel, which is life in the kingdom of God, but it is a description, more particularly, of the life of nameable individuals. These individuals are there in front of Jesus and in them he sees all those who will come to believe in him.

As in Matthew's version, there is a contrast between the way things are now and the way things are going to be when the promise of the kingdom has been fulfilled. But the Beatitudes assume the present reality of the kingdom, albeit in germ. They confirm the life that the disciples are already leading, a life which, on the face of things, is a pretty wretched one. By a misunderstanding, the Beatitudes have since been used to underwrite the *status quo*. Those words of Jesus, 'Blessed are the poor in spirit' (Matthew) or 'Blessed are you poor' (Luke), can be used as an excuse for doing nothing to alleviate the chronic distress of the poor. But Jesus is not really suggesting that wretchedness of various sorts guarantees eternal happiness. The Beatitudes can only be understood in the light of the kingdom of God which is breaking in. If a banquet has been prepared for anyone who wants to share it, then a hungry man is better off than a man who has just finished a square meal. He is in a position to enjoy the feast whereas the man who has recently eaten will only be able to toy with his food. The greater the need people have for the kingdom, the more will they be able to appreciate it. Matthew tries to show this by spiritualising the Beatitudes: Blessed are the poor *in spirit*. He seems to make Jesus concerned exclusively with people's interior dispositions, their general attitude and approach to life. It might follow from this that if we want to gain the blessings of the kingdom then we must go in for soul-culture, making ourselves poor in spirit in a purely interior sense. Luke's version, probably closer to the original, avoids the danger of this misunderstanding. He makes the recipients of the words of Jesus people whose lives are obviously poor, and he underlines his point by putting in a series of woes concerning people whose lives are visibly and observably of the other sort.

Being poor, hungry, sorrowful, hated and despised – all of these can be summed up in the first term: poverty. The Greek word used by Matthew and Luke is *ptōchos*, meaning not mildly impoverished (for that there was another word, *penes*) but completely destitute, a beggar, one who has to rely totally on the kindness of other people, a person who has nothing at all. Interestingly, Tertullian translates the word *mendici*, beggars, in contradistinction to the Vulgate *pauperes*. People who were poor in this sense were always despised in the Greek world as in the Jewish. Plato in the *Laws* says that

> there shall be no beggar in our state, and if anyone attempts to beg he shall be driven across the border by the country stewards in order that the land may be wholly purged of such a creature.[1]

In the Gospels, the widow woman who put two farthings in the temple treasury is described by this word, as is Lazarus in the parable, set down each day at the door of the rich man's house to beg and be glad of the scraps of food thrown to the dogs under the table. In the Letter of James we meet with such a man and see the sort of treatment he might get even from Christians at times:

> If a man with gold rings and in fine clothing comes into your assembly, and a poor man in shabby clothing also comes in, and you pay attention to the one in fine clothing and say 'Sit here, please' while you say to the poor man 'Stand there' or 'Sit at my feet', have you not made distinctions amongst yourselves and become judges with evil thoughts? (James 2.2–4)

And in the parable of the Great Banquet it is the poor in this sense, vagrants, who are invited in from the highways and byways. It is these poor whom Jesus now calls happy and fortunate above all men.

The witnesses converge on this point. As James has it:

> Listen, my beloved brethren. Was not God chosen those who are poor in the world to be rich in faith and heirs of the kingdom which he has promised to those who love him? (James 2.5)

[1] Plato, *Laws*, XI. 936.

Paul too has a strong sense of the poverty of the first Christians. Writing to the church at Corinth he says:

> Consider your call, brethren. Not many of you were wise according to worldly standards, not many were powerful, not many were of noble birth, but God chose what is foolish in the world to shame the wise, God chose what is weak in the world to shame the strong, God chose what is low and despised in the world, even things that are not, to bring to nothing things that are, so that no human being might boast in the presence of God. (1 Cor. 1.26–29)

Poverty here is real and observable, even though it has gone beyond the purely economic. In Paul's understanding of the term, the poor would be those in any way deprived – materially, physically, mentally, spiritually, sexually, relationally. In this, Paul is in continuity with the Old Testament where the *anawim* correspond to the *ptōchoi* of the New. The *anawim* were originally those who, being poor, had no prestige nor influence, and so stood to lose in law where judges were all too often open to the bribes of the rich or the pressure of the influential. Such people were typified by Uriah the Hittite whose wife was stolen by King David and himself then quietly put out of the way, or by Naboth, whose vineyard was taken from him by the king. These were the wretched of the earth, oppressed, downtrodden, pushed to the wall by the pressures of the society in which they lived, people with no hope of redress. Despite everything, such people could retain their integrity and their trust in God. They could accept humiliation with God rather than force their way in the world by entering the competitive society of their day on its own corrupt terms. In other words, they could live their poverty in such a way that they became an alternative society carrying in itself the germs of destruction of the dominant society. To do this was to run counter to accepted ideas of what constituted happiness and the blessing of God. In the Old Testament, wealth is frequently taken to indicate that a man is divinely blessed, whilst poverty can be taken as a sign of alienation from God. With the work of the prophets in particular, however, it was realised that this picture simply did not stand up to serious examination. To see what God really thought of riches you only had to look at the people he gave them to, people who, in order to make or keep their wealth, were prepared to make any number of compromises in the moral order and, as likely as not, to be callous towards those who were not themselves wealthy. As James goes on,

> Is it not the rich who oppress you? Is it not they who drag you into the court? Is it not they who blaspheme the honourable name which was invoked upon you? ... Come now, you rich, weep and howl for the miseries that are coming upon you. Your riches have rotted and your garments are moth-eaten. Your gold and silver have rusted, and their rust will be evidence against you and will eat up your flesh like fire. You have laid up a burning fire as treasure for the last days. Behold, the wages of the labourers who mowed your fields, which you kept back by fraud, cry out against you; and the cries of the harvesters have reached the ears of the Lord of hosts. You have lived on the earth in luxury and pleasure; you have fattened your hearts in a day of slaughter. You have condemned, you have killed the righteous man; he does not resist you. (James 2.6–7; 5.1–6)

In the Apocalypse too there is a lament by the kings and merchants of the earth, all shipmasters and seafaring men, those who traded in the wealth of Babylon the Great – the Roman Empire – over its destruction. Once again, it is the sense of the compromises people make in order to make money that accounts for the feeling that the rich cannot be blessed by God. The communal penury of Israel in exile made poverty a religious term: the poor were those who had remained with God. The experience was reinforced in the time of the Maccabees. At that time, those who stayed faithful to the law and traditions of the Jews suffered great hardship, while those who went along with the Hellenising policies of Antiochus Epiphanes did well for themselves. So it was that the poor became the faithful, those who trusted in God to save them. They resembled the slaves in Egypt who somehow managed to remain faithful despite frequent lapses from faith and were in the end saved from actual slavery in what was for the Old Testament the paradigm case of God's intervention, the exodus.

In neither Testament is there a denial of the worth of this world's good things, or any failure to desire them. The Jewish-Christian tradition in its classical (biblical) expression never attempted to deny that the world was God's good creation and

72

made for man. The longing for a time of peace and prosperity when every man would sit under his own vine and under his own fig-tree was only a little less materialistic than the Christian hope for the resurrection from the dead. But there were the hard facts of experience to prove that it was extremely difficult to be both prosperous and faithful. Whenever Israel was well-to-do it almost inevitably lost its faith in God, just as in the New Testament it seemed a rule that a wealthy church like the church in Laodicea would be a church poor in faith:

> You say, I am rich, I have prospered, and I need nothing; not knowing that you are wretched, pitiable, poor, blind and naked. Therefore I counsel you to buy from me gold refined by fire that you may be rich, and white garments to clothe you and keep the shame of your nakedness from being seen, and salve to anoint your eyes that you may see. (Apoc. 3.17–18)

And so there grows up in Israel and in the Church the sense that while material gifts are gifts of God, the deprivation of them may be the necessary means to the rediscovery of God. God can only be loved for himself when the temptation to worship the gifts and not the Giver is (perhaps forcibly) removed. The gifts can get in the way of the Giver. The gifts can certainly get in the way of one's neighbour, for riches are always to some degree divisive. The legend of the halcyon days of the Jerusalem church presents this in typical fashion. The unity of heart and mind of the first Christians was translated then into material terms:

> Now the company of those who believed were of one heart and soul, and no one said that any of the things which he possessed was his own, but they had everything in common. (Acts 4.32)

Ananias and Sapphira by refusing to enter wholeheartedly into this community of goods cut themselves off from the life of the Church and indeed from life itself.

The poverty of the early Church – including the fact that Christians were despised and persecuted – made faith a genuine possibility. But with the passage of time and the increasing respectability of the Church, a real threat to faith emerged. In the face of an increasingly acclimatised Church, many people took to the desert to preserve the possibility of faith, and equally many people undertook voluntary poverty with the same end in view.

This was not meant to be a denial of created goodness, though with some sectarian groups it took this form. Rather, it sprang from a sense that the time for wealth was not yet. Until the kingdom of God came in power, wealth was too dangerous for faith. The same thing had happened in the last centuries of Judaism before Jesus, and especially at Qumran. Josephus describes the Essenes in these terms:

> Contemning wealth, they admired a life lived in common. No man is richer than another man because it is a law that each one who enters the sect then surrenders his fortune to the community. All that is owned is owned in common; each one possesses a single patrimony.[2]

Neither here nor in the Jerusalem church was there poverty in the fashion of the Beatitudes. At Qumran (if without further ado we may identify the Essenes with that Dead Sea community), Josephus explicitly says that 'No one suffers the misery of poverty or enjoys the splendour of wealth'. In the Jerusalem church, too, 'there was not a needy person among them' (Acts 4.34). But equally, wealth as a divisive force was removed. The flight to the desert in Christianity's early centuries sometimes put the emphasis on genuine absence of any possessions as a necessary precondition for true faith in God, and sometimes on poverty as what was later to be called *vita sine proprio*, 'life without anything of one's own'.

There has always been an ambiguity in the tradition about which model to follow here. Should it be that of Christ the workman of Nazareth? Or Christ the wandering preacher, dependent on the generosity of well-to-do ladies, though often enough in real need as well? Or that of the Fourth Gospel where the followers of Jesus have a common purse, as befits those who have been given the new commandment to love one another? Or again, that of the Jerusalem church where there was not a needy man amongst them, even though they had all things in common? Paul seems to have opted for the first approach, though he insisted that he had the right to live on the alms of those to whom he ministered: the style of poverty he adopted voluntarily was chosen primarily for apologetic motives. Monasticism of the

---

[2] Josephus, *Jewish Wars*, II. viii, 3.

Benedictine variety, on the other hand, opted for the Jerusalem church model, attempting to live now as they did then. The Franciscan movement developed a mystique of poverty as part of the *imitatio Christi*. Once poverty had become institutionalised, then much of what we have been talking about so far became trivialised. It seems fairly meaningless for most (though not all) religious orders to be called poor. And yet poverty is so fundamental to the Church that if it is trivialised in one of its manifestations, it will appear in a purer form elsewhere. Again and again in the history of the Church, a new style of religious life has come into being and by its very existence condemned the failure in poverty of older forms of religious life.

In these closing years of the twentieth century poverty has taken on a quite new meaning. We have become aware of the colossal ramifications of wealth and poverty in the one world, with rich countries getting richer and poor countries getting poorer. It is true that in the Western world there are considerable numbers of people who have not got in on the act. Nevertheless their poverty is as nothing compared with the grinding poverty of peoples in Africa, Asia and Latin America. Any poverty in the Church which is going to measure up to the universal significance of the cross and resurrection must also measure up to these dimensions of world poverty. In this perspective, it seems obscene to talk about the poverty of most of our religious orders however good and Christian a thing it may be to live *sine proprio* – not making a distinction between our possessions and those of the nearest people to hand. The problem of whether Christians should live simply *sine proprio* or in real poverty as well is found today in a rather different form. Many Christians evidently wish to form alternative societies, following through the same inspiration that animated the founders of the traditional Orders, with sharing of goods and life in common. On the other hand, it can be argued that Christians are called to insecurity and discomfort and material impotence. In this perspective, it would be a betrayal of this call to attempt to work within the structures of this world as it now is. The Church, unlike secular society, lives by the End.

8

Bride of Christ

ONE of the more obviously metaphorical ways of talking about Israel which the Church used for talking about itself was that of *bride*, an image rooted in the Old Testament and developed in the New Testament and by the Fathers. The image of the Church as bride is hard for us to grasp properly, in that we are always trying to find some way of reducing its metaphorical and imaginative force. When the Church is described as a temple it is easy enough to find the points of comparison between a temple in the literal sense and the Church that we are. The image of the temple can be made to function as though it were a Homeric simile, detail after detail after detail. Mediaeval sermons for the consecrating of a church building would be a good illustration of this. In this case, we look for truth by a process of deduction. We abstract common features from temple and Church and find the truth of the image of the Church as temple in the end-product, in what we have deduced. The image of the temple lies, so to speak, alongside the independently accessible reality of the Church. The image supports and illustrates the truth of the thing itself. But if we are to enter into the thought-world of the Bible and the Fathers we should realise how time-conditioned this way of using an image is. For the ancient world, or that part of it we are concerned with, an image was not an illustration of some reality to which one had access independently of all images. An image was the reality itself expressed and represented. Perhaps the nearest approach we can make to this is by way of the relationship between words and thought. Words are not the clothing of thoughts. They do not form one possible expression of a thought that could have been expressed in quite different words. The words simply *are* the expression of the thought that has been expressed. In the fullest sense the words contain what they express. In the ancient world it would be true to say this also of the image, *eikōn*, of some reality.

In biblical thinking, the *eikōn* is not some functional representation of a reality already known, but an epiphany or manifestation of that reality. It shares in the being of the reality itself. The *eikōn* is not something you think up outside of the reality which it images; rather, it is the reality itself in one of its modes of being. Ancient thought did not build up images of reality. All reality was image-reality. This was so whether the image took the form of a person, of some plastic object, of a significant word or of a historical event. Somewhat similarly, in modern phenomenology, we grasp the essence of things not in the first place by way of abstraction from the universal to the particular concrete given, but by means of entering more and more deeply into the particular itself. The image is a way in which something is, rather than a mental construct made by human beings from outside the reality in question. So too for the Bible which speaks so often in images. These images, the parables of Jesus for instance, are not changeable clothing for some teaching which could be expressed in their absence. This sort of imagery is not a stylistic device. In speaking in parables Jesus was not accommodating himself to the simple minds of his hearers (though because of the way he taught in parables he was certainly more intelligible than he would have been had he taught in abstract fashion). Instead, he was renewing the revelatory character of being and re-establishing the symbolic significance of the world. For the Bible, creation is a word of God. God speaks things. Creatures are parables. And the parabolic language of Jesus, in line with the parabolic language of so much of the Old Testament, restores the voice of creation.

All this has to be born in mind when we are examining the image of the Church as bride of Christ. The temptation is to analyse the image in such a way that we build up a number of points of resemblance. But this makes the image allegorical rather than an image containing the reality to which it points. Interpretation of this sort has to be approached as one would approach the central image of a poem. The object of literary criticism, in providing background, cross-references and the like, can only be the poetic image itself in its own life. The point of it all is to let the image be. And so for this image of the Church as bride. The work of clearing the ground is there so that the image can be entered imaginatively, in the way appropriate to such an image.

The Church as woman, whether as girl or bride or wife or mother or widow, is an image rooted in the Old Testament and finding new life in the New. The Church as woman is more basic than the Church as bride. Practically all the books of the New Testament reflect it in some form. Interestingly enough, in the New Testament a bride is often referred to as *gunē*, a wife. The angel who appears to Joseph calls Mary his 'wife', even though it is only later that he takes his 'wife' to himself. In the Book of Revelation the great multitude in heaven says that 'the marriage of the Lamb has come and his wife has made herself ready' (Apoc. 19.7) even though the marriage has not in fact taken place at all. And one of the angels says to the seer, 'Come hither, and I will show you the bride, the wife of the Lamb' (Apoc. 21.9). This usage reflects the ordinary customs in Palestine at the time. According to Jewish law at this period, the bridegroom acquired his bride when they were betrothed. From the betrothal onwards he had full husband's rights over her, so much so that he could divorce her even though they had not strictly speaking been married yet. This is what lies in the background of the story of Joseph and Mary. It is important for the use of the image of the Church as bride to Christ as bridegroom, for in this use it is often hard to see whether what is in question is the Church's present situation or the Church of the eschatological fulfilment. Given this relationship between betrothal and marriage, it can be both. Although the marriage of the Lamb with the Church may not yet have come, the marriage supper being identified with the messianic banquet at the end of time, the Church can still be the wife of the Lamb in that they are betrothed even while the marriage is not yet fully celebrated. The Church can have already the obligations of a wife towards her husband, and Christ can already cherish the Church as a husband does his wife.

The principal part of the marriage ritual in Palestine was like those ceremonies described in the parables of Jesus in the Synoptics, such as the parable of the wife and foolish girls in Matthew 25. There are jollifications both in the house of the bridegroom and in that of the bride, but it is the bridegroom's house which is really important. When the bridegroom is ready he goes with his friends to the bride's house and takes her back to his own home, where the marriage banquet and marriage-bed are prepared. And so the picture is of the Messiah coming from his Father's home to take his bride back there for the marriage. By the stage the parable has reached in Matthew, it is allegorical: a point-by-point allegory of the coming of Jesus from heaven at the end of time to take the bride – the Church – he had already betrothed to himself at his first coming.

One important person in marriages who does not figure in this parable but appears elsewhere in the New Testament is that of the 'friend of the bridegroom', the 'best man' as we would call him. The best man usually acted as go-between at various stages in the courtship, and figured prominently in the cere- mony of betrothal. When the wedding took place he went with the bridegroom to the bride's house, and saw to the proper ordering of the procession back. He was responsible for the sexual propriety of the whole business. In the Fourth Gospel John the Baptist says:

> He who has the bride is the bridegroom but the friend of the bridegroom, who stands and hears him, rejoices greatly because of the bridegroom's voice. (John 3.29)

The reference is almost certainly to the voice of the bridegroom calling from the marriage-bed as soon as the marriage has been consummated, so that the best man can come and take pos- session of the *signum virginitatis*. So John is saying that, as the Lord's precursor, he is entirely happy to know that Christ has consummated the bridal relationship of God with the people, that he is glad, not jealous, at the success of Jesus.

But where does this image of a marriage relationship between God and the people, Messiah and the messianic community, originally come from? As far as God and the people are con- cerned, it is easy enough to say. From the time of Hosea onwards, the Old Testament uses the metaphor of the marriage of the Lord and Israel to express the covenant relationship of God to his people. Probably, covenant and marriage formulae had the same linguistic structure. Once the metaphor was accepted, it could be developed in the direction of, for example, betrothal. The time of Israel in the desert could be described as the time of the courtship of God and Israel; or the image of the joy of the bridegroom could be used for the time of salvation.

As a young man marries a virgin, so shall he who builds you marry you; and with the joy of the bridegroom over the bride, so shall your God rejoice over you. (Isa. 62.5)

In later Judaism, this imagery became very common, and the Song of Songs entered the official canon of Scripture drawn up at the Synod of Jamnia (in the year 90 in the Common Era) on the basis of its allegorical interpretation as a love-song between Israel and her God. With the increasing tendency in later Judaism to look for a decisive intervention of God in the future, a golden age still to come, the marriage imagery of God and Israel developed in the direction of making Israel's engagement not simply the Sinai period but the whole of the present age. This age, it was said, is the betrothal. The wedding will be in the days of the Messiah. Not that Jewish writers actually suggested that the Messiah himself would be the bridegroom: the marriage is between Israel and *God*. This is very different from the Gospels, where it is Jesus himself as Messiah who is bridegroom to the community which is his bride. However, it is only fair to mention the view of some critics, that while Jesus would have spoken of the times in which he was living, the messianic times, as the time of the marriage of Israel, it was the later Church who thought of him as bridegroom to the people of God as bride.

Can the sons of the bridechamber mourn as long as the bridegroom is with them? But the days will come when the bridegroom will be taken away from them, and then they will fast. (Matt. 9.15)

Outside the Synoptic Gospels there is a much more definite use of the image of Christ and the Church as bridegroom and bride. In the Second Letter to the Corinthians, for example, Paul says to the Christians in Corinth:

I am jealous over you with a jealousy of God; for I espoused you to one husband, that I present you as a pure virgin to Christ. But I fear lest by any means, as the serpent beguiled Eve in his craftiness, your thoughts should be corrupted from the purity and simplicity which is toward Christ. (2 Cor. 11.2-3)

Paul sees himself here as the best man, the marriage-arranger whose task it is to make man and woman belong definitively to each other. He looks forward to the eschatological marriage, the time when Christ will come as bridegroom to take his bride to himself. He is anxious that the bride will keep herself pure for her bridegroom, and impurity here means contamination by false doctrine, as the rest of the epistle shows. Purity of faith is compared here with purity of body: the Church will be a virgin at her marriage if she keeps faith with the one to whom she is betrothed. Keeping faith in Christ is in close relationship with keeping the faith about Christ, the faith Paul had taught the Corinthian Christians. The Church's task is to keep this faith inviolate.

In the Letter to the Ephesians, the thrust of the image changes somewhat. It becomes an illustration of marriage between Christians rather than something invoked in its own right. From its origins as a comparison with how things should stand between husband and wife, the author moves to perhaps the most profound use of the bride–bridegroom image in the entire New Testament.

> Wives, be in subjection to your own husbands as to the Lord. For the husband is the head of the wife, as Christ also is the head of the Church, the saviour of the body. But as the Church is subject to Christ, so the wives also to their husbands, in everything. Husbands, love your wives, as Christ also loved the Church and gave himself up for it, that he might sanctify it, having cleansed it by the bath of water with the word, that he might present the Church to himself a glorious Church, not having spot or wrinkle or any such thing, but that it should be holy and without blemish. (Eph. 5.22–27)

Here the custom of a pre-marriage ritual bath for the bride, Greek in origin but known also in Judaism, is being compared with baptism. Some commentators think that the writer to the Ephesians sees the Church as already cleansed by Christ, so that it is spotless; others, more weighty, hold that it is in process of purification, a process founded on the fact that Christ gave himself up for it. So much in the rest of the letter makes it clear that the author knew the Church to be quite certainly *not* spotless. But what matters for his present purpose is Christ's self-gift for the Church, and so he goes on:

> Even so, husbands ought also to love their wives, as their own bodies. He who loves his wife, loves himself, for no man ever hates his own flesh, but nourishes it and cherishes it even as Christ also nourishes and cherishes the Church, because we are members of his body. (Eph. 5.28–30)

Some manuscripts, not the best, add here the words 'of his flesh and of his bones', an indirect quotation from the Genesis account of God bringing to Adam the woman he has formed from Adam's rib, and Adam saying 'At last! Bone of my bone, and flesh of my flesh!' (Gen. 2.23). Despite its poor support in the manuscript tradition, there can be no doubt that this makes explicit what the whole passage implies in going on to quote the subsequent verse from the Genesis story: 'For this cause shall a man leave his father and mother and shall cleave to his wife, and the two shall become one flesh. This mystery is great; but I speak in regard of Christ and of the Church' (Eph. 5.31–32). The mystery in question is the mystery of male and female as such, inscribed into the very order of creation and already eloquent. What it is meant to be eloquent of, the author suggests, is the relationship between Christ and the Church, a relationship which is and should be expressed in the marriage of particular people in the Lord.

The eschatological reference of the image of the Church as bride of the Messiah finds its fullest expression in the Book of Revelation. There the multitude in heaven say:

> Alleluia! The Lord our God, the Almighty, reigns. Let us rejoice and be exceeding glad, and let us give glory to him, for the marriage of the Lamb has come, and his wife has made herself ready. And it was given to her that she should array herself in fine linen, bright and pure, for the fine linen is the righteous acts of the saints. (Apoc. 19.6–8)

The seer of the Apocalypse is told, accordingly:

> Write, Blessed are those who are invited to the marriage-supper of the Lamb. (Apoc. 19.9)

words used in the invitation to holy communion in the Roman liturgy. The author sees, in fact, the holy city, new Jerusalem, coming down out of heaven from God, made ready as a bride adorned for her husband. (Apoc. 21.2)

And the angel who shows him this city calls it 'the bride, the wife of the Lamb' (Apoc. 21.9). It is the Spirit and the bride who say 'Come!' at the end of the Apocalypse. Here too, as in the passage from Ephesians, there is an appeal to the order of creation as such. John sees a new heaven and a new earth, that is to say, a new creation, and in this new creation as at the first creation there is a man and his bride. The marriage of Christ and the Church is the goal to which all creation is moving, the end-result for which it was all planned.

So the image of the bride holds together the beginning and the end, and the time between, the eschatological pause. In the full scriptural perspective, the very existence of man and woman precisely as man and woman, is a great mystery, one of those hidden divine decrees which is revealed in a veiled manner in the course of time. The order of creation, and especially the mutuality in their sexuality of man and woman, is already part of the activity of God for us and for our salvation. It is a 'mighty word' of the God who is faithful, for though he may make all things new he is also true to himself and consistent in what he does. The unfolding of God's plan for man's salvation is the unfolding of what is built into the created order as such. If, as the New Testament comes to maintain, this is all 'in Christ' and 'for Christ', through whom all things were made, and without whom nothing was made, then it could fairly have been expected that one of the images for the consummation of all things in Christ that the Bible would use would be that of bride and bridegroom. But given the marriage customs of Israel, given that delay between betrothal and marriage and yet the beginning of definitive union with marriage, the image of the bride could be used both for the Church as it now is – pledged and committed to Christ and yet not fully his – and the Church as it will be. And given the reality of marriage as two becoming one flesh while remaining two, the image was patent of expressing both the solidarity of the Church with Christ, bone of his bone and flesh of his flesh, and the reciprocity of Christ and Church, the fact that the one is not swallowed up in the other. It is this image, finally, which enables the Church, in distinction from Jesus, to be thought of and experienced as a moral person, a corporate personality with its own inherent responsibility to Jesus, a responsibility of obedience and service, of keeping faith and keeping the faith.

We have been looking in all this at the Church as bride. I said earlier, however, that the more primary image which enables the Church to be bride is the Church as woman. In the Second Letter of John, the author addresses some local church as 'Elect Lady' (v. 1), and speaks of some other church as her 'Elect Sister' (v. 13). The First Letter of Peter refers to the Roman church as 'She who is in Babylon, elect together with you' (1 Pet. 5.13). This lady, this woman, whether the Church throughout the world or the church in a particular city, may be seen not as bride but as mother, a development of the image of the Church as woman which became very significant in the early Christian centuries and has remained an important part of popular piety towards the Church until our own day: 'our holy mother the Church'. This development, too, has its roots in the New Testament. In Galatians, for example, St Paul speaks of 'the Jerusalem which is above, our mother' (4.26) echoing and developing the words of Isaiah about the faithful mother city Zion. Once again, it is a way of talking about the Church as a moral person, distinct from Christ and not simply the 'whole Christ', yet in some way also distinct from any particular members of the Church. Just as in the parable of the wise and foolish girls, little attention is paid to the bride herself because the parable is addressed to Christians who are being exhorted to be ready for the parousia of the Lord when he comes for his bride, and in the parable they are to find themselves in the persons of her attendants, so too in the image of mother Church the individual members of the Church are thought of as children of the Church even though in point of fact there is no subsistent entity of the Church altogether distinct from the sum total of the individual members of the Church. And this brings us back to where this chapter began: the image has its own inherent laws, its own mode of being. It is in being held whole that its value lies. Then it shows itself as containing that which it alludes to, a true facet and face of the Church.

9

The Body of Christ

THE most immediate difficulty that presents itself in the matter of the Church imaged as the 'body of Christ' in the New Testament has to do with where we should start. Even in the earliest New Testament usage, the concept appears in a developed form, almost as a commonplace. Any attempt to go back beyond the writings as we have them must be very tentative, but an attempt there must be if the resonances of the language of this metaphor are to be sounded at all. The original and originating centre for Paul's usage (for it is with Paul and his disciples that we have to do) may well be the eucharistic body of Christ. The Pauline writings are all of them written from faith to faith. Paul's theology is a meditation in faith on the experiences of faith, on the experiential knowledge of the Lord Jesus Christ shared by the apostle and those to whom he wrote. We can surely allow that the primaeval experience of the post-Pentecost Church of its own communion with and in Christ was granted in the eucharistic event – the regular recalling of the Lord's Passover and the obeying of his command to 'do this, in memory of me'. It was here, in the Greek-speaking communities, that the language of the body of Christ came to birth, although it depended, surely, on the human will of the historical Jesus in his originating act at the Last Supper.

At this high point of the Eucharist, the source and goal of Christian living, believers were continually brought to concentrate their attention on the body of the Lord, that body which, as they all knew – for this was the primary good news that had been preached to them and which they had accepted – was risen and glorified, seated at the right hand of the Father. The sacramental realism of the New Testament makes it clear that precisely this body was the gift of the Eucharist. Christ had only one body, present in heaven and given to his own as their food. It seems reasonable to maintain that this eucharistic consciousness made possible the very early understanding of the Church as itself the body of Christ. Paul appeals to this as common knowledge in the First Letter to the Corinthians: 'Do you not know that your bodies are members of Christ?' (1 Cor. 6.15). So realistic is Paul in this matter that he can put into strict parallel being joined to the Lord in his body on the one hand, and being joined to the body of a harlot on the other. If as early as the writing of this epistle the faithful were expected to know that their bodies were members of Christ, then clearly the language of the community had already made communicable, as a conscious experience, the community of all with the uplifted body of the Lord really present with his own.

It is sometimes alleged that this idea of the body of Christ in Paul is metaphor purely and simply. Paul starts, it is said, with the idea of the ordinary human body being one and having many members. He develops it in much the way that the Stoic Menenius Agrippa applied a relevant fable by Aesop to the social order. But even though Paul may well be using quite consciously the language of the Stoics it seems clear that the movement of his thought is not from a common metaphor to its application. Rather, it is from a prior conception of Christians as the body of Christ to what this implies for their life together. Paul's is genuinely theological discourse. The foundation of the argument is the Christian experience itself:

> for in one Spirit were we all baptised into one body ... and were all made to drink of one Spirit. (1 Cor. 12.13)

The tense of the verb Paul uses insists on the primacy of the activity of God, which is the basis in the real order of the literary imagery that follows. Again, the opening section of this passage, 1 Corinthians 12.12 and following, shows that something more than a Stoic allegory is at issue here:

> For as the body is one and has many members, and all the members of the body, being many, are one body, so also is *Christ.*

The same notes are struck in a passage from the same letter which deals explicitly with the Eucharist.

The cup of blessing which we bless, is it not a communion of the blood of Christ? The loaf which we break, is it not a communion of the body of Christ? Seeing that there is one loaf, we who are many are one body, for we all partake from the one loaf. (1 Cor. 10.16–17)

The 'one body' which we all are can here be only the body of Christ, the pneumatic body seated in heaven. The realism of the reference is emphasised by the parallel Paul draws with the old Israel which in the desert ate the same pneumatic meat and drank the same pneumatic drink from the pneumatic rock that followed them, namely Christ himself. The remarkable *koinōnia* of Christians has its total cause in the *koinōnia* of each of them with Christ in the breaking of bread. Each one, in his *koinōnia* with Christ, is con-corporeal, *sussōmos*, with Christ and so with every other. So an offence against the community is a failure to discern the body, a judgment on the schismatic and the heretic.

In the deutero-Pauline writings there is precious little to suggest that here we are in the realm of metaphor. Indeed, only a mind over-influenced by the technical developments in the notion of the 'mystical body' in the High Middle Ages could think otherwise. The body of Christ is not a linguistic style which can be reduced, along with others, to a lowest common denominator which the language is 'about'. It is itself the common denominator, the very reality itself, and to this reality other styles of language are related as so many figurative expressions drawing out now one, now another implication of the Church's being the body of Christ. The author of the Letters can now talk time and again of 'the Church, which is his body', and still more unambiguously, of 'the body, the Church'; he can even refer without further ado to 'the body' or 'one body' and expect to be understood. Parallel usage shows that this body is none other than the body of the Lord himself who has passed over from being 'in the likeness of sinful flesh' to being 'in the spirit'.

But in what sense *can* the body of Christ have as its limbs other human bodies? What kind of conceptual picture could Paul have had of this body of Christ which is made up of many men as its members? Some light is thrown on this puzzle by the way contemporary rabbis speculated about the figure of Adam, or, more particularly of the 'two Adams'. In their strange way of thinking, the first Adam was created by God as a giant of enormous size, his span extending from one end of the earth to the other and reaching from earth to heaven itself. He was either androgynous or asexual. His body was formed from dust collected from all over the world. All subsequent generations were said to be truly 'in' Adam in a quite naive, literal way. His descendants were not simply in his loins, but different individuals were part of, and derived from, his members – his ears, hair and the rest. The glory of this pre-lapsarian condition was sharply contrasted with his condition after the Fall, when he was reduced to a length of one hundred yards, lost the glory of his appearance and ceased to be immortal. There is one Adam, but his two conditions differ *toto caelo*. In much of the Pauline literature we come across the idea that redemption is a new creation. The *Urzeit*, original time, has its strict corollary in the *Endzeit*, the final time of man's history. This suggests that, for Paul and his disciples, Christ's personal history reverses that of the primaeval Adam. In the days of his flesh he was circumscribed, alone, doomed to death; after his glorification in the Spirit he fills heaven and earth and calls mankind, and ultimately the whole cosmos, into one. In the Lord (Jesus Christ), as in the unfallen Adam of the beginning of time, there is 'neither Jew nor Greek ... neither bond nor free ... no male and female' (Gal. 3.28) because all are 'one man in Christ Jesus', all are one Adam. Of his glorious body all men are called 'members', being incorporated into the specific personal organism of the 'one new man' by the sacramental rites of baptism and the Eucharist.

But the body of this new Adam has not yet achieved its full stature, or so Paul would aver. In principle, the Christ fills all things. But in fact his body has still to be 'edified', to 'increase with the increase of God'. We have still to 'attain unto a full-grown Adam'. The body's unity and catholicity are still in a state of becoming. Into this body men are baptised in a rite that expresses and makes actual in the very bodies of the neophytes the present condition of Christ, fixed eternally as he is at the high point of his sacrifice, dead to the world and living to God. Baptism does not so much recall a past event as extend into a new member the mode of being of the whole body which is the ever actual realisation of the plan of God. As members of his body, believers always bear about in the body the putting to death of Jesus, that the life also of Jesus may be manifested in [their] body ... in [their] mortal flesh. (2 Cor. 4.10)

The whole Christian life, in its ethical striving as well as in its sacramental givenness, is baptismal. It is a progressive taking possession by Christ's paschal body of all aspects of the believer's existence. The body of Christ that rose from the tomb is the bud of new life in the Spirit. That body increases by subsuming the earthly man under itself and raising it to its own manner of existing. This will go on until the final flowering and fructification in heaven, the final apocalypse of the whole Christ.

For our citizenship is in heaven, from whence also we wait for a Saviour, the Lord Jesus Christ, who shall fashion anew the body of our humiliation that it may be conformed to the body of his glory. (Phil. 3.20–21)

To this building-up there contribute the apostolic institution and all the charisms of the Spirit, but most especially the Eucharist, the bodily-pneumatic Christ in the continuum of his earthly corporeity. This food is indeed eaten by the faithful but unlike ordinary food it transforms the eater into itself, not the other way round: 'Christ the panther: us he devours'.

If, then, 'the body of Christ' in St Paul does refer to the actual physical body of the Saviour raised in the Spirit, this can hardly help but have considerable implications for ecclesiology. The relation of the Church to Christ is not 'like' that of a man's body to the man himself. It *is* that of Christ's body to the Lord himself. The uplifted body of Christ is the sign and reality of the victorious grace of God in the world. It is the turning of God towards the world in Christ in order to reconcile the world with himself. It is the eschatological Peniel: the place where the agonising of the patriarchal man with God (as Jacob with Yahweh) wins blessing for the race, and constitutes him as the spiritual Israel. It is the embodiment, realisation and manifestation of the mystery previously hidden in the depths of the Godhead. It is the substantiation of the promise. The whole Johannine theme of the saving efficacy of the flesh of Christ, and the emphasis in the Synoptics on the function of Christ's body in his healing work can be brought in here to widen the perspective without betraying it.

Christ has only one body: he is not monstrous. That body is accessible to men in various ways: it is heaven, it is the sacrament of the Eucharist, it is the Church. All this, however, describes the body for the sake of those who are not yet attached to it. What can it mean for those who are already its members? Just as the body is in a sense distinct from Christ, so also is it in a sense distinct from his members and able to be set over against them. It is possible for the body to become an object for them, as it can for Christ, just as it is possible for a man to objectify his own body for himself. The hand can objectify the other members by pressing hard against them and so becoming aware of itself as hand and as member. How then may we explore our own belonging, in such an act of reflex awareness?

Two considerations may be brought in here: the relation to Christ of his eternal Father, and the tension in the New Testament between the already-given and the yet-to-be. Certainly, Christ himself is the Saviour of the body, but at the same time he is passively or receptively raised by the Father through the Spirit. 'God has made him both Lord and Christ, this Jesus' (Acts 2.36). Certainly, there is nothing now to be added to Christ in his glory by the Church. But at the same time his body has to be built up, its essential unity, holiness and catholicity progressively realised. The Church is the *plērōma* of Christ: the area into which he expands until he has subjected all things to himself. In this continuing process of the body's expansion in power of God there is a hint of how the one body can be on earth and in heaven, sinless and yet sinful, pilgrim and arrived. On such occasions as it is possible for a Christian to put the ecclesial Christ over against himself, then the Church can be seen (*pace* the last chapter) as the immaculate bride. Such occasions do not, it is true, perpetually offer themselves. For much of his time the Christian is likely to be more concerned with bearing the ecclesial Christ to the world than with his own confrontation by the Church-body of the Lord, for every Christian ideally bears in himself the dying and rising bodiliness of the Christ. In principle there is nothing in the Church as expressing Christ that there cannot be in the individual. This we see above all in Mary who supremely shares a *communicatio idiomatum* with the Church. Every Christian is to be a 'Church-man'.

It may be asked, 'On this realist view of the Church as truly

Christ's extended body, what becomes of the personal resurrection of Jesus? Would there have been a resurrection without believers?' Father Durrwell in his great study of the resurrection speaks of the body of the Lord rising from the tomb as a Church-body,[1] but it must surely be insisted that it rose as the personal body of Christ, who ate and drank with his disciples. If we are to have an ecclesiology that does justice to the New Testament as a whole and not simply to one strand within it, this problem must be faced.

One solution is the way of metaphoricisation followed (at any rate in part) by Pope Pius XII in his encyclical letter *Mystici Corporis*. There the Church appears as a body in rather the same sense that mediaeval jurists called the State the 'body politic'. In the case of holy Church, however, this body is unique in alone belonging to Christ, furnished as it is with 'institutions' – the divine sacraments – that no other body possesses. The pope's approach has indeed much to recommend it; yet considered as an exegesis of the Pauline texts it will hardly suffice. Neither will Rudolf Bultmann's more radically demythologising account serve our need.[2] Bultmann maintains that, contrary to appearances, *sōma* is not an essentialist term in Paul but an existentialist one. In other words, it stands for a way of being, and more particularly a way of being-in-a-world. Man's existence is always somatic, whether in a fleshly or a spiritual way. In speaking of the Church as the body of Christ, Paul means to say, according to Bultmann, that the Church is a way of being of Christ. This is coupled in Bultmann's theology with a lack of interest in the personal bodily resurrection of Christ from the grave. Again, this view offers some valuable hints in filling out St Paul's teaching, but it falls short because of its unconcern for the referent of Paul's language. This referent is, as we have seen, the personal physical body of the risen Lord which makes possible any way of being, any world, for Christ or the Christian.

It is indeed difficult to decide how far Paul's usage can be demythologised without remainder. It is not open to us to say that Paul was simply mistaken in his view of the nature of the body of Christ. That would be infidelity to the data on which our

[1] F. X. Durrwell, C. Ss. R., *The Resurrection: A Biblical Study* (ET London 1960).
[2] R. Bultmann, *Theology of the New Testament* (ET London 1952, 1965) pp. 192–203.

theology must build. We may say that the body of Christ is the *expressive organ* of Christ. It is the making manifest of the nexus of his presence to the world. So far so good, but this does little more than point to a mystery. The problem, we may say, rests; it is irreducible. The body of Christ reveals itself in sacrament and liturgical assembly, in icon and martyrdom, but all these manifestations are referred in faith and only in faith to the underlying and unimaginable reality of the body of Christ. This suggestion may offer more to us than at first appears. For are we not aware, through a body's 'accidents', of that body offering itself palpably before us, even though the body is known only in those accidents – in the way it inserts itself into the *omnitudo realitatis*, the totality of being?

IO

New Creation

OUR final 'primal metaphor' for the Church is unlike all the others in yet another way. The Church is the community which resulted from the activity of God in Jesus, the community which exists in order to commemorate that activity by its life and worship. All the various images of the Church we have contemplated show us different facets of what this activity brings in its train. But there is, in conclusion, a mode of reference which speaks in terms not of the effects of that divine activity, but of the activity itself. The Church, it says, is a new creation.

Creation has a very distinctive place in the biblical tradition. If the truth be told, 'nature' and 'providence' are not biblical terms at all. For the biblical God *creates* the material world and the destinies of men, and he does so by a word, that is to say, freely. In the first chapter of Genesis we read, time and again, 'God said ... and it was so'. As the thirty-third Psalm puts it,

> By the word of Yahweh were the heavens made, and all the host of them by the breath of his mouth, For he spoke, and it was done. He commanded, and it stood fast. (Ps. 33.6, 9)

The Hebrew doctrine of creation speaks of the absolute sovereignty of God with respect to the material world and to the world of man. The linguistic expressions suggest that God is some kind of artist in creating. He produces something outside himself. The world is not an emanation from God, it does not come oozing out of him. And so the words used for this divine activity connote the fashioning or shaping of a piece of furniture, or the founding of a city. There is one word which in the Hebrew Bible is used only with God as subject: the word *bara*, normally translated by our English 'create'. Outside the Hebrew Bible the word is used for chiselling or shaping some material into an artistic form: in the Bible it denotes the way in which God makes creation exist, 'exsist', come forth from nothing. At his word the universe comes to

93

be manifest, it steps into the light. Near the beginning of the classic film *Lawrence of Arabia*, there is a fine graphic illustration of this point when the rider of the camel comes into focus out of the heat and haze of the desert background. This concept of creation by a word rather than any kind of emanation distinguished biblical thought from that of other ancient writings. This is so even though, once the distinctively biblical conception was sufficiently rooted, other ways of talking could safely be employed in a poetical way in Scripture.

For the primary world-view of primitive peoples seems always to have been one in which man and not-man are bound together in a single significant order. Even the gods are part of a moral system which includes man. It is a major transformation in the human understanding of man and the world for man to come out from nature and to stand over against nature, so that nature becomes something simply physical or, perhaps, physical-and-aesthetic. When this happens man no longer looks at God-nature but – with the Hebrews – at God without nature. Once we can conceive of the possibility of God without nature, it is not that great a step to think of nature without God, no matter how certain we may be that nature owes its existence to God. If it is there by the word of God, then it has a certain independence of God. In our dealings with nature, we are not immediately having to deal with God. Nature may be used, not venerated. This Hebrew breakthrough prepared the way for the possibility of secular politics, of erotic love, of modern technology: in a nutshell, of a radically demythologised world where woods and streams are not inhabited by fairies and sylphs. At least in principle, the Hebrew breakthrough rules out any form of superstition, for superstition depends on seeing the universe, or particular elements in it, as bringing luck to man, whether for good or evil. In the Hebrew pattern of thought, the universe is the result of a deliberate and conscious act of the will of God, calling into being things outside himself. For this reason, the natural things of the world have a real, self-contained, intrinsic being, just because the creative will of God is being-giving. To create means to communicate being. The creative power of God finds expression in the very autonomy and intrinsic effectiveness of created things, which can intensify their existence by affirming it or weaken it by negating it. On the basis of our freedom as created beings, we can

94

resist or further our self-actualisation, for creation and creator are radically apart. No part of creation, and not the whole of creation either, is any part of God. Nevertheless, creation is open to God: it points Godwards. This is the basis of natural theology, of any attempt to establish points of contact between God's revelation and our total human experience. Creation is responsive to God, in such a way that everything that exists beckons towards him. Not that the existence of God can be proved in the manner of a geometrical theorem, for this would deny the voluntary nature of creation. Geometrical proof would be possible only if creation were necessary.

The world, therefore, is created in such a way as to be free. The more some element of the created world is, the freer it is. And yet at the same time everything that is depends on God and the word of God for its existence, not only at the beginning but at each ongoing moment.

In the Bible this word *bara*, and other words for 'create', are not only used to refer to the material existence of objects and people. They can also point to God as he brings into being some new situation, a new pattern of relationship within what already exists. One might even say that the word *bara* always has something of this aura of novelty about it, and that this is what gives it its full significance in the opening chapter of Genesis. *Bara*-activity is always characterised by being new, unexpected, unpredictable, freely willed, not restricted in any way by what has been until now. And so for example there is in Exodus the following text:

> And Yahweh said, Behold I cut a covenant; before all thy people I will do such marvels as have not been created in all the earth or in any nation. (Exod. 34.10)

Or again in Psalm 51:

> A clean heart create in me, O God. (Ps. 51.10)

But the primary use of this creation vocabulary comes in the oracles of Second Isaiah, and it is from him that an understanding of the original creation took its rise. The 'new exodus' spoken of in Isaiah 41 is a creation of the Holy One of Israel. For Yahweh is the 'creator of Israel'. As the prophet insists,

95

> Thus says the Lord who created thee, O Jacob, and he that formed thee, O Israel. (Isa. 43.1)

From the experience of being formed and reformed as a people, and indeed as a remade individual ('a pure heart create in me, O God'), Israel comes to extend the concept of creation by the word and will of God to the whole universe. The argument does not run from God as universal Creator to his power in respect of his people, but from the experience of the God who creates his people and does new things for them and with them there derives a refusal to limit his power in any direction at all.

In the New Testament, the pattern of thought about creation which we have found in the Hebrew Bible is accepted, but there is at the same time an emphasis not on what God once did but on what he is doing now. With reference to the first creation, to the universe as it exists now, the New Testament says on a number of occasions that the work of God then and now is not independent of Christ but has him always in view. We may regard this as a very remarkable assertion about a man who had been crucified less than thirty years before the earliest of the New Testament letters was written. In the First Letter to the Corinthians we find Paul affirming:

> To us there is one God, the Father, of whom are all things, and we unto him; and one Lord, Jesus Christ, through whom are all things and we through him. (1 Cor. 8.6)

Similarly in the Letter to the Colossians:

> He is the image of the invisible God, the firstborn of all creation; for in him were all things created, in the heavens and upon the earth, things visible and things invisible, whether thrones or dominations or principalities or powers; all things have been created through him and unto him, and he is before all things, and in him all things hold together. (Col. 1.15–17)

The writer to the Hebrews calls Jesus

> a son whom God appointed heir of all things, through whom also he made the ages, who being the effulgence of his glory and the impress of his substance, upholds all things by the word of his power. (Heb. 1.2–3)

Finally, there is the prologue to the Gospel of John:

> In the beginning was the Word, and the Word was with God, and what God was, that the Word was. All things were made through him, and without him was not anything made. What was made was life in him. . . . He was in the world, and the world was made through him. (John 1.1–4, 10)

Here too, as in the Old Testament, the move is from an experience of creation in Christ, an experience by the first Christian generation of something so novel, unexpected and *ex nihilo*, that it seemed right to call it a work uniquely of God himself. From that experience, as from Israel's experience of the exodus from Babylon, the thought of the New Testament writers panned back to the first creation. Just as now God did this altogether new and unexpected thing through his Word, personally identified with the man Jesus of Nazareth, so all creation from the beginning came to be seen in the light of Jesus. Jesus came to be understood as the directing principle through which God made everything there is, and for whom he made all that is, the goal and purpose of creation as such. There are certain parallels here with the Stoic notion of the *logos* as the form of God's self-expression in all things; but only somewhat distant parallels. More immediately, the New Testament is moving in a realm of discourse close to that of the Wisdom Books of the Old Testament. There Wisdom, more or less personified, became the link between creation and redemption, the 'master-craftsman' who was with God when he made the universe and then lived amongst men as the Torah, the divine plan for the world poured out on creation. But this too provides only a certain kind of parallel. The basic move is from the experience of the altogether new and unexpected activity of God encountered in Jesus to seeing all that is in the light of Jesus. The New Testament represents the continuous work of God in creating and recreating through Jesus of Nazareth as effected by the word of Jesus who is himself the Word of God. This is especially clear with those acts of creation in the Gospels which go by the name of 'miracles' although that word itself is rare in the New Testament. In the Fourth Gospel it is clear that the re-creative work of Jesus is part of God's ongoing work of creation. After Jesus has told the paralysed man at the pool of Bethsaida to take up his bed and walk, we read:

The Jews persecuted Jesus because he did these things on the Sabbath. But Jesus answered them, My Father is working even until now and I am working. For this cause, therefore, the Jews sought to kill him, because he not only broke the Sabbath but also called God his own Father, making himself equal with God. (John 5.16–18)

In its most thoroughgoing form, the work of God in Jesus is called a new creation destined to be as extensive and all-inclusive as the first. As the seer of the Apocalypse has it:

And I saw a new heaven and a new earth, for the first heaven and the first earth are passed away, and the sea is no more.... And he who sits on the throne said, Behold I make all things new. (Apoc. 21.1, 5)

This is echoed in the Second Letter of Peter:

The day of the Lord will come as a thief; in the which the heavens shall pass away with a great noise, and the elements shall be dissolved with fervent heat, and the earth and the works that are therein shall be discovered. Seeing that these things are thus all to be dissolved, what manner of persons ought you to be in holy living and godliness, looking for and hastening the parousia of the day of God, by reason of which the heavens being on fire shall be dissolved and the elements shall melt with fervent heat. But according to his promise we look for new heavens and a new earth in which righteousness dwells. (2 Pet. 3.10–13)

The creative work of God, in other words, cannot have to do with any area less than that of his original creation, held in being as that is by the Word who was made man in Jesus. Creation is not a stage-setting for the drama of salvation but already itself in some sense a saving act of God. Even the creation which we experience as fallen is upheld by the word of God which makes all things new. The goal of all that is will be refashioned in Jesus and find its true significance in him. It will be set free from its bondage to meaninglessness.

For the created universe waits with eager expectation for God's sons to be revealed. It was made the victim of frustration, not by its own choice but because of him who made it so; yet always with the hope that the universe itself is to be freed from the shackles of mortality and enter upon the liberty and splendour of the children of God. Up to the present, we know, the whole created universe groans in all its parts as if in the pangs of childbirth. Not only so, but even we, to whom the Spirit is given as first-fruits of the harvest to come, are groaning inwardly while we wait for God to make his sons and set our whole body free. For we have been saved, though only in hope. (Rom. 8.19–24)

The resurrection of Jesus is the first-fruits of this hope for the recreation of the whole universe: this is what the Eucharistic Prayer of Hippolytus of Rome means when it says that Jesus 'revealed the resurrection'. Although we have been saved only in hope, we have nevertheless been saved. Although we look for new heavens and a new earth in which righteousness dwells, there has already been a new creation.

The New Testament texts on this are few but significant. A passage in the Second Letter of Paul to the Corinthians has it that

If any man is in Christ, a new creation; the old things passed away; behold they are become new. (2 Cor. 5.17)

This literal translation shows the extreme compression of Paul's language and thought here, but the general sense is clear enough. The new man in Christ is not only new in himself, as though he were a solitary being independent of any nexus of relationships. Rather, through him the chaos of human existence begins to bear some sort of order. In the sixth chapter of Galatians, the new creation language is a way of relativising anything less than creation as a whole. Any division within the world subsequent to the creation cannot be compared in significance to the unity and wholeness worked by the creative and re-creative Word:

Far be it from me to glory except in the cross of our Lord Jesus Christ, through which the world has been crucified to me, and I to the world. For neither is circumcision anything nor uncircumcision, but a new creation. (Gal. 6.14–15)

The same stress is found in the Letter to the Ephesians, this time à propos of the single most significant distinction in the ancient world, that between Jews and Gentiles:

Now in Christ Jesus you who were once far off are made near in the blood of Christ. For he is our peace, who made both one and broke down the middle wall of partition, having abolished in his flesh the enmity, the law of commandments in ordinances, that he might create in himself of the two one new man, making peace, and might reconcile them both in one body to God through the cross, having slain the enmity thereby. (Eph. 2.13–16)

A little later, the author returns to his theme:

Put away as concerning your former manner of life the old man, which is turning corrupt after the lusts of deceit, and be renewed in the spirit of your mind, and put on the new man, which is according to God, created in righteousness and holiness of truth. (Eph. 4.22–24)

In Ephesians, therefore, we find a picture of the ongoing activity of God in a work so radically new that it can be called a re-creation. This re-creation takes place in the body of Jesus, and can be put in strict parallel with the creation of man as such, made as he was in the image and likeness of God. This likeness is restored in the man Jesus, especially in the manner of his dying, and it is being progressively pursued in the moral lives of Christians. The 'former manner of life' (Eph. 4.22) which the Ephesian Christians are to put away has been described earlier as 'walking as the Gentiles walk, in the futility of their mind' (Eph. 4.17), in the *frustration* of their minds, that same frustration to which, according to the Letter to the Romans, the creation has fallen a victim. This re-creation is God's activity alone, although it is achieved through Christ:

By grace you have been saved through faith, and that not of yourselves; it is the gift of God; not of works, lest any man should glory. For we are his workmanship, created in Christ Jesus for good works, which God prepared beforehand that we should walk in them. (Eph. 2.8–10)

Here God even prepares the good works which Christians should walk in. But this being re-created by God in no way diminishes personal freedom and responsibility, as we see from the way the author calls on his hearers to set their lives to rights. And so the wheel comes full circle, for in Isaiah there is the same exhortation to bring one's life into conformity with the new thing that God is creating, and an equal insistence on its being wholly the work of God.

> Yahweh, you will ordain peace for us, for you have also wrought all our works for us. (Isa. 26.12)

The fourth and last New Testament text on the new creation is from Colossians and it is much of a piece with all that we have seen:

> Put away anger, wrath, malice, railing, shameful speaking; do not lie to one another, seeing that you have put off the old man with his doings and have put on the new man, which is being renewed unto knowledge after the image of him who created him, where there cannot be Jew and Greek, circumcision and uncircumcision, barbarian, Scythian, bondman, freedman, but Christ is all and in all. (Col. 3.8–11)

Here too the new creation is most fundamentally the creation of one new man, begun in the humanity of Jesus who is the nucleus of the new mankind and its continuing progenitor.

Man and his destiny remain, then, the goal of the second creation as of the first. The world is a human world, finding its meaning in man. Because man misses his true direction, the world as a whole goes awry. It is made subject to futility, to frustration. When, in the person of Christ, man recovers his true vocation, the renewal of the whole creation can begin. Man as a new creation cannot leave untouched the reality of the world in and from which he lives. A really new humanity must mean a new world. Isaiah saw this in his vision of the new world of messianic times, where a new man is set at the heart of a new cosmos.

> The people who walked in darkness have seen a great light. ... For unto us a child is born, unto us a son is given. ... And there shall come forth a shoot out of the stock of Jesse, and a branch out of his roots shall bear fruit, and the Spirit of the Lord shall rest upon him. ... And righteousness shall be the girdle of his loins, and faithfulness the girdle of his reins. And the wolf shall dwell with the lamb, and the leopard shall lie down with the kid, and the calf and the young lion and the fatling together; and a little child shall lead them. ... For the earth shall be full of the

knowledge of Yahweh as the waters cover the sea. (Isa. 9.1, 6; 11.1–2, 5–6, 9)

As for Isaiah, so for Paul, creation can only be restored to what it was first meant to be when men have been re-created through the Spirit of God. It is the way a man stands with God which decides, in the last analysis, what sort of a person he is. In the life, death and resurrection of Jesus, God has changed this relationship with man. And so the new world of the eschatological vision is there in the world of the present whenever God is active for human salvation. In such situations God is bringing to completion his own work of creation through the Word in the Holy Spirit. This work was so transformed by the event of Jesus that it could be called a new creation, even though the whole creation was already in the Word which, when translated into humanity, was and is Jesus of Nazareth. The Church is the first-fruits of creation, the sphere in which God's work moves towards its final completion.

PART TWO

Focussing the Church:
The Sacraments

11

What is a Sacrament?

ONE of the most famous statements of the Church Council which met in the 1960s stands at the head of its constitution on the Church.

> The Church is the sacrament or instrumental sign of intimate union with God and of unity for the whole human race.[1]

The Church as a sacrament is, then, both sign and instrument, both manifestation and means. In this the Church is like Christ himself who is also in tradition called the sacrament or mystery of God. Christ and the Church can both be spoken of as the sacrament of God's saving work on man's behalf: they are the epiphany and the means of the activity of God, the visibility of grace, the gracious God whom eye has not seen nor ear heard. They are God's graciousness made visible, tangible and audible. It is because we are as we are, creatures of flesh and blood, that we need such tangible sacraments. God's saving work is worked out in concrete terms; if it were not then we would not be touched by it and so it would not be a saving work for us.

The Jewish-Christian tradition to which we belong sees this as quite basic. It is a tradition which sees God at work in the processes of history where grace has its local habitation and its name. God meets man not in the realm of ideas but in the reality of man's flesh. As the Bible story unfolds, it becomes increasingly 'not a theology for man but an anthropology for God', in the words of the Jewish exegete Abraham Heschel.[2] The great promise made to Abraham and his seed was the promise of what he as a nomad wanted more than anything: children, and somewhere to settle down. He was to be redeemed out of the possibility of total oblivion into his son Isaac. The pattern continues in the story of the exodus, which is a redemption from quite un-

[1] *Lumen Gentium*, 1.
[2] A. J. Heschel, *The Prophets* II (New York 1962; 1971), pp. 1–11, 48–59.

metaphorical slavery into equally un-metaphorical freedom. This remains the New Testament pattern also, as we wait for what the apostle Paul calls the 'redemption of our bodies' (Rom. 8.23). This progressive humanising of man (the transfiguration of the body and all that entails in terms of sexuality and society) is also the progressive revelation of God. There is a history of Immanuel, of 'God with us', which moves through God's speaking to men by way of cosmic events or generalised historical happenings – earthquakes, storms and gentle breezes; through, as a second stage, the particular historical events of the escape of Jewish slaves from the land of Pharaoh, and their return from another bondage in Babylon by the wholly unexpected courtesy of a pagan ruler – the fulcrum here being the land, as the pledge and incarnation of God's promise; to what, finally, the New Testament calls 'these latter days', when God has spoken to us in a Son, a man in whom the fulness of the Godhead 'dwells bodily'.

And so we can talk about Jesus of Nazareth as the revelation of God: God for us, the face of God, *Deus ad nos*, the man whom God lived and lives, the man for God and the God for man, God's way to be human. Jesus of Nazareth is the revelation of God: first of all, simply as man, as someone who shares the human gene pool. In line with what the early Church worked out, an orthodox understanding of Jesus wants to say that from the first moment of his individual existence he is God, the incarnation of God in the flesh and blood we all share. This involves, naturally enough, his continuity with his mother and through her with the whole Jewish race. He was born into a particular time and at a particular place, within a particular national and religious tradition. But he is in continuity with all mankind too, and this is Luke's point in tracing his family tree back to Adam, just as Matthew had traced it to Abraham. Jesus is one of us, and so in continuity with the world of nature as we ourselves are. He comes from 'the dust of the earth', to use the language of Genesis spelt out scientifically by Darwin in the nineteenth century. Simply in being a man, Jesus recapitulates in himself the long evolution of human history, all the dispersed peoples of the *humanum* back to Adam, all tongues, all races. For us men and for our salvation he was *made*: he was created into the creation which he then showed had been made through him for us men and for our salvation.

But like any man he had his own history to create; he had to become himself. He had a plan to enter into, a biography to write. And in the end that history took him outside human history: like any man he had to die. And in dying he left the fellowship of man; in his mode of dying he was forcibly thrust outside the human community, even though he accepted this of his own free will – as it says in the Second Eucharistic Prayer of the Roman rite. He freely chose the destiny that awaited him. In the resurrection he began a new history and that new history was more human than the previous one. This history on the other side of the death of his body showed what the body is for. It is the risen Jesus, more human, more bodily, than he was before his death, who is the revelation of God. From the first moment of his conception Jesus is to be talked about as perfect God, but it is only in the high-point of his resurrection that he has become God-for-us in the most thoroughgoingly human way imaginable. The Father constituted him Son of God in power by raising him: there is something definitive about this moment in the story of God with us. For revelation is not simply God speaking; it is also man receiving. It is a 'got-it' or achievement word, referring to the whole process whereby a person reveals himself and is encountered by another in the mode of his revealing. So Jesus is the revelation of God from both sides: the dialogue between God and man, God speaking and man answering, and man speaking and God answering. In his one ministry Jesus fulfils both sides of the historical dialogue between God and man. He is the single Mediator between God and man or, better, the single Immediator, the one in whom there is no distance between what it means for him to be God and what it means for him to be man, God and man reconciled in the unity of a single *prosōpon*, person, as the ancient definitions of faith have it. Or in a different idiom still we may say with Karl Barth that Jesus Christ does not simply reveal the covenant between God and man; rather, he *is* it.[3]

Sacramentality is rooted in Jesus as the dialogue, conversation, meeting between God and man, and between man and God. By 'Jesus' we mean this particular man who was made in all things like to us, sharing our history and making a new history for us,

---

[3] K. Barth, *Dogmatics in Outline* (ET London 1949; 1982), p. 69.

indeed in his risen life *being* that new history. This represents a very definite option amongst religious traditions, many of which would see salvation in terms of liberation from the particularities of human existence in time and space. As Professor Mary Douglas puts it in her book *Natural Symbols*:

> Devotion to the sacraments depends on a frame of mind which values external forms and is ready to credit them with special efficacy.[4]

She speaks of the traditional Catholic understanding of the real presence in the Eucharist as emphasised in, for example, Pope Paul VI's letter *Mysterium Fidei* as

> a doctrine as uncompromising as any West African fetishist's that the deity is located in a specific object, place and time under control of a specific formula. To make the deity inhabit a material object, whether shrine, mask, juju or piece of bread, is ritualism at its starkest. The condensation of symbols in the Eucharist is staggering in its range and depth. The whole circle of bread encompasses symbolically the cosmos, the whole history of the Church and more, since it goes from the bread offering of Melchisedech to Calvary and the Mass. It unites the body of each worshipper to the body of the faithful. In this compass it expresses themes of atonement, nourishment and renewal.[5]

And she draws out here a fundamental presupposition of the Catholic view of sacraments:

> It is based on a fundamental assumption about the human rôle in religion. It assumes that humans can take an active part in the work of redemption, both to save themselves and others, through using the sacraments as channels of grace – sacraments are not only signs but essentially different from other signs, being instruments.[6]

She also points out that such non-verbal symbols are capable of creating a structure of meanings in which individuals can relate

[4] M. Douglas, *Natural Symbols: Explorations in Cosmology* (London 1970), p. 9.
[5] *Ibid.*, p. 47.
[6] *Ibid.*, pp. 47–48.

to one another and realise their own ultimate purposes. It is here that the crisis of sacramental belief and practice may be situated in the West in our own time.

For if we are to be able to celebrate and appreciate sacraments properly, we must have faith in the worthwhile nature of external activities, of given words and gestures, of the material universe. And this is difficult for those of us who have had a highly verbal and personalist upbringing, who distrust external expression and value a man's inner convictions at the expense of what he actually says and does. If we place too high and exclusive regard on 'sincerity', on spontaneity, the speech that flows straight from the heart, un-premeditated, irregular, we shall find it hard to make sense of sacramental forms. As Professor Douglas warns:

> The body may come to represent an alien husk, something from which the inmost self needs to escape, something whose exigencies should not be taken too seriously. It can and even must be transcended if the individual encased within the body is to fulfil his unique potential for experience.[7]

In this fundamental cleavage of our time, the body or flesh always represents the wider society, just as the flesh and blood of Christ tie us inescapably to the givenness or particularity of the Jewish and the Catholic Christian traditions. Mind and spirit are where the emphasis is put by those who are concerned principally for their individual wholeness or for the well-being of the particular sub-group to which they belong. But sacramental practice declares that

> spirit works through matter, that spiritual values are made effective through material acts, that body and mind are intimately united.[8]

The sacramental view of the world is prepared to sacralise the flesh; those who oppose it count it blasphemy to teach the intimate union of Godhead and manhood. A European turning to Oriental faiths, in this perspective, is someone rejecting the Christian gospel of God taking flesh. If we are to make sense of the sacraments then we must take seriously both the faith of the early Councils that Jesus is God and man in the unity of a single

[7] *Ibid.*, p. 158.
[8] *Ibid.*, p. 162.

person, and an anthropology which accepts that the proper thing to do with the body – whether the individual body or the body politic – is to transform and transfigure it rather than to opt out of it.

It is only in this way that we can properly speak of Jesus as what Augustine calls 'the sacrament of God', and Augustine's modern disciples among the Catholic theologians of Germano-phone Europe call the *Ursakrament*, the 'primordial sacrament'. Jesus, as the French sacramental theologian Père de la Taille put it, has placed himself in the order of signs; and the Church as in some sense the body of Christ partakes of that quality of being the instrumental sign of the activity of God and of man's response. The whole life of the Church comes thereby within a sacramental horizon. The seven sacraments are certain privileged points at which we can see the whole life of the Church as sacrament. Seven here is a mystical number, a number of fulness. If one wished to say there was some particular number of sacraments, that number could only be seven. Things can be arranged to ensure that the sacraments emerge as seven, neither more nor less. There is no overriding reason, for example, why baptism and confirmation should not count as one sacrament rather than two, while conversely the diaconate, presbyterate and episcopate might well be three rather than one. The word 'sacrament' or its Greek equivalent *mystērion* is used liturgically of such things as the incarnation, the transfiguration and the whole complex event of Easter. Devotionally, in popular parlance, we speak of meditating on the 'mysteries' of the rosary – and we might equally well call these 'sacraments'. To say that Jesus or his Church is the sacrament or mystery of God is to say that he or it is God's proper activity, not something ancillary to his basic work. This is how the term 'mystery' is used in the mediaeval plays, and it is close enough to the intention of the Second Vatican Council in calling the Church 'the universal sacrament of salvation'.

The Church and the seven particular articulations of the Church's life that normally go by the name of sacraments are meetings, dialogues, covenants, speakings and answerings, in microcosmic mirroring of Christ himself. The sacraments 'speak' not just in words, in phonemes, but in gestures: in eating and drinking, washing and anointing, making love and caring for the flock of Christ, and in passing on forgiveness. The divine 'speaking' of the sacraments comes over in the particular human way we speak in them. For conversations at their best are not merely exchanges of information: they are the substance of friendships, in which as much is achieved by silence as by words. So much depends in significant human encounters on the creation of an atmosphere and a mood: what Michael Polanyi would call 'the tacit dimension'.[9] The speaking that we do in liturgical situations is as often as not what recent English philosophers of language have come to call 'performative utterance', the making of statements which create a new situation rather than inform us about an existing one. The sacramental encounter is the whole of the sacramental celebration in which the word is the soul and sense of the sacramental gestures.

If we are to raise the question of truth or falsity in relation to the sacraments, it is the whole celebration at which we must look. In such a celebration there is a nebula of meaning of a pre-theological kind, and sacramental theology exists as a 'second-order' elucidation of this nebula. What is true or, conceivably, false about a sacramental occasion is not any one of its meanings or possible frames of reference, nor any one theology of the sacraments to the exclusion of all the others. The reality of Christ shows itself – if it *does* show itself – in ways which cannot be exhaustively expressed in concepts and so need such imaginative representation. The ritual gestures of the sacraments, many of which are rooted in the human will of the historical Jesus, are bearers of a meaning which cannot be adequately stated in words. By their very nature the images are multivalent and enable the whole man to grasp the ultimate reality of the things of God. This is another reason why one must have confidence in the validity of external behaviour and not demand 'sincerity' as a non-negotiable minimum. The command is not, 'Say this!' but 'Do this!' The sacraments are human activities played out before God in the fellowship of his people and in this way are pregnant with God's own activity. Such human goings-on as eating and drinking, making love, serving one another, caring for the sick, even conducting legal proceedings, undergo a transmutation of

[9] M. Polanyi, *Personal Knowledge: Towards a Post-critical Philosophy* (London 1958); *idem*, *The Tacit Dimension* (London 1967).

meaning by being situated within the context of the gospel. They preach Christ more eloquently than words would do; and the preaching of the word of God *is* here the word of God: the sacraments, in the Thomistic tag, 'effect what they signify'.

Theological understanding of these miniature dramas relies on tokens of participation rather than techniques of observation. Our sharing in the sacraments is a *Gestalt* wherein aesthetic, ethical, psychological and historical elements are fused inseparably together. Because a sacrament is a celebration, blood, imagination and intellect run together in it. Sacraments may be called a 'mythical' way of being in the world: a myth being not merely a tale told but a reality too great for literal language being lived out. In myth, thought, feeling and action are integrated, just as they are in interpersonal disclosure where more is accomplished through symbolism than through propositional speech, more through gesture and action than through formal statement. And as in the beginning, myth is not so much an object of thought as the necessary precondition for thought, so to speak sense about the sacraments we must first have celebrated them aright. To celebrate aright is to abandon oneself to the internal rhythms of the sacrament, to trust in the efficacy of the rite in its wholeness, its simultaneously intellectual and emotional 'mythopoeic' immediacy. Sacramental celebration involves sharing, forgetting our own individual existence in order to find it again. Celebration means letting ourselves go into the mood and movement of the sacrament, not imposing ourselves upon it but allowing it to work in its own way.

It is only as people who participate in sacraments that we can theologise about those same sacraments. Here only believers are rational: and faith here includes listening and contemplation. We ought not to forget the etymology of that word 'contemplation': the key word *templum* is originally a defined space within which we live and move for the duration of this particular activity. In the confined significant space of the sacramental action we let go, let God be God and abandon ourselves to his gracious action coming to expression there. In so celebrating we are not simply manifesting the life of faith that is in us. We are to some degree creating ourselves as believers. In our celebrations there should always be some alienation effect, some challenge to our self-understanding rather than simply a confirmation of what we understand ourselves to be as individuals or as groups. But this is not to imply that we can cut loose from sacred tradition, from the past of our community or from present Catholic practice in the wider Church. To do so would be to cut away the ground of our own understanding, the condition for our thinking faithfully about the sacraments. Tradition is essential to us. Man is not organised like an archaeological mound, in strata; as he grows he makes the past part of all future time, and every environment that he has ever experienced into part of the present environment. Tradition is the sense of the total past as now, and the time-scale of the sacraments is what the Rumanian phenomenologist of religion Mircea Eliade has called 'concentrated time', the time of a heightened intensity outside of ordinary time.[10] In this *temps fort*, time is intensified as it is in the art of theatre or cinema, where a play or film rarely occupy the same length of clock-time as the clock-time they portray. The language of the sacraments is also intensified by images, and we cannot bypass the biblical and traditional images to arrive at some imageless Christian truth, for there is none. But if we cannot divorce ourselves from the past, no more can we do so from the rest of the Catholic present. It is the contemporary Great Church which teaches us how to celebrate. It is the Christian community, catholic and apostolic, synchronic and diachronic, that pre-defines for us the fundamental symbolic apparatus of words and gestures with which we lay hold of the gospel. The rôle of the Church is much like the rôle of art in the writings of the lay Dominican poet and artist David Jones, for whom art bestows on human beings a special insight, *not*, however, through some sort of mystificatory magic, but by way of patience, craftsmanship and mental alertness within the bounds of an organised discipline.

This is not to say that we should renounce any exercise of critical imagination *vis-à-vis* the Church's current ways of doing things in some respects. In a given historical epoch, we may find ourselves obliged by the gospel to present quite fundamental challenges to current ways of celebrating the sacraments or the hidden or overt assumptions which underlie some current pattern. The sacraments need the word, not only the word *of* the

---

[10] M. Eliade, *Patterns in Comparative Religion* (ET London and New York 1957), pp. 388–409.

sacraments but words *about* them. For their own health they need the activity of sacramental theology which is itself one primary way of understanding the Church. For the Church exists in and through its sacraments.

I 2

Baptism

IN the traditional way of talking about sacraments in the stricter sense, it has been customary to speak of sacraments of initiation, sacraments of return and sacraments of state, with the Eucharist fitting in some way into each of these divisions. I intend to follow this general schema, and to begin with the sacraments of initiation: baptism, confirmation and in some sense the Eucharist. More than any of the other sacraments, baptism and confirmation are sacraments of entering into an experience, the experience which has made Jesus of Nazareth who he is, the 'only sacrament' as Augustine puts it. We were saying in the last chapter that Jesus of Nazareth has made a new history between man in the world and God, a new history on the other side of death which puts a man outside the old human history. Into this new history we must in some way enter. We must enter into the 'name' of Jesus, into what Jesus has become through experiences he underwent, experiences which are open to us also to share in some degree. As in any process of initiation, this implies that the old situation will no longer sustain us. We must either move or perish. But also, as in any initiation rite, the moving is a painful experience, involving the relinquishing of a particular past. When a person is being initiated into a tribe or a school or a fraternity, he discovers that he is no longer at home in his prior situation. He must break with an old solidarity, at least in some areas of life, and the more significant the group into which he is initiated the more areas of his old life he must break with. In the interpretation of marriage in the Book of Genesis, for example, it is said that a man will leave the most fundamental structure of the ancient world, the extended family or tribe, and make a new community with his wife. The sacraments of Christian initiation involve just such a relinquishing and affirmation, and in the case of baptism in particular both the New Testament and Catholic tradition insist that this relinquishing and affirmation is 'necessary to salvation'.

There has been a tendency in the history of theology to go on making this statement even though no one believed it to be true in any ordinary sense of the words that compose it. From quite early times, people were saying that some sort of baptism is necessary to salvation, but they went on to distinguish various kinds of baptism. St John Damascene, for instance, the great Greek theologian who attempted to sum up the whole Eastern patristic tradition, talked about as many as eight different sorts of baptism. More usual is a distinction of three: baptism of water, baptism of blood and baptism of desire (what St Thomas Aquinas calls *baptismum flaminis*, 'baptism of the spirit'). This tradition is too well rooted to be dismissed, but perhaps we could also investigate what we mean by 'necessary' as well as by 'baptism'. Leaving baptism its central and normative denotation, the baptism of water in the name of the triune God, what is involved in claiming necessity for it? Very often we use the exact words of the New Testament but invest them with a meaning they did not carry there, rather than try to keep the language pure by using new terminology as new situations arise. Something of this sort has occurred with the concept of necessity to salvation. It seems clear from the great variety of applications of 'must' words in the preaching of Jesus and the apostles that a univocal interpretation of the 'must' of baptism is not possible.

It was necessary for the Christ to suffer and to rise from the dead. (Acts 17.3)

We had to make merry and be glad, for this your brother was dead and is alive again, was lost and is found. (Luke 15.32)

I must be about my Father's business. (Luke 2.49)

You must be born again. (John 3.7)

After the Pentecost sermon in the Acts of the Apostles, the crowd ask Peter: 'What shall we do?' (Acts 2.37), just as Paul, after his experience on the Damascus road asks 'What shall I do?' (Acts 9.6 [in certain manuscripts]). In the Fourth Gospel, indeed, the Jews have already asked Jesus himself, 'What must we do that we may work the works of God?' (John 6.28). And what response do we find? Peter tells his hearers, 'Repent and be baptised every one of you in the name of Jesus the Christ' (Acts 2.38). Paul is told,

'Arise and go into Damascus, and there it shall be told you' (Acts 9.6); when it is, Ananias lays hands on him, restores to him his sight and baptises him – or has him baptised. Jesus tells the Jews, 'This is the work of God, that you believe on him whom he has sent (John 6.29). So a complex activity of repentance, faith and going under the waters is called for. One may speak of each of these elements as including the other two. Repentance is specifically Christian only if it springs from faith and finds expression in going under the waters. Faith without renunciation is no faith, for faith always involves both understanding and behaviour: one believes the truth and does the truth; faith acts through love. Similarly, baptism without either faith or repentance is scarcely baptism at all. Tertullian, Ambrose and Augustine with so many of the Fathers speak of baptism as 'the sacrament of faith', but then again, as Augustine remarks, 'the sacrament of faith is faith'. baptism is the *body* of faith. It is necessary to salvation insofar as it is the answer to my own personal question, confronted by the person, work and claim of Christ, 'What must I do to be saved?' When a person has reached the stage where he can ask that question as his own personal question, an 'existential' question, a refusal to act on the answer entails losing his integrity, his chance of salvation, of wholeness and healing and ultimate identity.

The baptisand commits himself to doing this thing which is absurd in the sense that it could so easily have been otherwise ordained, so contingent a thing is the rite itself. That one should be baptised, baptised in water, depends on a particular series of choices in the course of the history of God's dealings with a particular group of people, and with the particular Man, Jesus of Nazareth. The sheer givenness of the requirement that a person be baptised is principally responsible for the fact that a constantly recurring catechetical reading for those preparing for baptism in the tradition is the story of Naaman the Syrian. Naaman's predictable reaction to Elisha's command to dip himself in the river Jordan was

> Are not Abana and Pharpar, the rivers of Damascus, better than all the waters of Israel? Could I not wash in them and be clean? (2 Kings 5.12)

But his servants said to him,

'If the prophet had commanded you to do some great thing, would you not have done it? How much rather, then, when he says to you, Wash and be clean.' So he went down and dipped himself seven times in the Jordan according to the word of the man of God, and his flesh was restored like the flesh of a little child, and he was clean.(2 Kings 5.13–14)

The Fourth Gospel hints at the same sort of 'absurdity' in its story of the healing of the man born blind, told by Jesus to wash in the pool of Siloam. For the Jewish-Christian tradition, healing, sight, and insight come from commitment to a particular tradition with its own rites and customs: truth is specific before it is universal.

We must enter then into the particular experience of the particular man, Jesus of Nazareth, and more particularly still into that part of his experience which more than any other has made him what he is, Lord and Christ, namely, his being killed and being raised. We are baptised into the name of the Father, the Son and the Spirit, as the Matthaean formula has it, but also and more simply, elsewhere in the New Testament, 'into Christ'. In baptism the name of the *Kyrios Christos* is invoked over the baptisand. The language of invoking a name calls forth the actual happening of salvation in Christ in the life and being of the candidate. He is associated with Christ; he is crucified with Christ, raised with Christ, set in heaven with Christ. He is put where Christ is. Like any language, but in a strengthened way, the language of the baptismal rite binds time and makes possible a contemporaneity of the once-and-for-all event of the past and the present of the baptisand. Baptism is one of the growing points at which God conforms the life of the Church to Christ, what the late John A. T. Robinson used to call a 'hot-spot of the new creation'. The baptisand enters into the experience of Jesus not speculatively but sacramentally and morally. Baptism is the gestured and spoken representation, in water and word, of the fate of Jesus which he made his destiny by freely accepting it. We accept it as our fate, and so make it our destiny, our salvation.

This is obvious enough when the sacrament is typically celebrated, not for the newborn child whose ancestors have been Catholic for centuries, but for the adult convert from paganism or unbelief. Within the Catholic tradition we are not at liberty to question the validity of the baptism of children below the age of reason, although we may wish to question its pastoral value in many cultures. When we call a sacrament 'valid' we are maintaining that it possesses at least a minimum of symbolic consistency with the sacrament as celebrated through the ages and throughout the present Catholic world. And in our tradition we must say that the baptism of an infant by the pouring of water does possess such a consistency. But we will understand what baptism is about when we see the rite as celebrated in the classical ages of the Church. We still possess catechetical instructions from patristic times which show us how it was done. The baptisand was required to strip naked, to make no pretences, to appear as he really is: the same sort of concern, this, that accompanies nakedness in the modern theatre. Like a newborn child or like Christ dying on the cross the candidate is accepted by the community and its God with all his rôles stripped away, without support from those rôles that clothes express and foster. After baptism he was given a white garment, as a symbol of his having 'put on Christ', a Pauline image which is derived in the first place from the putting on of clothes but which perhaps has more in common with putting on weight, for the latter changes the personality even more. In the West until the later Middle Ages, baptism itself consisted of being totally immersed in water, water which the liturgy of baptism identifies with the waters of chaos, and of the great Flood, the waters of the Red Sea and the waters of the Jordan, as well as the water that flowed from the side of the crucified Christ. The Eastern churches have not ceased to practise baptism in this form, and the modern rite of the Latin Church encourages us to follow suit. As Cabasilas puts it:

> Those who imitate, as it were by a picture, by means of certain signs and symbols, the death which he truly died for the sake of our life, he renews and recreates by these very acts and makes them partakers of his own life.[1]

In being baptised, a person offers to the Lord the imitation of his own death, and God's answer is resurrection. He is baptised into the waters of a particular tradition, and yet we would do well to remember that those waters are also identified by the liturgy itself with the waters from which all life emerged, the waters which are

[1] Nicholas Cabasilas, *The Life in Christ*, I. 5 (ET Westchester, N.Y. 1974), p. 49.

also potentially lethal for all life. In being baptised it is not only a matter of leaving one history to take on another, it is also a question of being baptised into the universal fate of the world. One goes down into the waters that threaten every man. One accepts one's fate in the faith that Christ has accepted the universal fate of man, and in the hope that God will draw us out of that fate into a new destiny, just as he drew Christ up from the waters of death.

Water itself has a whole complex of valencies, and each of them has its own significance here. In this sacrament we enter into contact with water; more fundamentally, we are immersed in it. In this act of immersion in water there are three primordial human activities or passivities: that of being bathed, that of drowning, and that of emerging from circumambient water, of being born – for all life on this planet begins from water. The sacramental activity itself speaks of a comprehensive act of reception and initiation, and these three basic elements single out particular effects that take place, rather in the way that the various ceremonies of the full baptismal rite – clothing with the white garment, being given the lighted candle, and so forth – spell out in their own way various secondary aspects of what baptism means and effects. These human activities are not necessarily assumed directly from their merely biological or utilitarian functions. As we have them in baptism they have already passed through the mediation of the religious traditions of Judaism. Judaism knows, for example, of ritual washings and not merely functional washings, of cleansing from a kind of defilement that is not visible and external. In the Letter to the Hebrews (6.2) we read of Christians receiving instructions about 'baptisms', in the plural, and Judaism does in fact know the concept of baptism as a means of entry into the covenant.

Let us look at these three valencies in a little more detail, examining first the valency of washing. In the Letter to the Ephesians we hear:

> Christ loved the Church and gave himself up for her, that he might sanctify her, having cleansed her by the bath of water with the word, that he might present the Church to himself glorious, not having spot or wrinkle or any such thing, but that she should be holy and without blemish. (Eph. 5.25–27)

The picture here is of the washing away of sin imaged as a stain, as dirt. Non-personal images for the relationship between man and God are out of favour nowadays, often enough for good reasons. And yet there is surely a need for such non-personal language in this area to respond to the depersonalisation which what we call sin produces. Images of defilement are too deeply rooted in the human psyche for them to be simply reducible to the breakdown of friendship.

Secondly, there is the valency of death by drowning. It is interesting that in profane Greek *baptizein* has the sense of 'to destroy' or 'to perish'. The significance of this image as a basic human passivity is modified by various stories in the Jewish tradition, notably those of Noah's flood and the crossing of the Red Sea. In both these cases the waters are selective in what they drown and what they let through, being rendered so by God's will. Eight people are saved in the ark with Noah; the children of Israel pass through the Red Sea dry-shod. On the other hand, the evils of the first creation are drowned, and the Egyptians (the 'idolaters') perish. There is also the story of Jonah, whom the New Testament sees as an indicator of the fate of Jesus. In his psalm, death is death by water like the death of the sun each night in the western sea. What is not drowned is what God chooses out for his own, what he 'hallows'. In baptism, however, it is the whole man who is drowned, his whole past which is called into question, even condemned. All is immersed in the destructive element, as when a man drowns it is commonly believed that his whole life flashes before his eyes offering him the opportunity of repentance. The whole man is baptised because the whole man is sinful. Sin is not incidental to man but is what situates him as unbaptised. Equally, therefore, it is the whole man who is claimed for Christ, the whole individual man and the whole body corporate. The unity of the Church comes from its being baptised into the one death and resurrection of the one Christ: it receives its solidarity through undergoing that experience with him.

Finally, baptism revalorises the image of birth, of emergence from surrounding and sustaining waters. When the creation story in the Book of Genesis speaks of the dry land emerging from the waters, it seems likely that the picture is that of islands of land appearing when the Nile floods began to recede each year: a new creation from out of chaos. The New Testament, however, in speaking of a new 'genesis' whenever anyone is in Christ, is thinking more immediately of the rabbinic teaching that through conversion the proselyte attains a wholly new existence. One cannot become a Christian by birth, but only by rebirth. Those who fail in their once-bornness want a second chance to be born. To ask for baptism means recognising that human existence is not in order and that it needs to be re-aligned. In bringing a child to be baptised, parents are already loosening their hold on him, acknowledging the relativity of their rights in his regard. Baptism means a new set of relationships, new brothers and sisters, the choice of God to be my God. Any such choice is an act of essential self-definition, like the choice of a spouse or of a friend. In being baptised a man enters into that relationship with God which is characteristic of Jesus of Nazareth, or rather, which *is* Jesus, for as St Thomas remarks, within the Trinity the persons *are* relationships, and Jesus according to the Catholic understanding of him is a trinitarian person, the person of the Word. So now Jesus is the place where the newly-baptised person stands, and the 'Our Father' is the first prayer he prays. The font is grave but it is also mother. It is both tomb and womb, as Cyril of Jerusalem told his catechumens so long ago.[2] The circumambient water from which he emerges is the principle of the world, the archetype of the cosmos. It is the image of the font as womb that lies behind the image of the Church as mother. That image is graphically expressed in the ancient rite of the Easter Vigil with its ritual copulation between the paschal candle (which is the risen Jesus) and the waters of the font, completed by the pouring on to the font of the semen-oil which is the Holy Spirit.

Baptism is, therefore, the primary sacrament of initiation, of entering in. This is not just the first of a series of moments, consecutively and qualitatively alike, but a moment which (like the prologue of a play) is qualitatively different as well as chronologically separate. The prologue is not just one structural part of the play but the moment at which, having seen the setting and actors, the opening words bring the burden of the play to bear on the audience. In an important sense we can never get beyond our baptism, because it is the sacrament of the whole Christian life, a life in faith and in the community of faith. Just as during our

[2] Cyril of Jerusalem, *Mystagogical Catecheses*, 2.

lifetimes there are certain moments which sum up years and years apparently ordered to those moments in advance, so in baptism the reverse occurs. The waters of baptism are the well which the Jesus of the Fourth Gospel speaks of as 'springing up to eternal life', the image of that internal font that we read of in Ignatius of Antioch: 'water living and speaking in me and saying, Come to the Father'.[3] Lived conformation with Christ is daily and terminal dying to self, but in baptism we envisage that this will involve and anticipate the kind of result to be obtained: the kingdom. We become master of our own death by accepting it in advance, sacramentally, and by entrusting it into the hands of God. This is why martyrdom can be spoken of so early in the tradition as 'baptism of blood'; baptism in one's own blood which because of faith is the blood of the Christ who shares our flesh and blood. In the teaching of Pope St Leo, after all, the body of the man who is baptised *becomes* the flesh of the crucified. Baptism in blood is the expression of a total fidelity to the confession of one Lord made in baptism, a total acceptance of the sword of the word of God which divides us from our own culture. There is a deep truth in such legends as the story of the virgin-martyr Thecla of Iconium: throwing herself into a pond full of ferocious sea-lions she exclaimed 'In the name of Jesus Christ I am baptised in this wild womb'.[4] Baptism of blood is the true dying in faith imaged in the baptism of water.

As we come up out of the waters of the font we enter into a new situation, pre-defined by the tradition of the Church and by the Church's Lord, and contemporaneously co-defined by the present Christian community. It is this community, past and present, apostolic and catholic, which gives us our identity and will sustain us in that identity, making it possible for us to grow up, to undergo and live through later crises of identity. It is a community in which all talk the same language, which is why the articulation of faith is so important in baptism. We are asked point-blank, 'Do you believe in ...?' And we answer, 'I do believe'. We answer in that way because our ears have been opened to hear and to accept, and our mouths to give back the confession of the faith. The responses to these questions fired at

---

[3] Ignatius of Antioch, *To the Romans*, VII.
[4] *Acts of Paul and Thecla*, II. 34.

us as we stand in the waters of the font go together to make up the Creed in its primary form. The original function of the Creed is to express and create unity, the unity of the community of the confessing word. But the Creed is also the form of our worship of God: our conversation as a turning towards one another is the common glorification of God. Faith thus calls for fellow believers, while the whole Church calls for its *symbolum* in the original sense, its complementary 'other half', for God.[5]

---

[5] See also G. Preston, O.P., 'Death by Water', *New Blackfriars* 52. 619 (1971), pp. 553–558; *God's Way to be Man*, pp. 35–39.

13

Confirmation

IN the previous chapter we considered baptism as the primary sacrament of initiation. But as we noticed in the chapter before it, on sacramentality in general, it is not always clear why the sacraments have been divided up in the way we now know. Why, for example, should the diaconate, the presbyterate and the episcopate count as only one sacrament, although they are normally separated by a considerable lapse of time and many people are deacons without ever becoming priests, or priests without ever becoming bishops, and at least in the early centuries often became priests without having been deacons, or bishops without having been deacons and priests? A similar query arises here in connection with baptism and confirmation. We think of it as obvious that baptism and confirmation should constitute two separate sacraments, since in our practice the two are separated by just such a lapse of time. But so are the diaconate and presbyterate, or presbyterate and episcopate, yet we think of these as one sacrament, the sacrament of order. Even more to the point, there are many Catholic rites in which it is unknown for a person to be baptised without being immediately confirmed. Originally, Christian initiation was a single process. Water baptism was followed by a ceremony of 'sealing' or chrismation, by anointing or laying on of hands, and then by communion. This seems to have remained the practice of virtually the whole Church until around the year 1100. Just occasionally in the early centuries, there was a separate rite from baptism as part of Christian initiation, but this seems to have been confined to those baptised outside the Church as visibly and institutionally formed. Leo the Great advocates this, on the grounds that, while baptism may not be repeated, the Spirit is only given within the Catholic Church. In the Eastern churches it has always remained the case that when a baptised man who has been in schism wishes to become an Orthodox Christian he is reconciled by a ceremony identical with

confirmation in other churches. In the reformed rite for the
admission of a validly baptised person into full communion with
the Catholic Church, as promulgated for the Western patriar-
chate in the wake of the Second Vatican Council, the normal
means of such admission is confirmation, or (if the person has
already been confirmed outside the visible unity of the Church)
the laying on of hands, the old gesture of confirming. So, normally, confirmation is the reconciliation of such a person into full
Catholic communion, a point to which we shall come back
later.

Increasingly, people will come to be baptised and confirmed in
a single liturgy, for more and more people will be baptised as
adults, rather than as children. The present discipline of the Latin
Church allows the one who baptises an adult to confirm him or
her there and then, in order to keep the unity of the sacraments of
initiation. When this happens, there is no pressing need to distinguish between baptism and confirmation in terms of their
effects, water baptism doing one thing, chrismation another and
Holy Communion yet another. This perhaps gives us the clue to
how we should see confirmation anyway. It is not terribly pro-
ductive to investigate the distinctiveness of the first two sacraments in terms of their effects. It leads to embroilment in what
have proved fairly unanswerable questions such as whether or
not the Holy Spirit comes to a baptised but unconfirmed person,
and if he does then why should the person be confirmed; if he
does not, then what is the status of a Christian who does not have
the Holy Spirit of God? If we return instead to the basic significance of sacraments, we may get further forward. The history
of Jesus, as the primordial sacrament into whose inner story we
must ourselves enter, is mapped out in the Pentecost sermon
ascribed to Peter in the Acts of the Apostles as follows: Jesus was
crucified, died and was buried; on the third day he rose again in
accordance with the Scriptures and finally,

> being therefore exalted at the right hand of God, and having
> received from the Father the promise of the Holy Spirit, he has
> poured out Holy Spirit on us. (Acts 2.33)

Full Christian initiation means entering into that story whole and
entire, not simply into the death and resurrection of Jesus but
also into his being filled with Holy Spirit and pouring out that

Spirit onto his brethren. To speak of Jesus' Passover to the Father in terms of these three discrete moments, Good Friday, Easter and Pentecost, is natural to us because it is the way in which the liturgical celebration of that Passover in the Church's year has developed. We celebrate the death and resurrection of Jesus over the paschal *Triduum*, and fifty days later we celebrate the pouring out of the Holy Spirit. But there is an equally canonical way of talking about this according to which everything is compressed into a single day. If the one scheme is Lucan, then the other is equally certainly Johannine. On Easter Day, in the Fourth Gospel, Jesus both is raised and breathes out Holy Spirit on his disciples, giving them the power to forgive the sins of others.

In the light of this we can set up a model: Good Friday and Easter are to Pentecost as baptism is to confirmation. This enables us to make sense *both* of the custom of a single rite of initiation, a Johannine way of doing things, *and* of the practice of separating the rites by a time-lapse, the Lucan picture. In the light of this model, we would not regard confirmation as necessary to salvation, even in the sense of 'necessary' explained in the last chapter. It is not so necessary because a man who has been baptised has entered into the Christian mystery. Having died with Christ, he has risen to a new life with Christ. But the only life of Christ to which he could have risen is the risen life of Christ, which is a life in the Holy Spirit. So the man who has been baptised but not confirmed does not lack the Holy Spirit in all his power. And yet the full process of Christian initiation always includes a rite additional to that of immersion in water, a rite thought of as bearing some special relation to the Spirit. If a man is to enter properly into the history of Jesus, to live through the experience of Jesus, then both matter. The baptism in water has reference to the death and resurrection of Christ; the rite of anointing or of laying on of hands has reference to Pentecost. Both matter, insofar as we should always think of them in terms of fulness, rather than of minimum conditions for validity. It is not that the unconfirmed Christian cannot enter into the full blessing of Pentecost, but simply that the Spirit-rite in Christian initiation is the way entering into Pentecost is normally expressed and effected. The Spirit-rite is the Pentecost of the individual believer. Approached by this route we can see that it is not by any means absurd to delay confirmation, even perhaps by more years than is customary now in the Church of the West. Children who are baptised but not confirmed are very much in the position of the apostles between Easter and Pentecost. They have an experience of the risen life of Jesus, which is a Spirit-filled life, but they are not yet called or sent forth. It would not make sense for them to rush babbling out onto the streets. They are in a kind of latency period, rather like the period between five and seven in a child's life in general, a time of calm, stability and consolidation where body and psyche await their activation, gathering strength for the uprush of adolescence. Confirmation, as St Thomas says, is the consummation of the sacrament of baptism, just as, in the liturgical tradition of the Church, Pentecost is called the consummation or crown of the mystery of Easter.

This particular model of the relationship between baptism and confirmation enables us to cope with the equal standing in the Church of both the Western and the Eastern practice with regard to the discipline of the sacraments. In one way or another, both East and West insist that the bishop has an important part to play in the Spirit-rite in Christian initiation. The Council of Trent spoke of the bishop as the ordinary minister of the sacrament, the Second Vatican Council as its originating minister. When the Eastern and Western practices parted company, the East opted to maintain the unity and fulness of the rite of initiation by having presbyters confirm, even though this ran the risk of obscuring the ecclesial significance of the sacrament of the pentecostal gift. For the Holy Spirit and the unity of the Church, visibly expressed in the bishop, necessarily belong together. They attempted to maintain some link between the bishop and confirmation by insisting that a person could be sealed only with chrism that had been consecrated by the bishop, or even by the patriarch. The West on the other hand chose to maintain the relationship between the Spirit and the Church community by insisting that normally only bishops should confirm, even though this ran the risk of breaking the one rite of initiation and diminishing its fulness. Historically, it led to the posing of complex theological problems, and to a practical downgrading of the Spirit-rite, so that the only way of ensuring its celebration in many countries was to insist that only a confirmed person could receive Holy Communion. Now in the Western Church we have seen a shift of emphasis. When there is a pastoral need to underscore the unity and fulness of Christian initiation, especially in the case of previously unbaptised adults, this aspect is highlighted by confirmation at the hands of the same man who baptised them. But when, on the other hand, there is a pastoral need to underscore the relationship of the gift of the Holy Spirit to membership of the wider Church then it is the bishop who confirms, being the man who stands for the whole *Catholica*. Probably this situation can be judged the 'best of both worlds'. The rite itself says, 'N., be sealed with the gift of the Holy Spirit': in these words, which date back to the fifth century and are common to East and West alike, we can find an expression for both ways of looking at the sacrament. It is the seal on the previously received gift of the Spirit, and it is the gift of the Spirit itself.

The gesture that lies at the heart of confirmation has long been that of anointing with oil, even though no reference can be found in the New Testament to any such external anointing. It may well be that it found its way into Christian initiation from sources outside the Judaeo-Christian tradition, but caught on rapidly because of its congruence with what the Holy Spirit represents. A bath followed by anointing and a meal occurs in non-religious contexts in the *Odyssey*, for example: anointing with oil was a common part of the preparations for sharing a festival meal in the ancient world. Once the gesture of anointing was established as part of the ceremony of Christian initiation, then its potent symbolism began to exercise a considerable effect. There was the memory of the way the people of the New Testament had used anointing for various functions, especially those of priesthood and kingship. When Aaron was anointed priest by Moses this followed a ritual bath, and the same practice was observed for many of the kings. The New Testament too spoke of the whole Christian people as a race of kings and priests. The specific anointing of priests (in the sense of presbyters) and kings (in the sense of sovereigns) is subsequent in Christian history to this basic anointing of every Christian to be king and priest. There is also the solitary biblical example of the anointing of a prophet in the cycle of narratives concerned with Elijah. All Christians were supposed to be prophets – so what more appropriate way of expressing this than by anointing them with oil?

Much more significant than any of these considerations, however, was the case of Jesus himself, the Jesus whom the Church professed to be Messiah, *the* 'Anointed One' of Jewish tradition. The New Testament has preserved accounts of the physical anointing of Christ by Mary of Magdala and perhaps by some other unnamed woman, but these were secondary to the witness that he had been anointed by God with the Holy Spirit. If a man were to enter into the full experience of Jesus of Nazareth, then he too had to be anointed with the Holy Spirit. There were different ways in which Jesus had been so anointed. The infancy narratives of Luke's Gospel traced his very conception to the work of the Holy Spirit. All four Gospels speak of the Holy Spirit coming down on him at his baptism in the Jordan. The Epistles say that he offered himself to God through the Holy Spirit on the cross, and that God raised him from the dead by the Holy Spirit. But in the Pentecost sermons, Peter says that

> being therefore exalted at the right hand of God, and having received from the Father the promise of the Holy Spirit, he has poured out Holy Spirit on us. (Acts 2.33)

The Jesus who was always a man of the Spirit, always led or driven by the Spirit, becomes at Pentecost the Jesus who gives the Spirit. Conformity to Jesus, entering into the full experience of Jesus, means becoming not only a person who is guided by the Spirit, but also someone who gives the Spirit to others. It is in this perspective that we can see how the story of the disciples in the upper room in the twentieth chapter of the Gospel of John is truly a Pentecost story. The disciples are not simply the recipients of the Spirit but those given authority to forgive sins, and so givers of the Spirit to others. Christianity, then, is not only a religion of the saved but a religion of saviours: those who give the Spirit as well as receive it. The Fourth Gospel contains a deliberate ambiguity when it records:

> Jesus said, Whoever believes in me, as the Scripture says, 'Out of his heart shall flow rivers of living water'. This he said of the Spirit (John 7.38)

The 'heart' in question is the heart of Jesus, and the heart of the believer, who like Jesus is a Spirit-giver. The New Testament is full of the way in which the same language is used both of Jesus and of the believer: both are lights of the world, shepherds, and ultimately saviours, even though the believer never ceases to be dependent on Jesus. The ritual of confirmation makes this point very strongly.

The consecration of the chrism on Maundy Thursday must be regarded as part of that ritual. In that prayer the oil on the altar is identified with the oil of the Promised Land, the oil which makes a man's face shine, making him happy with the oil with which prophets, kings and priests were anointed, with the Holy Spirit himself with whom God anointed Jesus. Not for nothing had Irenaeus called the Father the Anointer, the Son the Anointed and the Spirit the Anointing. It is from Christ Jesus, as the prayer says, that chrism takes its name; and it is the Father who is asked to make this chrism a vehicle of his grace, to conform Christians to Christ himself. Interestingly, the liturgy says that God anointed not only prophets, priests and kings but also martyrs. The origin of this statement is unknown, but it must have reference to the way martyrs were seen in the early Church as the typical Christians, the most obvious examples of the way each Christian was prophet, priest and king. The implication is that every Christian is to share in the work of the gospel, in spreading the Holy Spirit whom he himself has received, the good odour of Christ spread in the world by other Christs as the chrism is perfumed in the making.

The sacrament of confirmation, then, signifies and effects a conforming of the baptised (dead, buried and raised) Christian to the Christ of Pentecost. As the Apostolic Constitution on the Sacrament of confirmation of Pope Paul VI puts it, 'The sacrament of confirmation somehow perpetuates pentecostal grace in the Church', taking up the theme of the decree of the Second Vatican Council *Ad Gentes*, 'on the Missions':

> By the sacrament of confirmation, a man's bond with the Church is made more perfect, and those who are confirmed and enriched with the special power of the Holy Spirit are thus more strictly obliged as true witnesses of Christ to spread and defend the faith by word and deed.[1]

---

[1] Paul VI, 'Apostolic Constitution on the Sacrament of Confirmation', in International Commission for English in the Liturgy, *The Rites of the Catholic Church, Revised by Decree of the Second Vatican Ecumenical Council and Published by Authority of Pope Paul VI* I (New York 1976), p. 292.

St Thomas speaks of this obligation as being '*quasi ex officio*', and says that the character of the sacrament – consecration for mission – is the very reality of confirmation. It is noteworthy how constant this stress on consecration for mission has been in the tradition: the Council of Florence, for example, says:

> the effect of this sacrament is that in it the Holy Spirit is given for strength, as he was given to the apostles on the day of Pentecost, that is, so that the Christian may boldly confess the name of Christ.[2]

It is always by talking of Pentecost that we talk of confirmation.[3]

[2] H. Denzinger, *Enchiridion symbolorum, definitionum et declarationum de rebus fidei et morum* (Freiburg 1991[37]), 1319.
[3] See also G. Preston, O.P., 'Death by Fire', *New Blackfriars* 53. 622 (1972), pp. 124–129; *God's Way to be Man*, pp. 27–34.

14

Eucharist

To talk about the sacraments of the Christian Church, it is necessary, as we have seen, to talk first about the only sacrament, Jesus of Nazareth, the at-one-ment of God and man, the one person in whom there is no gap between what it is to be God and what it is to be man. The sacraments in the narrower sense of the classical seven are to be seen as so many ways of entering into the 'name' of Jesus; Jesus as he has been made what he is by the history he has enacted and undergone. The work of God towards men is one and undivided: God speaks only one Word, and the continuing process of the Christian life consists fundamentally in our growing up in all things into Christ. That life is a matter of letting God abolish the inner space in the whole Christ, Head and members, between what he is and what he is to be. For the time being, however, our relationship with Christ is differentiated. We may think at one point of what it is to enter into the sacrament of Jesus, and so have to concern ourselves with what we call sacraments of initiation, baptism and confirmation. But then again, for one reason or another we may fall away from our total adhesion to the whole Christ, and in such a situation we must needs attend to sacraments of return. In addition, there are certain ways of living out the life of Jesus in our daily existence which are so much a focus of the way Jesus is that they too can be called sacraments, the sacraments of state, marriage and ministry. And yet further to all this, there is the possibility of considering Jesus simply as God's sacrament, the only sacrament, the mystery of God's grace and man's response. In thinking of Jesus, as in thinking of anyone, we do not always have to be thinking of some particular aspect of him. More normally, we will want to think of him whole, in the round, globally. The sacramental way of celebrating Jesus in this manner is called the Eucharist.

It is not that the Jesus who is globally celebrated in the Eucharist is other than the Jesus whose activities are celebrated in the other sacraments. But the person in his own right subsumes all his activities while remaining unexhausted by them. He subsumes them: what we spell out in celebrating the other sacraments is there *in toto* in the Eucharist in that Jesus himself is there. But the person is not exhausted by the sum total of his activities. And it is here that the Eucharist differs from the other sacraments. In all the other sacraments, the sacrament consists of activities (though this must be carefully qualified in the case of marriage and ministry, two sacraments which have been closely associated traditionally with the Eucharist in this regard). In the Eucharist the sacrament exists even outside its being activated, even though it only exists by virtue of the activity of taking, breaking and sharing, so that there would be no eucharistic presence in bread and wine that had not been taken and given thanks over, the bread broken, and both bread and wine specifically intended to be eaten and drunk. The Eucharist is not simply the sum total of what is celebrated in the other sacraments, any more than any person is simply the sum total of all his activities. But all the sacramental activities of Jesus are in principle included in it. That is why it is appropriate for all the sacraments to be celebrated or initiated within the context of the Eucharist.

In this sacrament there is, for instance, continual entry into the life of Christ, and so people are baptised during the course of the Mass. Some of the patristic writers speak of how each communicant is baptised anew in the eucharistic cup, that vessel which has typically the same female rôle as the font. In the Eucharist there is also forgiveness for sins committed after baptism. Nicholas Cabasilas, the great fourteenth-century Greek theologian whose *Commentary on the Divine Liturgy* was so highly valued at the Council of Trent, begins that book by saying that

> the aim of the celebration of the Holy Mysteries is the sanctification of the faithful, who through these mysteries receive the remission of their sins and the inheritance of the kingdom of heaven.[1]

St Thomas teaches that since the whole point and deepest reality of the Eucharist is love, and since it is by love that sins are blotted out, it is beyond question that the Eucharist remits sins. This does

[1] Nicholas Cabasilas, *A Commentary on the Divine Liturgy* I (ET London 1960), p. 25.

not simply touch what Thomas, and much of the tradition after him, would call 'venial' sins. He envisages the situation of a man who really has committed a mortal sin but judges that he has not, and is not in fact attached to that sin as such. Although at first he may not be sufficiently contrite, when he comes to the sacrament of the Eucharist with devotion and reverence, he receives from that sacrament the grace of charity which makes his contrition perfect and so brings him the forgiveness of the sin in question. In saying this, Thomas is only taking up a very ancient tradition, witnessed to in, for example, the *Ecclesiastical History* of the Greek Christian historian Sozomen. According to this, if a person undergoing canonical penance cannot be absolved in the ordinary way by a presbyter, it suffices to give him the Eucharist before he dies. That is, for him, full reconciliation with God and the Church. And so the theologically (though not statistically) typical way of celebrating the sacrament of penance may be said to be while the Holy Eucharist is being celebrated: that is the time, above all, when people should be reconciled to the Church. In the Eucharist there is also healing: many of the prayers after Holy Communion in the Roman rite ask for the healing of the body as one of the effects of this sacrament. In a number of eucharistic prayers, that same healing is prayed for during the invocation of the Spirit on the congregation. So it is altogether appropriate that the sacrament of healing should be celebrated during the course of the Eucharist – as is often done nowadays. Again, in the Eucharist there is the great example of service: my body *for* you, my blood *for* you. The Fourth Gospel has no account of Jesus doing anything with bread and wine the night before he died, but finds it fitting to speak of the inner significance of the Eucharist by giving us a story of Jesus serving his disciples by washing their feet. And so people are commissioned for service within the celebration of the Eucharist. The Eucharist is the sacrament of love, that love which is expressed and brought about also by married couples: and so people are usually pledged to each other for a lifetime of love during the Eucharist. And in the Eucharist there is the fulness of the Holy Spirit, for there can be no Eucharist without the presence of the Holy Spirit in all his power. The account of the actions of Jesus at the Last Supper that we find in some eucharistic prayers says, for example, that Jesus took the cup, gave thanks over it and filled it with Holy Spirit.

135

The word *koinōnia*, 'fellowship', in the New Testament is used both of the Holy Spirit and of the Eucharist; we are told that in one Spirit we were all baptised into one body. The modern Greek rite expresses this by pouring boiling water into the consecrated chalice, what it calls *zeon*, water and fire in one. Ephrem of Syria makes a connection between the body of Christ and the Holy Spirit when he writes

> In your Bread is hidden the unconsumable Spirit; in your Wine dwells the undrinkable Fire; Spirit in your Bread, Fire in your Wine – exalted marvels, which our lips received.[2]

And so appropriately the pentecostal sacrament, confirmation, is celebrated within the context of the Eucharist.

And yet, to repeat, there is something special about the Eucharist which is more than the sum total of the other sacraments. The person of Jesus around whom the Eucharist is centred is what he is as a result of what he has done and undergone, and supremely of his being killed and raised to life. Dead to sin, he lives unto God. He is 'dead to sin', to this present age which is characteristically an age that falls short of the glory of God; he is 'alive to God' in the life of the age to come. His present is our future, a future which we can enter into only by passing through the death that divides that future from our present. Here and now that death can only be baptismal dying, by that rite which is the sacrament of faith *par excellence*. And so if we are going to celebrate the person of Jesus who lives beyond this present age, this must be a celebration in faith, as seeing what is not seen. Jesus is not part of the furniture of the world; he is not to be met with in the ways in which we meet each other. He reveals himself only to faith. Or rather, it is only in creating faith that he reveals himself. In the appearance stories of the New Testament it is manifest that the risen Jesus could not be sought for in the way we might set up an expedition to search for an unknown animal, known as yet only by rumour but not scientifically observed. In the stories of the resurrection appearances, Jesus always presents himself when and where he himself chooses. Part of what we understand by sacraments is that Jesus of his own choice has covenanted to manifest himself, to make himself known, when

[2] Ephrem Syrus, *Hymns on Faith*, X. 8.

his people engage in certain styles of behaviour: when for example they feed the hungry and clothe the naked, or when they take bread and wine and give thanks over them and share the gifts. He has covenanted to come to his people in such situations, such faith-encounters, through and only through that human activity which is the gift of God that he creates in us, namely faith. It is not that he is present because of our faith, but that he is present always to our faith. The eucharistic presence of Jesus is a presence given to believers, to those who accept that word by which he tied himself to these actions with bread and wine. 'This is my body, this is my blood' are words of administration addressed to people, not to elements; not isolated or magical sayings but words spoken within the context of a relationship of a particular kind, the relationship of faith. So we can say that Jesus in the Eucharist is present at the table rather than on the table, present *to us* – as the Council of Trent and the Roman Canon put it – to us who are already acknowledged as being in the communion of the Holy Spirit, standing in a relation of peculiar intimacy with him by virtue of our being baptised. One of the most primitive ways of inviting the people to share in the Eucharist is with the words *Sancta sanctis*: 'Holy things for holy people', 'the Gifts of God for the people of God'. We are already the people of God when we gather to celebrate the Eucharist; the Eucharist is the domestic worship of the household of faith; the gifts have to be made holy for us who are holy, made fit for us so that we can be made fit for them. So the Eucharist is properly shared only amongst the members of Christ, those who already by one Spirit have been baptised into one body. These two must be placed in their proper order: first the indwelling presence of the Holy Spirit (as in the old expression, 'being in a state of grace'), and then the presence of Christ as given to those who share Holy Communion. Faith is the context in which we encounter Christ, for it is faith and faith alone that gives us the necessary expectations presupposed by any meeting with him. The set of expectations that faith gives us is a readiness for an encounter with Jesus on the basis of his word of promise to be where we meet to celebrate the Supper, to be present as Lord of the Feast.

Here too is part of the implications of such a New Testament expression as 'the body of Christ'. The eucharistic bread is called the body of Christ, as indeed are we ourselves. The chalice is filled with the fruit of the vine, but the faithful activity of Christians is also called (in John 15) the fruit of the vine. The eucharistic gifts are the body and blood of Christ but the congregation that eats and drinks them is the body of Christ, living with the life – the blood – which he poured out for them. And so Augustine can properly say to his people, 'There you are on the paten, there you are in the chalice.'[3]

So when we celebrate the sacrament which is the real presence of Jesus we can fairly expect to find it all somewhat ambiguous. There is necessarily a touch of vertigo about celebrating someone who is dead to this present age and alive to God in an age that we as yet have very little idea of. The sacramental symbols with which we celebrate have an ambiguity arising from the way they are qualified within the eucharistic rite, an ambiguity over and above that which all things have in being parables only in potency, awaiting their proper specification. The sacramental signs are signs of a real absence to those who do not have faith. And for those who do have faith, they are also signs of an absence, that kind of absence which is in itself a mode of presence, as in a house where someone has just died. Even for those who do have faith, life in the world takes on its meaning through the celebration of the Eucharist as life in a world to which Christ is dead. That is what is involved in the Church's articulation of its faith in terms of transubstantiation. That teaching insists that we must live within the linguistic community of the New Testament, a community founded on and still centred by the Scriptures: we submit to that discipline of celebration which the Bible sets in order. But the doctrine of transubstantiation also stresses that we must not try to draw any logical conclusions from this, or bring in extraneous questions from another realm of discourse. 'This is my body; this is my blood': we are required to give our assent, Amen, Yes, to that, to the offer of the gifts as the body and blood of the Lord. But we must not go on to imagine that if we break the bread we are breaking the body of Christ, nor even that if we touch the bread we are touching the body of Christ. We must say that this is the body of Christ, but not that the body of Christ is round, whitish-brown, or even here-and-now. At root, transubstantiation insists that we play the eucharistic game properly. It is

[3] Augustine, *Sermon* 209.

an attempt to keep the *logos* out of the *mythos*, logical considerations out of sacramental ones. The glorified Christ is present by his glorified body, that is, the body which is altogether and only the body as subject and not at all the body as object. The body is present in a way which negates the limitations of the presence of the non-glorified human body to other men and to the world, and which transforms the conditions of that bodily presence as we know it, normally involving as that does a distance between one man and the next, between a man and the world, and between a man and himself. But this sort of presence can only be signified: the 'accidents' of bread and wine *remain*. The substantial presence of the glorified Christ does not act in the way that substances as we know them in the world act; it remains always other than the world and the believer. Part of what it means for the body of Christ to be a 'glorified' body is for it to be able to be represented in this sort of way.

And the signs are themselves signs of brokenness, rather than wholeness. They point away from the here and now towards the time and place in which Christ is lifted up, the time and place of Calvary. The signs are signs of sacrifice and loss, signs of disappointment. Each Sunday when we assemble we hope and pray for the coming of the Lord, and each Sunday to date we have been disappointed. He does not come in the way in which we hope that he will come, though come he does. The signs are not outside the sacrament; they are not veils masking the sacrament's reality; it is in and through the signs that the reality appears and the Lord reveals himself. Because Jesus at the Last Supper placed himself in the order of signs, the sacraments effect by signifying. In the Eucharist we are not to seek an encounter with Christ outside the sacrament's own internal modalities. The signs are broken bread and poured-out wine, bread and wine *sumendus et bibendus*, 'to be eaten and drunk'. The bread is interpreted as the body of Christ given for us, broken for us, broken in pieces for us; the wine as the blood of Christ poured out for us and for all men so that sins may be forgiven, shed, sprinkled for the life of the world; bread and wine separately given, interpreting the death of Christ as a voluntary death. The expression 'poured out' all through the Old and New Testaments is a sacrificial expression: a word belonging to the technical language of sacrifice. It is through a sign of *sacrifice* that we have access to Christ. The Last Supper before, the Mass after Calvary interpret that unique, once-and-for-all event as being concerned with us: 'Here your affair is being treated of'.

But the Lord's death is presented to us, for us to share by and through the sign of a meal. 'When we eat this bread and drink this cup we placard the death of the Lord until he comes' (1 Cor. 11.26). The human activity of eating and drinking finds a new value which it had been awaiting until the moment Jesus enacted his prophetic sign at the Last Supper. By this sign, he had set in motion the events of that night and the Good Friday that followed; by it, too, he had committed the future. Through this sign we see that it is Christ who is the source and support of human life: not only sacramentally but in all the other ways in which we feed on him. There is a table of the Word as well as a table of the sacrament, and the same food is provided at both. Ignatius of Antioch tells us that faith is the flesh of Christ, the substance of the Christian life, and that the blood is love, the energy that courses through the veins and arteries of the life of the Church-body of Jesus. With the flesh and blood of his word as with pure food and drink, writes Origen, he refreshes all mankind.

'When we eat this bread and drink this cup we placard the Lord's death until he comes'. Not for ever, but for the time being. Whenever we do it, we do it in the knowledge that it is only a passing phase. We look forward to the time when sacraments will be no more, when God will be all in all. Whenever we eat and drink it, it is always as *viaticum*, food for the *via*, the way through. A proper celebration of the Eucharist will always let this appear. There will be times when it will seem appropriate to celebrate the Eucharist triumphantly, with pomp and ceremony. But the signs are broken signs, and as in Brechtian theatre there must always be some distancing, a style of acting in quotation marks. At the Eucharist we should always behave as people who see that the signs are signs of a Jesus who is for ever dead to the present age, even though alive to God. The Eucharist is always the sacrament of the dying, of our dying now and of our terminal dying.

This is why the Eucharist and martyrdom go together: the death of the martyr approximates as closely as possible to the death of Christ. Indeed, in his dying the martyr may be said to become the Eucharist. Ignatius of Antioch, being taken from the

East to Rome to suffer martyrdom in the Colosseum, speaks of that pure oblation of Malachi's prophecy which is brought from east to west.

> I am the wheat of God, and I am to be ground by the teeth of the wild beasts so as to be found the pure bread of Christ.[4]

In the legend of St Lawrence, Lawrence speaks to Pope Sixtus II as he is led out to martyrdom, and compares his approaching death with the Eucharist:

> It has never been your custom to offer sacrifice without a deacon.[5]

Those of the English Catholic martyrs who were priests used to kiss the scaffold on which they were about to be hanged as they kissed the altar on which they were about to offer Mass. The psalm of the eucharistic cup is the psalm of martyrdom:

> What shall I render to the Lord for all that he has done for me? I will take the cup of salvation and call on the name of the Lord. (Ps. 116.13)

Perhaps the best expression of this comes in the letter that a group of early Christians wrote to the other churches to tell them what had happened to their old bishop Polycarp. When he was bound to the stake he pronounced the eucharistic prayer over himself:

> Lord God Almighty, Father of your well-beloved Son, Jesus Christ, I bless you that you have counted me worthy of this day and of this hour, so that I may be counted amongst the martyrs and may take part in the chalice of your Christ for the resurrection of eternal life, in the incorruptibility of the Holy Spirit. May I then be received in your presence today as a sacrifice rich and acceptable. For this and for all things I praise you, I bless you, I thank you, I glorify you, through the eternal and heavenly high priest, Jesus Christ, through whom to you, with the Holy Spirit, is glory now and in the ages to come. Amen.[6]

[4] Ignatius of Antioch, *To the Romans*, IV.
[5] Cf. *Butler's Lives of the Saints*, revised and supplemented by H. Thurston, S.J., and D. Attwater, III (London 1956), p. 297.
[6] *Martyrdom of Polycarp*, XIV.

The letter goes on:

> When he had pronounced the Amen and finished his prayer, the executioners lit the fire. A great flame sprang up and we saw a wonder: the fire formed as it were an arch, and it surrounded the body of the martyr. And he himself in the midst appeared not like flesh being burned but like bread in an oven.[7]

It is in martyrdom that what is given obscurely in the Eucharist receives its full reality – the presence in his people of the *Christus passus*, the Christ who died and who rose again.[8]

---

[7] *Ibid.*, XV.
[8] See also G. Preston, O.P., 'The Eucharist: Development or Deviation?', *New Blackfriars* 51. 601 (1970), pp. 269–273; 51. 602 (1970), pp. 317–321; *God's Way to be Man*, pp. 82–91; *Hallowing the Time*, pp. 132–135; 'The Feast of Christ's Body and Blood', *Doctrine and Life* 31. 6 (1981), pp. 366–370.

15

Marriage

JESUS is God with humanity taken to himself, the Word of God made and become flesh, become world and history, created into the creation. But not in an instant, as though one could have a full understanding of the incarnation by speaking of the deepest implications of the annunciation of the angel to Mary. With no uncertainty or quibbling, the Catholic tradition insists that from the first moment of his conception in the womb of Mary Jesus of Nazareth must be called God; and yet the Church's Scriptures also include Paul's assertion that he was 'constituted Son of God in power by his resurrection from the dead according to the Spirit of holiness' (Rom. 1.4). Only by being lifted up and glorified did he become 'Son of God in power', God for us, the face of God turned towards us. And that is because only at his resurrection did he become fully human, truly 'in the image'. All men are human, but One is more human than others and that One is God. We as yet are not fully human, but Jesus is already so: in him what is for us a project is even now realised. Originating in the same gene pool is a necessary substratum for becoming human, and whatever shares the flesh and blood of that animal which is the human race cannot be treated as non-human, or without human rights and dignity. Yet this is a rather vestigial way to be human: for humankind is more than a common structure of tissue. It is something to be achieved, or, better, received. For us to be saved is for us to enter into the name of Jesus, the story of the progressive humanisation of God. According to that story, the Son of God became Son of Man so that the sons of men might become sons of God. We have to make that project our own, each of us individually and the whole race corporately. We have to accept that task laid upon us to grow up in all things into him who is the head, to be in the image of God, indeed in some sense to *be* him who is the image of God in person.

The Church is the sacrament which expresses, celebrates and

effects the immediation of all men in the new humanity which is the humanity of God. Christ and the Church form one mystical person, one body, the whole Christ. As some ancient manuscripts of the New Testament say in the course of the Letter to the Ephesians, 'We are members of Christ's body, of his flesh and of his bones'. The Church is Christ's way of being in the world, Christ revealing himself in numerous forms, not only as the sign of a datum of salvation already achieved, but also as means for the *agendum*, for the project, for what is to be done. Christ is still in process of becoming all in all. And so when the Fathers speak of the prayer of Christ in our present, they describe him as praying for the resurrection of his body. For Augustine,

> Since ... the whole Christ is Head and Body ... the members of Christ understand, and Christ in his members understands, and the members of Christ understand in Christ, that Head and members are one Christ. ... We are with him in heaven through hope; he is with us on earth through love.[1]

Christ, we may say, is the nucleus in the sense of 'nucleus' that we meet with in chemistry and biology; he is the exemplary unity which actively draws disordered free elements into its own pattern of organisation. In this way, the whole Christ is the sacrament of salvation for the whole of mankind.

Now of the Church as body of Christ, just as of the eucharistic bread as body of Christ, it must be said that the whole is in all its parts. When the eucharistic bread is broken, the body of Christ is in no way divided. When the global community of the Church is separated, the body of Christ is similarly in no way sundered. Any part of the whole is as much the way in which Christ is present in the world as the whole itself. So whenever and wherever the Church meets together, there is the whole Church, since there is Christ. The smallest gathering possible is itself the Church, in that according to the promise of the historical Jesus whenever two or three are gathered together in his name, there he is in the midst of them; and where Christ is, there is the Church and the Holy Spirit and all grace. The gathering together of even two people in the name of Christ is therefore the Church just as intensively, although clearly not as extensively, as the Great

---

[1] Augustine, *Narrations on the Psalms*, LIV. 3.

Church throughout the world, the *Catholica*, is the Church. Such a gathering of even two people in the name of Christ is the Church in a particularly intensive and pure way when those two are gathered together for the whole of their lives, accepting the project of a love like that of Christ himself. A married couple form what the Second Vatican Council calls an *ecclesia domestica*, a 'house church', a notion which goes back at least to Augustine and has its roots in the New Testament itself. Husband and wife are the smallest unit of the Church, a micro-church as John Chrysostom puts it, the fundamental cell of the Church. So fundamental a cell are they that they can be called a sacrament of the Church, using the genitive here both subjectively and objectively. They are both a sacrament which pertains to the Church and a sacrament which is the Church. They are what Chrysostom calls elsewhere an icon of the Church – and an icon actually re-presents what it depicts. In their life together the married couple incarnate the Church and focus it, both as gift and task, *datum* and *agendum*, salvation and saving mission and commission. It is because the married couple actually *is* the Church that it is properly called a sacrament.

The Scriptures see marriage as rooted in creation, in the very nature which we all share. When Christ is questioned about divorce, he sets aside the Mosaic legislation and returns to the account of creation in Genesis, where Adam, man, mankind, is made androgynous.

> God made man in his own image, male and female made he them. (Gen. 1.27)

In his God-induced ecstasy, Adam is made *vis-à-vis* himself; and in the love of man and woman Man recovers his original unity of one flesh. The unity in which mankind is made is recovered in the mutual giving of two lives, of two centres of consciousness. That is: the grace of God is not something simply to fall back on in moments of guilt and sickness (as the sacraments of return – penance, anointing – might suggest). Nor is the grace of God something to appeal to when we are made aware of our fundamentally flawed or inadequate existence (as we might think if we thought only of baptism and confirmation). Rather it is encountered and experienced at the heart, core and centre of daily life. According to St Thomas, it is not so much the giving of marital consent as the living out of that consent which signifies the union of Christ and his Church. It is the whole of married life that is the efficacious sign, the dedication of man and woman in partnership to the Christian mission. St Robert Bellarmine seems to have been the first to make that comparison of the sacramental duration of marriage with the sacramental duration of the eucharistic elements which has become a commonplace in modern theologies of marriage. Neither marriage nor the Eucharist are sacraments only in the moment of their coming to be – at the words of institution or when the marriage vows are exchanged – but as long as the sign remains. In a similar way, the Second Vatican Council talks of marriage as a conjugal and familial community, a community of life and love, building partly there on the Roman legal definition of marriage as *consortium omnis vitae*, a 'fellowship in all living'.[2]

In marriage there is meant to be expressed and effected that uniting of the human race in Christ in which people are not fused by their union but rather every person finds fulfilment through others, as the human race finds its fulfilment in Christ and Christ finds his fulfilment in the human race. This sort of fulfilment is part of what the Bible means by 'glory'. 'Glory' is how a person matters, the weight he carries in the world, his significance. The wife is the glory of the husband, and the husband the glory of the wife. The sense of 'glory' as splendour becomes fused with this in the Greek rite of marriage in which crowns are held over the heads of bride and groom and continually criss-crossed throughout the ceremony to indicate how each is the crown of the other. Shakespeare speaks of the fabulous phoenix and turtle:

> So they loved, as love in twain
> Had the essence but in one.
> Two distincts, division none:
> Number there in love was slain. . . .
> Either was the other's mine.[3]

So St Thomas speaks of marriage as a two-in-one way of life, a single life and lifestyle: *individuae vitae consuetudo*.

Marriage expresses the Church precisely by being in the first place a natural institution, an activity rooted in the first creation.

[2] Cf. *Lumen Gentium*, 40; *Gaudium et Spes*, 48–52.
[3] W. Shakespeare, *The Phoenix and the Turtle*.

This natural institution, however, can be experienced in the Lord Jesus; indeed, it retains its full validity only when it is at least potentially open to being so experienced. This is the basis of the so-called 'Pauline privilege' in which the Church takes literally the advice given to the Christian community in Corinth by its apostle:

> To the rest I say, not the Lord, that if any brother has a wife who is an unbeliever, and she consents to live with him, he should not divorce her. If any woman has a husband who is an unbeliever, and he consents to live with her, she should not divorce him. ... But if the unbelieving partner desires to separate, let it be so. In such a case, the brother or sister is not bound. For God has called you to peace. (1 Cor. 7.12–13, 15)

When one partner, in other words, is not prepared to allow the natural institution of marriage to be even potentially open to finding the fulfilment of its meaning in expressing and effecting the love of Christ for the Church, then the marriage even as a natural institution ceases to be such. The so-called 'Petrine privilege' depends on the same sort of argumentation. A marriage between an unbaptised person and a baptised person, though entered into with the full agreement of the whole Church, can be set aside if it proves an obstacle to marriage finding its full significance. The prohibition of divorce between Christians is based on the assumption that it is not possible for a marriage entered into and experienced in Christ to be rejected without the whole Christian understanding of the love of Christ for the Church being *ipso facto* rejected.

As marriage is a natural institution which can be experienced in the Lord Jesus, so when two married pagans are baptised, their previous marriage is thereby confirmed in Christ and by that very fact becomes a sacrament in the strict sense. For centuries there was no church marriage at all in the sense of an ecclesiastical ceremony. When there did begin to be a Christian ritual of marriage, the ceremonial referred marriage back to its natural origins. For example, the bishop would give the bride's right hand to the groom, and so bring the wife to her husband in an explicit harking back to the story of God bringing Eve to Adam in Eden. As some forms of marriage put it,

As the first man, Adam, took Eve to be his wife in the paradise of Eden, so I, N., take you, N., to be my wife.

Until the end of the Middle Ages people in England were married outside the church building, in the secular world. (Given English weather this meant in effect in the church porch!) Only when the marriage had been entered into and witnessed to, did the couple go into church to receive a blessing on their union, to have it made explicitly Christian. Even now according to the rites of the established Church of England, people are married outside the sanctuary, going into it to have their marriage blessed in the name of Christ. Catholics have lost a great deal by situating the *whole* marriage ceremony in the centre of the Mass: lost the expression of how Christian marriage gives a deeper expression to human sexuality as such, lost the ritual enactment of the goodness of sexuality in its own right, of the goodness of the first creation. For as the ancient nuptial blessing words it, marriage was the only institution which did not lose its primordial blessing during the great flood.

Christian marriage is meant to give a deeper expression to human sexuality as such. This sexuality is the most obvious indicator of the fundamentally communal character of human existence, of how people are made for one another. The Judaeo-Christian tradition insists that marriage is part of that natural order which God created and saw was very good. Other religious traditions have tended to sacralise sexuality when they have not despised it, and there are many modern attempts to do both. But our tradition wants to say that man is a sexual being in a sense far deeper than is the case with any other species. The words 'male and female created he them' are not used for any other part of the created world. In contradistinction to even the highest primates, men and women know a sexual life which is not a marginal erotic function. The whole of their existence carries sexual implications. By its very nature sexual union between human beings so absorbs and expresses the whole personality that it becomes thereby an entirely unique kind of self-revelation and self-commitment. So lust is destructive of selfhood and of community, a sin of the spirit against the body. Kierkegaard has a dictum to the effect that the body is given to the soul in order to refine the soul. Marriage as a personal and loving relationship of the sexes is

148

creative of community and is itself community. The Church in miniature which is marriage in Christ points all human strivings towards their true goal, the growing up in all things into the measure of the stature of the fulness of Christ. Marriage, the principle within the world for the perpetuation of mankind on earth, is also, in faith, an instrument of salvation, for the directing of mankind to Christ.

In another way of putting it, husband and wife are to become one flesh. Marriage must be open to husband and wife becoming one flesh with one another and one flesh and one spirit with Christ, members of his body. One flesh in somewhat the way in which a violin and a bow are one musical instrument, or a key and a lock one mechanism. The wife, says Paul, is the husband's own body, and one must add that the husband is the wife's body, and the one flesh which they form is the body of Christ. The wife is the husband's way of being in the world; and the one flesh which they form is Christ's way of being in the world, his expressive form, the nexus of his presence to creation. Husband and wife become one single life, as Eve is aboriginally Adam's flesh; the man knows himself in knowing his wife and she herself in knowing her husband. Marriage more than any other sacrament engages the whole of life: going to bed together and washing up together as well as sharing the flesh of Christ in the Eucharist. The canonisation of marriage as a sacramental structure in the Church mercifully prohibits any departmentalisation of the Christian life as between liturgy and living, sacraments and ethics.

In the whole of their lives together, husband and wife have the task laid on them of ministering Christ to each other. Each has to play Christ to the other, even when one is an unbelieving partner. 'The unbelieving wife is consecrated through her husband,' says Paul (1 Cor. 7.14), and the unbelieving husband through his wife. It is primarily by sacrificial love that they so minister Christ, in that marriage is not so much a self-acquisition as a self-giving and self-emptying, willingly accepted as Christ willingly accepted his passion. This, for St Thomas, is how marriage is a sacrament. For him, any sacrament must be rooted in the passion and death of Christ, and marriage is rooted there by its love, a kenotic kind of love like that of Christ himself. The specifically Christian kind of love called *agapē* can include and transmute

149

other kinds of love; more often than not it is only realised when it does so include other loves, the love of eros and the love of friendship. Marriage, says Chrysostom, is the sacrament of erotic love as it is the sacrament of the love of friendship. Marriage contracts the immensities of all kinds of loving. The love of marriage, in being *agapē*, is not a Don Juan love but a covenant love, what the Second Vatican Council calls a *foedus matrimoniale*, a love 'till death do us part or the Lord shall come', as our Baptist brethren put it. It is a bond or chain, *vinculum caritatis*, as is the Eucharist. Part of the task and commission laid on married couples is that of being faithful throughout life to each other: for better, for worse; for richer, for poorer; in sickness and in health. If one partner is to minister Christ to the other, then the love involved must not be made dependent on the other being worthy of such love. One entrusts himself to mankind in the Church. The micro-church of marriage is to be as forgiving as the macro-church: 'What can separate us from the love of Christ?' (Rom. 8.35).

This kind of emptying love is that of the martyr to Christ. So many of the sacraments find their ultimate reference in martyrdom. All through the Book of Revelation, marriage and martyrdom go together, and in later Church history the same kind of language has been used of both. The crowning of bride and groom in the Greek rite is called a *stephanōsis*, and deliberately linked with the name of Stephen, the 'crowned one', the first and typical martyr. This is how marriage comes to be another rite of initiation, another crisis of identity, of death to the past and birth to new life. 'A man will leave father and mother and will cleave to his wife' (Gen. 2.24): he will have to discover a new identity in being-with, in co-existence. Man was called to such being-with from the beginning. 'God created the co-existent', as Cyril of Alexandria put it. The Christian husband and wife share in the kenotic love of Christ the martyr in rejecting the manipulation of sex by society and equally in renouncing that domination of the other which is so common a part of the sexual affirmation of life. In their love husband and wife are called as each other's Christ to let the full humanity of the other appear, the humanity of the pure of heart. These are they who have become virgin in and through their sexual love in marriage, for sexuality here has ceased to be in any way demonic and has become altogether personalised. So marriage as a *con-iugium*, a joint yoke, is not part of the order of the day, but comes from the order of the last day, of Christ's present which is our future. The love of marriage is an *anamnēsis* of Christ's future coming.

Marriage must not become what the French call an *égoïsme à deux*, a 'mutual egotism', any more than the local church may properly become a mutual admiration society. If it is not actively nuclear, missionary, it is nothing. The purpose of marriage (in one very significant strand of Catholic tradition its primary purpose) is to pass over into the larger community of a Christian family. As the Second Vatican Council teaches:

> In the house church, parents by their word and example should be the first preachers and heralds of the faith to their children.[4]

And so there come together the three so-called 'goods' of marriage: children, fidelity, sacrament. In the Thomist scheme it is the sacrament that ultimately matters, the couple as sign of the love of Christ and the Church for each other. But in the present age, it can only be such a sign if it is also a means to the building up of the body of mankind into the body of Christ. In the age to come, all that will remain will be the love. Being children of the resurrection they will neither marry nor be given in marriage because there will no longer be any need to make up the ravages of death by the propagation of the human race. The bond will remain but in the transfigured conditions of the age to come. Glorified, it will be the only human grouping that will survive, unlike the nation or the ministry: no longer a means for the propagation of the love of Christ but simply an expression of that love. It will no longer be what it is *for*: the christianising of each other, of the children and of the world, *ecclesia congregans*, but simply what it *is*, a community of love, *ecclesia congregata*.[5]

---

[4] *Apostolicam actuositatem*, 11.
[5] Cf. *God's Way to be Man*, pp. 68–73.

16

Ministry

THE primordial sacrament of man's salvation, as we have seen, is Jesus himself. In him God and man are reconciled, personally and immediately but not as yet universally. God has reconciled humanity to himself; Christ has made peace by his blood on the Cross. But that reconciliation still needs extension and increase – an extension into ever new areas of the lives of those who have already turned to Christ, and an extension of a sort which will include ever more people. In the words of an ancient collect, 'May your Church grow in numbers and holiness'. The sacrament of that is the Church which as a sign simply *is*, and as an instrument *is for*. As we saw in the last chapter this is also the case with the smallest church, the married couple who give the *Catholica* a local habitation and a name. What marriage and the Church *are* is love: the love between God and man which Jesus personally is; what the Church and marriage *are for* is the upbuilding of each other in love, and self-surpassing in love: in children, and in mission and ministry to the whole world. When Christ has been formed in all men, then that ministry and mission will cease. The Church will cease to be *for* anything and will simply *be*. The weekdays of work will give place to the eternal sabbath of contemplation; the forty days of Lent will give place to the fifty days of the one day of Easter. But until then, until Christ who is our life appears and we also appear with him in glory, the ministry and the mission necessarily remain. Until then, people have to bring Christ to others, both in that church which is intensively but not extensively as much church as the *Catholica* is, and in the *Catholica* itself. And that aspect of the life of the Church we call ministry is also held to be a sacrament, the sacrament of Order.

The people of God is not an undifferentiated mass: it is an ordered body. It possesses a hierarchical structure, always remembering that the hierarchy is basically the whole ordered body and not some group of people within the body. That is how 'hierarchy' is used in the writings of the fifth-century Syrian Father who used the pseudonym 'Denys', and from him the word and concept entered Christian thought. In the people of God different individuals have different functions *vis-à-vis* one another: they minister to one another. They are not simply *with* each other as they will be in the kingdom; they are *for* each other. These different functions are actions of Christ, ways in which Christ ministers to us, he who in his historical existence came among us as 'one who serves' (literally, who 'ministers'). Peter baptises, Paul baptises, even Donatus baptises – but it is Christ who baptises. Peter ministers, Paul ministers, even Donatus ministers – but it is Christ who ministers. The Church may be one flesh with Christ, but it is also over against Christ. Christ is the head *vis-à-vis* the body; Christ is the husband *vis-à-vis* the wife. The heart of marriage is the one flesh: that is why the sign will continue in the kingdom as a reality. The heart of the order is the '*vis-à-vis*': that is why the ordering of the Church will cease when God becomes all in all. Then Christ will no longer need to be the *vis-à-vis* of his Church, or even to be king of his people. As Paul puts it:

> Then comes the end, when Christ delivers the kingdom of God the Father after destroying every rule and every authority and power. For he must reign until he has put all his enemies under his feet. The last enemy to be destroyed is death. For 'God has put all things in subjection under his feet' [a citation from Psalm 8]. When it says 'All things are put in subjection under him', it is plain that he is excluded who put all things under him [that is to say, God the Father]. When all things are subjected to him, then the Son himself will also be subjected to him who put all things under him [the Father] that God may be all in all. (1 Cor. 15.24–28)

Even Christ's kingship is only a ministry for the time of building up, for the time of warfare and struggle against the authorities and powers. When God, who is Love, is all in all, then even that ministry will cease; Christ will no longer be the *vis-à-vis* of the Church but will stand together with the Church before the Father in the Holy Spirit. Until then, however, there is a polarity of Christ and the Church. For the time being, they are each other's counterpart or *Gegenüber*. Until then, there is a reciprocity of the Church and Christ. Until then, Christ is amongst us as one who serves; he is with us under the modality of ministry. And because we are as we are, in order for him to be present he must be represented and represented, imaged, in ministry, the appropriate modality for a time of building up. His washing the world's feet must find its icon.

All this is typified when the Church comes together to make Eucharist. Not that the Church is only being Church when it celebrates the Mass; but that is nevertheless the most typical situation in which it is Church. The *Institutio Generalis* of the Roman Missal describes the Mass as 'the action of Christ and the people of God hierarchically ordered'. In its most typical manifestation during the present epoch, the Church is not a haphazard conglomeration of people but an ordered or ordained assembly. The General Instruction goes on:

> Everyone in the eucharistic assembly has the right and duty to take his own part according to the diversity of orders and functions. Everyone, whether minister or layman, should do all that which and only that which pertains to the gift he has to exercise, so that from the very ordering of the celebration it may appear how the Church is constituted in her different orders and ministries.

And this is to be done

> not to add external splendour, but to signify in a clearer light the mystery of the Church, which is the sacrament of unity.[1]

The New Testament itself had already spoken of such a variety of orders and ministries. It speaks of diverse forms of services, in which the Church as the body of Christ is organically structured. We read of Christ as

> the Head, from which the whole body, nourished and knit together through its joints and ligaments, grows with a growth that is from God. (Col. 2.19)

The imagery here is taken from the medical science of Hippocrates and Galen, according to which the joints and ligaments, the sensitive and motor nerves of the entire body, are derived

---

[1] *General Instruction on the Roman Missal*, 58–59.

from the head. The Church, then, is being compared to the space in which Christ communicates to the body of believers his own Passover experience of death and resurrection. Christ contains within himself all the subsequent development of the Church rather as (to mix our metaphors) the apex of a cone contains within itself the whole of the subsequent projection of the cone. And so the ministries are in dependence on the one ministry of Christ.

The ministries and orders are listed in the twelfth chapter of the Letter to the Romans as follows:

> having charisms that differ according to the grace that is given to us, whether prophecy, according to the analogy of faith; whether ministry, in the ministering; whether the one teaching, in teaching; or the one exhorting, in the exhortation; the one sharing, in simplicity; the one taking the lead, in diligence; the one showing mercy, in cheerfulness. (Rom. 12.6–8)

In the First Letter to the Corinthians we are told that

> God placed some in the Church, firstly apostles, secondly prophets, thirdly teachers, then powers, then charismata of healings, helps, governings, kinds of tongues. (1 Cor. 12.28)

Earlier in this same twelfth chapter of 1 Corinthians we find another somewhat different list of ministries, a clear indication that Paul did not regard the number, kinds and ranking of ministries as particularly fixed.

> To each person is given the manifestation of the Spirit to profit with it: for to one through the Spirit is given a word of wisdom, to another a word of knowledge according to the same Spirit, to another faith in the same Spirit, and to another charismata of healings in the one Spirit, and to another operations of powers, and to another prophecy, and to another discernings of spirits, and to another kinds of tongues, to another interpretations of tongues. And one and the same Spirit works all these things, distributing to each one separately as he purposes. (1 Cor. 12.7–11)

In the Letter to the Ephesians there is yet another list:

> To every one of us was given grace according to the measure of the gift of Christ ... and he gave to some apostles, to some

prophets, to some evangelists and pastors and some teachers, for the perfecting of the saints, for the work of ministry, for building up the body of Christ. (Eph. 4.7, 11–12)

Elsewhere in the New Testament and especially in the Pastoral Epistles we read of *episkopoi*, *presbyteroi* and *diakonoi* which could be translated as 'bishops', 'priests' and 'deacons', although this would give the wrong feel. Interestingly, these three are never mentioned in the same place.

Judging by this evidence, therefore, ministry in the Church is an almost infinitely varied functioning. There are many different functions noted in the New Testament and no suggestion that even the sum of these lists would exhaust the possible forms of ministering. The ordering of the Church is in no way presented as the division of the Church into simply two classes, clergy and laity. Insofar as words in any way equivalent to our 'clergy' and 'laity' are used at all, there is a single *klēros* and a single *laos*, one people of God which is at once his *klēros*, 'portion', 'inheritance', and truly his *laos*, his 'people'. As Peter tells his fellow presbyters,

I, the co-elder, exhort the elders among you, shepherd the flock of God among you not as exercising lordship over (God's) *klēros*. (1 Pet. 5.21)

For Gregory the Great it is love that makes the Church a *concors diversitas*, a concordant diversity, a diverse concord. In the service of this love there can only be a distinction of functions, not of rank in any secular sense. Each Christian exercises some ministry; each person in some way ministers Christ – or rather, Christ ministers through each person, and he ministers as he wills.

Each believer, then, plays Christ in some way to each other believer. All Christians are called to be what Paul describes as 'fellow-workers with God': not clergy working with God in regard to the laity as such, but each minister as a fellow-worker with God in regard to those whom he serves. For St Thomas, Christ is the exemplar of all ecclesiastical offices, and so every minister of the Church in some way plays Christ, *gerit typum Christi*. The Council of Trent left open the question of whether or not the so-called minor orders are to be regarded as sacramental.

(Thomas was clear that they were.) According to the Fathers of Trent

> The hierarchy consists of bishops, presbyters and ministers [not deacons!].[2]

The strict division in some recent Church documents on the minor ministries between clergy and laity, in which orders in *any* sacramental sense *at all* are restricted to deacons, priests and bishops, can only be seen as a regression from the New Testament picture which is also the picture of tradition. It is not that one would wish to restrict the idea of the Church's ordered life to the traditional eight forms; rather, the traditional eight forms witnessed to the vast range of possibilities of ministry in a way in which the recent restriction does not.

There is a deeply Catholic notion that the minister of the Church acts *in persona Christi*, 'in the person of Christ'. The present Roman Missal, for example, speaks of the priest who presides at Mass as playing the part of Christ: *personam Christi gerens*. The minister acts the part of Christ, and so plays Christ, not in the sense of the theatre of illusion but in the sense of the theatre of Brecht. In that latter kind of theatre the actor thinks of himself not as impersonating the character he is playing but as narrating (in words and gestures) the actions of another person. To say here of an actor 'he did not merely act Lear, he *was* Lear' would be a devastating criticism. This implies a deliberateness of action, a consciousness of the presence of the audience, an acknowledgment of the reality of the situation. In Brechtian theatre the study of human nature is replaced by the study of human relationships. The main concern is not the characters but the story in which they are involved. The story is the centre-piece of the performance. It is the sequence of events which constitutes the social experiment of the play. There is a trust in the validity of external behaviour and not an overpowering concern for 'sincerity'. Characters are such precisely as acting and reacting on each other. The emphasis is not on the inner life of characters but on the way they behave towards one another. Basic attitudes are what Brecht calls *gestus*: the whole range of the outward signs of social relationships, including

[2] H. Denzinger, *Enchiridion*, 1770.

deportment, interaction, facial expression and gesture. *Gestus* is the stylised expression of human interaction. Language itself is to be 'gestic': certain kinds of speech contain the appropriate *gestus* and almost force the actor to assume the correct stance, the correct tone of voice. The actor, to repeat, never becomes the character he is playing, never tries to give the impression that he *is* Lear, but enables the audience, those whom he serves, to find themselves confronted by the character in his own independent reality. Surely this is very much what is meant when a Christian by his ministry is said to 'play Christ' to others. He plays him by outward and visible signs. The Mass, like daily living, is not meant to be a passion play, but an attempt to embroil the whole of humanity in the story which stretches from Genesis to the Apocalypse.

All ministries are an integral part of the sacrament which is the Church. The ministries let the dialogical structure of Christian existence emerge. The God of the Judaeo-Christian tradition is the God who speaks, addresses people, calls, invites a reply. At the heart of the Gospel there is also a personal challenge and encounter. The parabolic mode is crucial: man is invited to enter the structure of a story, to find his own matter treated of in the comic or tragic form of a parable.

Let us look in conclusion at those ministries which are on any showing, however, the most crucial – that of the apostle and its continuations and forms of assistance in the bishop, presbyter and deacon.

The *apostle* is the one who has the fulness of Christian ministry in himself and who in a quite special way plays Jesus. 'As the Father has sent me,' says Jesus to the apostles, 'even so I send you' (John 20.21). Jesus is the apostle sent by the Father and he himself in turn sends out the Twelve. The notion of apostleship, of being sent, covers the whole distance, it seems, between God and the world. The apostle represents Jesus to the Church and to the world, principally by speaking for Christ. He is 'an ambassador for Christ'. Of the Hebrew functionary who stands behind the New Testament apostle it was said that 'a man's *shaliach* ['apostle'] is as the man himself'. The Word of God which the Church hears comes to the Church from without, mediated to it by the apostles and apostolic men. The Church is not its own construction but receives itself from the dead and risen Christ. The apostle coming to the Church from without stands for the divine initiative and transcendence.

And the apostle in his turn sends out others. Primarily he sends the *bishop* who thus also comes to the Church from without. The rite of ordination by the laying on of hands means that the bishop, even though he may properly be elected by the Church in which he is to serve, also stands for the otherness of God, for the Word which comes to the Church from without and forms a tradition. This fundamental situation is expressed and realised in the celebration of the Supper, by the dialogue of the assembly with a president who is given to it from without and so represents the Christ who was sent to that assembly by the Father. That is, the president is Christ's ambassador, whom the assembly receives rather than gives to itself. The president is the 'vicar of Christ', the representative of the sacrificing, sanctifying, preaching Christ. He it is who has the function of the Word, the task of creating community. The early-second-century document called the *Didache* says

> You shall honour as the Lord him who speaks the Word of God to you, for where the lordship is spoken, there the Lord is.[3]

But we remember at once here that this is *Brechtian* theatre: the actor is not the character he represents; no more in the Catholic tradition do we confuse person and ministry. So in the purest Western way of celebrating the Supper, the bishop never addresses Jesus (he is playing Jesus) but speaks only to the Father and to the congregation. The people acclaim Jesus in such acclamations as the *Kyrie*, the *Benedictus*, the *Agnus Dei*, and most of the *Gloria*. The bishop is honoured as Christ in his relationship to the people, though once again he is never confused with Christ. For example, in a primitive basilica, it is the bishop – not the altar – who is attended by lights and incense. But always there are alienation effects: the bishop, for example, prays openly and specifically through Christ.

All the other orders refract the fulness of the function of the apostle and bishop as vicar, representative, of Christ. When the bishop is not available, then the *presbyter* takes on the function of the bishop. The *deacon* plays the part of Jesus in reading,

---

[3] *Didache*, XI. 1.

actualising the words of Jesus in the gospel, and thus polarises the congregation and Jesus, body and head, addressing the Church from without. (This is why the reading of one's own Missal while vernacular Scriptures are read aloud is so perverse.) And here we can enter a reference to the wider circle of ministries: so for those who read any of the Scriptures, those who lead the singing, those who show others to their places with the welcome of Christ, those who ring the bell to summon people with the call of Christ, those who give the bread of the Eucharist to others – all of these are making the dialogical structure of Christian existence manifest in a structuring which is a prerequisite of any sacramental activity. Everyone, however, both ministers and is ministered to – even the bishop, in whom there appears as much of the apostolic function as can be transmitted. He too is a hearer with the hearers, as someone ministers the Word to him. In many rites, his deacon brings him the sacrament – another alienation effect in good Brechtian style. The apostle always remains a disciple. As Augustine puts it, 'I am a bishop for you, but a Christian with you'.[4]

All this is in the function of the mission of the Church *militant*. Here we have, according to St Thomas, the point of all sacramental character. The mission of the Church is

> for the perfecting of the saints to the work of ministry, to the building up of the body of Christ, until we all arrive at the unity of the faith and of the full knowledge of the Son of God, at a complete man, at the measure of the statute of the fulness of Christ. (Eph. 4.13)

This task is not only intra-ecclesial but extra-ecclesial. The ministry and mission of the Church must be to the whole world. To exercise a ministry *in medio ecclesiae*, 'in the midst of the Church', should be to mirror and represent one's extra-liturgical activity. Paul, for example, speaks of his missionary work as 'a liturgy for Christ Jesus to the heathen' (Rom. 15.16). Doing one's liturgy demands a certain consistency. So the bishop who represents Christ to the people of God must represent him to the world. The martyr-bishop is an ecclesial ideal in that he shows forth so strikingly the consistency of his liturgy: so too the

---

[4] Augustine, *Sermon* 46, 2.

martyr-deacon. The ministry is task and project, the struggle to be consistent in the performing of liturgy. The Church is ordained in a multiplicity of ways just as the Church's service of the world is multiple. But however one serves the world, one serves it in series with one's intra-ecclesial ministry. Not all ministries to the world will be represented in any obvious way in the liturgical assembly for most of the time; yet everyone in the Christian assembly *has* a ministry. Sometimes this will be on an *ad hoc* basis, as with the prophesying of Amos; sometimes for a shortish period of time, as people in the helping professions, for instance, change their jobs. Sometimes, on the other hand, it will be for life, as in the case of the bishop in whom the sign is so full that it necessitates a lifetime's commitment. A sound lived theology of episcopacy would not tolerate a bishop retiring or even moving to another diocese. But whichever ministry is ours, each ministry is meant to speak Christ until he comes, to continue what Père Yves Congar called the series of the world's incarnations, *sequentia sancti evangelii*. Every ministry structures the Church as Christ's *vis-à-vis*, playing him, allowing him to appear. When he *does* appear, then ministry will cease: the Church will cease to be ordered, to be ordained, and will simply *be* in love. We are told to pray that he comes quickly![5]

---

[5] Cf. *God's Way to be Man*, pp. 73–75.

17

Second Repentance

IF one could imagine an altogether smooth Christian life, one would think of a person initiated into Christ by way of baptism and Confirmation, continuing to share in the eucharistic life of the Church until his dying day and slowly but surely developing life in Christ in the world before God. In asking for baptism such a person would have acknowledged that his life was out of true, that he was not where he should be, nor where he had been made to be. He would have found in the overarching biblical story from Genesis to Revelation an interpretation of his own existence as displaced, and in being initiated into Christ would regard himself as having returned to where he was meant to be. He might have found the story of the prodigal son, especially as interpreted in the early Christian centuries, a good image of himself. The prodigal son goes to a far country, far from the home of the father who is God. That far country is the present situation of mankind. In becoming man it is to that far country that the Word of God goes. There was nowhere else where he could have become man, because man was nowhere else than there. As St Bernard says, 'The Word took flesh, not the flesh of Adam before the Fall but *my* flesh'.[1] And St Paul, taking up Second Isaiah's picture of the Suffering Servant, goes so far as to say that he was 'made sin' for us. There, in that far country, he prayed to God. There he recapitulated in himself the whole body of mankind, and from there he returned to the Father. He arose (literally) and went to his Father. He returned by way of exodus rather than by ecstasy, for what stands between the world and God in the Judaeo-Christian tradition is not a contradiction, not a metaphysical distance, but a revolt. The world is estranged from God not by its nature but by its choice. There is a history of estrangement, and so the return is also in history and by historical choice. Jesus initiates the return to the house of the universal

[1] Cf. Bernard, *Sermon 4, For the Vigil of Christmas.*

Father: inaugurating a new humanity he becomes the return of man to God. Now, in the Father's house, he is man returned to God, man's return to God made concrete. In his very person he is the sacrament of that return. Insofar as other men become part of him do they also return. Because this return is by way of exodus rather than ecstasy it can be commemorated, shared and celebrated.

In being baptised, a person enters into that great return of humanity to God which Christ is, the Jesus who is personally the embrace of the returning Son and his Father. It is not that Jesus is simply the first of a long line of men and women who will win through to the same sort of at-one-ment with God. He is not simply an example. He *is* the meeting of God and returning man, and so, in order to return to God ourselves, we must get involved with him in some way. This is what we do in the sacraments of initiation. We say that we become members, limbs, organs of the body which died, was raised and entered into glory and (to use the imagery of the parable) was clothed with the best robe and the ring and the shoes of the Holy Spirit. In baptism, confirmation and the Eucharist we become involved in that by assimilation, rather than imitation, feasting on the fatted calf. From that point onwards, the baptised man should be living the risen life of Christ, albeit in faith and not in full reality. We are told to look forward to the appearing of Christ, who will make what is hidden in our lives appear. Until that happens, it remains possible for us to lose our hold on the resurrection life of Christ. There remains depths in our personalities which still have to be converted and which we can refuse to bring to the light. To the extent that we are altogether converted, we might fairly expect the risen life of Jesus to appear in our bodies, as in an atypical way it does in people like the nineteenth-century Russian hermit Seraphim of Sarov whose body once glowed with the uncreated light of the transfiguration. But we are not yet living altogether the risen life of Jesus. Our bodies are still 'of the earth, earthy' (I Cor. 15.47); we live in our hearts in this present age as well as in the life of the age to come. We can opt out of the life of that age and consent to live as those for whom the death and resurrection of Jesus are not the ultimate meaning of existence. It is possible to make any number of compromises with the present ordering of the world rather than to make what we possess in promise more and more of a reality. It is possible for us in partial or more complete ways to lose our faith.

The most obvious example of a time when this can happen is a period of persecution. In such periods in the age of the early Church people sometimes stayed firm and confessed their faith in Christ, but sometimes they denied it. They made some public gesture, often enough a small one in itself, which denied that the life, death and resurrection of Jesus were what made sense of existence for them. Persecutions, however, always come to an end, and people often enough regret what they have done. In their heart of hearts they are sorry that they did not have the courage to stand up for the faith of Christ even at the cost of their lives. They want to return. What is to be done, when somebody who was in all respects a Christian before the persecution began denied that he was still a Christian during persecution and at the end of the persecution wished to resume the Christian life? The Letter to the Hebrews is absolutely clear about what can – or rather what cannot – be done with such a man.

> It is impossible to restore to repentance those who have once been enlightened, who have tasted the heavenly gift, and have become partakers of the Holy Spirit, and have tasted the goodness of the word of God and the powers of the age to come, if they then commit apostasy, since they crucify the Son of God on their own account and hold him up to contempt. (Heb. 6.4–6)

In the early days this was the position of the majority of the Church. Much as they might have been concerned with the fate of those who had apostatised under persecution, they were even more concerned with the well-being of the whole Church. They were afraid that if it was possible for people to resume their Christian life after apostasy, the next time there was persecution yet more people would deny the faith and the Church would be lost. Nevertheless, as time went on and the numbers of Christians increased, there was an almost inevitable diminution in fervour, which meant that when fresh persecutions broke out the percentage of Christians who might deny their faith was likely to climb higher. A bitter controversy divided the churches over how such people were to be treated. Great names left Catholic communion over it. The Roman church (the local church of the city of Rome) quite early took the line that it was possible for people who had denied the faith to be re-admitted to communion, at least on one occasion, and with very stringent conditions attached to their reconciliation. The Roman church was indeed the most important of the churches which came to maintain a position which might seem diametrically opposed to that of the Letter to the Hebrews, teaching that a man who had once repented, 'returned', in baptism, and had been enlightened and tasted the heavenly gift, could fall away from Christ, publicly deny what in baptism he had received and *still* come back, repent, return. This church and the churches that sided with it took their stand on the infinite mercy of God, and held to their position through serious wrangles and schisms. God, they maintained in effect, was sufficiently God to receive a person back twice. For some time they were rather less sure about whether this could apply a third time, but it seems that the problem here was more pastoral than precisely theological. Eventually it was agreed that people could be reconciled, in principle, as many times as they lapsed and repented. Such return was not an easy business for the penitent. He had to join a special category of Christians, and might be deprived of the Eucharist for many years, even until he was on his deathbed. From the time of his repentance until the end of his life he might be required to abstain from marital relations and business transactions. Even so, he was the object of special pastoral care and solicitude, and prayers were offered for him during the liturgy. The prayers over the people during Lent in the Tridentine Missal originate in this practice of praying over the penitents.

Persecutions in the Roman Empire came at last to an end, though there has never been a time in Christian history when some of the faithful might not be called upon to witness with their lives to the truth of the gospel. But when persecutions became for most a thing of the past, a new situation came to be. People became increasingly aware that there were more ways of apostatising than by burning incense before the emperor's statue, that it was possible to loose or lose one's hold on the new risen life of baptism in more places than a court of law. One such way was by a certain style of life. Adultery was the obvious example. Christian marriage was a sacrament of Christ and his Church, even before the days when people thought in a technical way about what counted as a sacrament and what did not. To live in public adultery – not at all the same as committing secret sexual sins – was publicly to deny this Christ–Church relationship. Murder was the other major sin which was regarded as severe enough to cut off a person from the new life he had been given in baptism. But from adultery and murder as from apostasy in the strict sense, a man could return: he could repent and be reconciled with the Church. From these two sins also there was the possibility of a third repentance also, and of a fourth and fifth.

One more step was needed before our present situation with regard to this sacrament was reached. After a considerable struggle the Church had come to see that there is no limit to the mercy of God, no sin being beyond forgiveness even for the baptised. By a more gentle process the Church came to see too that no sin was too small to be forgiven, and that in principle both great and small sins are forgiven in the same way. When men's minds turned in a more precise way to the consideration of what was strictly a sacrament, a privileged celebration of the encounter between God and man we call Jesus Christ, they saw that this 'second repentance' was one of them. It is the way of return to God for people who have already returned once, in baptism. God has given his Church the power to forgive sins committed after baptism, not just sins enacted before baptism and forgiven and forgotten in baptism itself.

Forgiveness can be celebrated, though it does not always have to be celebrated. When people have apostasised in the strict sense, they have never been allowed simply to slip back into sacramental communion with the Church. Public denial of Christ means public reaffirmation of Christ, even if now the publicity in question need be no more than that of one other person, with both people in confessional darkness. If a person denies Christ in a minor way, then he cannot return except sacramentally. We might look to begin with at second repentance in the strict sacramental sense. I suggested when we investigated baptism that a proper sense of the modalities of the sacrament comes across best when it is thought of in its ideal form of celebration, not some truncated form. Baptism celebrated for adults on Easter night is more conducive to reflection on that sacrament than what happens in the case of a sickly infant in hospital. The full form of the sacrament of second repentance is not the one-to-one encounter in the darkness of a box (something invented by St Charles Borromeo during the Catholic Reformation), but the sort of thing that went on in the Roman Pontifical where public penitents were expelled from the Church on Ash Wednesday by a weeping bishop and led back by him in a ritual dance on Maundy Thursday, to be reconciled by a long preface which extols the mercy of God and calls it down on these particular penitents. The one-to-one encounter has its origins in the 'tariff' system of penance originally practised in Irish monasteries and taken by missionaries from those monasteries on their evangelising journeys across Europe. In the late sixth and early seventh centuries, the older system of public penance and the new Irish system existed side by side, rather uneasily. A Council at Toledo in 589 said:

> We have heard that certain people in certain areas of Spain do penance for their faults in an unworthy manner, and not according to the canonical prescriptions, that is, each time they sin they seek the priest's absolution. And so, to put an end to such a presumptuous and scandalous way of going on, this holy Council ordains as follows: penance is to be given according to the ancient official forms. The sinner who repents of his sins is first to receive a number of times the laying-on of hands in the *ordo paenitentium*; he is forbidden to receive communion. When his time of expiation is completed, as the bishop of the place judges right, he is to be readmitted to the eucharistic communion. As for those who fall back into their faults during their time of penitence, they are to be punished severely according to the prescriptions of the ancient canons.[2]

And yet around the year 650 a Council at Chalon-sur-Saône said:

> Concerning penance to be performed for sins – penance which is the remedy of the soul – the bishops judge that it is useful for everybody. We unanimously want an expiatory penance to be imposed on sinners every time they confess.[3]

[2] III Synod of Toledo, Canon 2; cf. B. Poschmann, *Penance and the Anointing of the Sick* (ET Freiburg and London 1964), p. 124.
[3] Synod of Chalon (*c.* 650), Canon 8; cf. B. Poschmann, *Penance and the Anointing of the Sick*, p. 132.

This text clearly assumes what the Toledo text denies, some form of frequent confession.

Over the course of the centuries a wide variety of ways of taking account of man's sin and God's forgiveness have been practised in the Church. Today we are once again at a turning-point in penitential practice, and it is far from clear in what direction we shall move. In the first place, since the high Middle Ages there has been some sort of acknowledgment of sin at Mass, usually at the beginning of Mass, although that is by no means obviously the right place. In the present Roman Mass, the whole assembly joins in acknowledging their sinful state, and this is followed by the *absolutio sacerdotis*, where the priest uses the old optative form of sacramental absolution which gave way during the twelfth century in the sacrament itself to an indicative formula: 'I absolve you'. Then there are the Ash Wednesday ceremonies, in which everyone puts himself in the position of the public penitents of the ancient Church, accepting the ashes which formerly were imposed only on the heads of those who were entering the 'order of penitents'. In certain situations there are general absolutions, in time of war, for example, or on sinking ships. Recently, penitential services, with or without an opportunity for individuals to make a private confession, have become popular in many places. And there remains the form of private confession and absolution which originated in the Irish monastic milieux of the early Middle Ages. The separated Eastern churches have some styles of celebrating penance which appear very strange to Western Christians. They do not have the same certainty that we have had in distinguishing between strictly sacramental and strictly non-sacramental celebration of the forgiveness of God. But the Decree on Ecumenism of the Second Vatican Council makes it clear that for Catholics such celebrations must be entered into without any doubts as to their equal standing with Western ways of doing things.

The Code of Canon Law of the Latin Church till recently in force states that

> In the sacrament of repentance, by a judicial absolution granted by a legitimate minister, sins committed after baptism are remitted to a believer who is rightly disposed.[4]

---

[4] Canon 870.

But this must be a performative utterance – a declaration of what in future shall count as the sacrament in question. Until shortly before the time of St Thomas, there was certainly no judicial absolution but rather a prayer or the expression of a wish – and yet there can be no doubt that the sacrament was celebrated. The legitimate minister is nowadays taken to be a bishop or a priest delegated to the rôle by the bishop (a priest with 'faculties') but there have been long controversies in the past about the sacramental status of confession to a layman, a very common practice during crusading times and regarded by many theologians as of obligation in the absence of a priest. So what we are left with from the Code is the rightly disposed (that is, repentant) believer, sins committed after baptism, and absolution. Confession in the sense of the detailing of individual sins is not an absolute requirement, as we see in the case of a believer who is too ill to do so, or when a general absolution is in question. A person who has in some serious way denied his baptism is required by the Church to celebrate his repentance in a one-to-one encounter in which the other one is a priest, but apart from that (for those conscious of mortal sin) literally vital requirement, other sins are not the more surely forgiven by going to confession than by taking part in the public penitential rite or, more simply, making a devout communion – though the Church encourages, on ascetical grounds, regular recourse to sacramental penance. The reason why is that it is Christ himself who is the forgiveness of sin; he is the return to the Father; and as long as a man is in Christ he is forgiven. He cannot be in Christ and not be forgiven. He cannot live in the Spirit, who is himself the remission of all sin and forgives all sins and removes all impurities (as Origen says), and not be forgiven. What is required, normally at least, is simply that the sin and forgiveness aspect of the Christian life be taken seriously.[5] We may finish, then, with a quotation from another Council at Chalon-sur-Saône, this time in 813:

> Some say that a man should confess his sins to God alone, others that he should confess to priests. Both customs, in use in the Church, are a source of great blessing. Thus we confess our sins to God alone – to God who alone can blot them out – and we say with David, 'I have made my sin known to you, I have not hid my

[5] Cf. *God's Way to be Man*, pp. 40–47; *Hallowing the Time*, pp. 150–154.

iniquity; and you, Lord, have forgiven the guilt of my sin'. On the other hand, according to the instructions given us by the apostle, we confess our sins one to another, in order that we may be reconciled. Confession made to God alone purifies us of our sins; that which we make to priests teaches us how to purify ourselves of our sins. God, the author and dispenser of health and salvation, grants us pardon, by the operation of his invisible power, and by the work of the doctors of the soul.[6]

---

[6] Synod of Chalon (813), Canon 33, with an internal citation of Ps. 32.5; cf. B. Poschmann, *Penance and the Anointing of the Sick*, p. 140.

18

Healing

JESUS Christ is the sacrament of human salvation. In English, unfortunately, 'salvation' is a very ecclesiastical word: not the sort of word you would normally hear outside a church building or the coteries of the pious. 'Are you saved?' is the question sectarian evangelists are supposed to ask you in the street. But the equivalent words in Greek and Latin are far from churchy. *Salus* in Latin, *sōtēria* in Greek, both mean 'healing'. Jesus as *Sōtēr* or *Salvator* is Jesus as healer, as Good Samaritan, as the physician of the human race. More strongly, we can speak of him as man's forgiveness – a forgiveness which is a person rather than simply being what a person does. To speak of Jesus as Saviour is, at root, to speak of him as the healing and health of mankind. He is humanity healed, saved, restored and re-created, the First Adam taken up into the Second.

One of the features of the far country in which the human race lives is that it is a disease-ridden and demon-haunted country, a land with sickness in the atmosphere, in the sphere of the 'prince of the power of the air' (Eph. 2.2). In the kingdom of God, on the other hand, there is to be, so the prophets and the New Testament witnesses assure us, no sickness. The kingdom of God is a healthy terrain. Now St Paul is found in his Letters telling Christians that they are a colony of heaven: in other words, that their homeland is the kingdom of God, the 'Father-land'. The suggestion is that the proper thing for them to do is to live as colonials typically live: in a way that springs from the thought-patterns of where they really belong, rather than from those of the natives amongst whom they have settled. But Christians are always tending to go native, to adopt the ways of living and thinking of the world around them. They are inclined to live as though they belonged to the present evil age, to the kingdom of darkness. One way of doing so is what we speak of as sin. In the last chapter we saw how that is exemplified in the man who has been untrue to his *patria* and so is excluded from that image of the kingdom which is the Eucharist until such time as he repents and receives again the Holy Spirit whom he has grieved and driven away by his sins. Another way in which we tend to go native is by falling sick. Insofar as we sin, we show that the resurrection of Jesus has not taken full possession of us; insofar as we fall sick, we show that the salvation or health which Jesus is has not as yet taken full control of our lives.

We must note straightaway that this is not a question of my individual sickness being a penalty for my individual sin. That would be altogether too atomising. But insofar as there is sickness amongst men, it is a sign that we are still in the far country, that we still need to return to God. Perhaps we need to be on our guard against making too hard and fast a distinction between sin and sickness. Sickness is obvious enough, for all the world to see. Even though we know a good deal about psychosomatic illness, we tend to forget that it would be equally valid to speak of it as 'somatico-psychic'. When someone is ill, it is the whole person who is ill. Conversely, when someone sins it is the whole person who sins. We should do well to recognise that it is not only in the case of illness, but also in the case of sin, that we need to grasp the importance of the external and the visible. We spend perhaps too much energy in thinking about degrees of guilt where sin is concerned, about the extent of the individual's responsibility, and the quality of their sincerity, and not enough in recognising the empirical reality of what the person does or fails to do, paying inadequate attention to what happens in the public arena. Whether our deviant behaviour takes the form of sin or of sickness, it is more pressing to heal the deviant than to analyse the cause of the deviance, always allowing for the fact that to analyse causes *may* be the first step towards reintegration. At the beginning of the story of the man born blind in the Gospel of St John, Jesus diverts the attention of his disciples from the 'Why?' of cause to the 'Why?' of purpose, away from questioning the genesis of the disease and towards questioning themselves about what they are to do. The internal link between sin and sickness is a very strong one, and both are expressed within the Christian community in very much the same way. The sinner is excluded from the Eucharist and the sick person is excluded from the Eucharist: not both in the same way, but both in some way. The sinner may take part in the public celebration of the Eucharist but he may not receive the sacrament itself. The sick man may receive the sacrament itself but is not able to take part in the public celebration of the Eucharist. When a person is in either situation (he may, of course, be in both) the pastoral care of the Church is called for. The sick person or the sinner needs to be reconciled to the community and to that image of the community's future which is the eucharistic sacrifice and sacrament. The future of the community is the kingdom of God come in power, and in that kingdom there will be no more sickness just as there will be no more sin. According to the imagery of the Book of Revelation, death and hell are to be thrown into the lake of fire, and the leaves of the tree of life will be for the healing of the nations. Sin is a sign of the continuing dominion of darkness, and sickness is also a sign of that reign. And as there is a sacrament for the forgiveness of sin, for the reconciliation of the sinner to the eucharistic fellowship of the Church, so there is a sacrament for the healing of those who are sick, for reincorporating them into the Christ who is man's return to God and who thereby is not only the forgiveness but also the health of mankind.

According to the Old Testament prophecies, the eyes of the blind are to be opened, and the ears of the deaf unstopped; the lame man is to leap like a hart and the tongue of the dumb sing for joy. The prophets say that the latter days will be days of healing. And when Jesus comes, he comes to heal. As the Gospels report, Jesus in his earthly life opened the eyes of the blind, unstopped the ears of the deaf, made the lame man leap and the tongue of the dumb sing for joy. In the seer's vision of the new Jerusalem, we read that

> God himself will be with his people; he will wipe away every tear from their eyes, and death will be no more, neither shall there be mourning nor crying nor pain any more, for the former things have passed away. (Apoc. 21.3–4)

Sickness belongs to these 'former things', to our present which is the past of Jesus, not to our future which is his present. Our true present should be the present of Jesus, but when we sin or fall sick we show that we are not contemporaneous with it. Sickness is the situation of the far country and when we find ourselves there we should want to return, to seek health, to become up-to-date with our true selves. Nowhere in the New Testament do we find people being encouraged to reconcile themselves with their sickness, to put a good face on it and accept it as the will of God for them. In the story of Jesus' encounter with a leper in the first chapter of St Mark's Gospel, we are told that Jesus was moved with *anger* at the man's leprosy, and reached out his hand to heal him. There is something indecent, *indecens*, not fitting, about a Christian being ill. The sickness of a Christian is the anti-sacrament of the sin of us all. One man's sickness, like one man's sin, focusses our common distance from the kingdom of God. The Council of Trent makes the vital connection between these two when it calls anointing

> the culmination, the consummation, of repentance and indeed of the whole Christian life which ought to be a continual repentance.[1]

and so in truth a continual turn and return.

So the sick Christian should strive to be freed from his sickness and the whole community has a duty to help him towards this. In the introduction to the present rite of the sacrament of healing we read that

> it is part of the disposition of God's providence that a man should fight strenuously against any and every infirmity, and seek with all the powers at his disposal for good health so that he can fulfil his function in human society and in the Church. And it is not only the sick man himself who should fight his illness, but doctors too and everyone who is in any way concerned with the care of the sick.[2]

This is part of the task which Jesus has committed to the Church. In the Gospels we read

> Jesus called to him twelve disciples and gave them authority over the unclean spirits to cast them out, and to heal every disease and every infirmity. (Matt. 10.1)

and again

---

[1] H. Denzinger, *Enchiridion*, 1694.
[2] *Rite of Anointing and Pastoral Care of the Sick*, Introduction, p. 3; cf. *The Rites of the Catholic Church* I, p. 582.

These signs will accompany those who believe ... they will lay hands on the sick and they will recover. (Mark 16.17–18)

and yet again

The twelve went out and preached that men should repent and they anointed many sick people with oil and healed them. (Mark 6.12–13)

Throughout the Acts of the Apostles comes story after story about healing. Paul speaks of 'healings' as one of the charismatic gifts of the Holy Spirit, and even goes so far as to suggest that it is because people have been celebrating the Eucharist improperly that many Corinthian Christians are weak and ill, and some of them have died. In the (pre-Conciliar) ritual for the consecration of a church, where the church of bricks and mortar is being regarded (more than ever) as an image of the Church made up of living stones, there occurs the following prayer:

In this your house, Lord, by the grace of the Holy Spirit may the sick be healed, may the weak recover, may the lame be healed, may lepers be cleansed, may the blind recover their sight, may demons be cast out. In your goodness, Lord, grant that in this place the ailments of all who are ill may be driven away and the chains of all sin be struck off.

The sacrament of healing in the strict sense is rooted in the advice of St James:

Is any one amongst you sick? Let him call for the elders of the Church, and let them pray over him, anointing him with oil in the name of the Lord; and the prayer of faith will raise him up; and if he has committed sins, he will be forgiven. (James 5.13–15)

Note the words: 'Let him *call* for the elders'. It is assumed that the sick man is at least housebound, that he is cut off from the eucharistic assembly. The sacrament of healing, like the sacrament of second repentance, is intended primarily for those who are obviously cut off from the eucharistic fellowship of the Church. In the discipline of the Western Church there has been something of an insistence that the sacrament of healing should not be celebrated for a person who is not seriously sick, even though the sacrament of second repentance has been advocated for people who have not sinned seriously. In the Western tradition there have even been times when it has become almost exclusively restricted to people so seriously ill that there was practically no hope for their recovery – though not until the twelfth century did the liturgy of the sacrament begin to manifest a concern with preparing a dying Christian for immediate entry into heaven. In the East, on the other hand, the sacrament is at times administered to everyone who happens to be in the church, rather in the same way that in many modern Catholic parishes on the feast of the martyr St Blase all those present come up to have their throats blessed even though they may never have suffered from an ailment of the throat in their lives. Presumably, just as the sacrament of second repentance can properly be celebrated even for sins which do not require its celebration, so there is no *absolute* reason why the sacrament of healing should not be celebrated for those whose sickness is not in any way serious. It is a pastoral rather than a strictly theological matter. We must note, however, the insistence of the Council of Trent that the sacrament of healing is to be administered to the sick but *especially* to those who appear to be in danger of death; the Second Vatican Council reaffirmed that ruling.

The matter of this sacrament is anointing with oil. The sacrament has the human shape of care for the sick, of medical aid, parallel to the human shape of eating and drinking together which the Eucharist assumes and transvalorises. In the ancient world, anointing with oil played a major part in the care of the sick. Even in modern medical practice many of the substances used in caring for the ailing have an oil base. The Bible witnesses to this use of oil for healing in Old Testament times. We read in Isaiah of 'bruises and sores and bleeding wounds which are not pressed out or bound up or softened with oil' (Isa. 1.6). In the Book of Leviticus we come across oil being used for the purification of lepers after they have been cleansed. The Good Samaritan pours oil and wine into the wounds of the man who had fallen amongst thieves. In Judaism oil was applied medicinally with a view to healing for sciatic pains, skin afflictions, headaches and wounds, and also magico-medicinally as a means of exorcism. In Jewish as in Hellenistic practice these two often went together, in that medical anointing had the character of a victorious action in expelling demons. There are any number of references in the literary sources to its use for afflictions which have psychic manifestations or causes, anointings of those thought to be possessed, for the healing and release of people believed to have been bewitched. In the New Testament itself there is often a link forged between the work of demons and sickness. Jesus speaks of a cripple as 'this woman, a daughter of Abraham, whom Satan has bound these eighteen years' (Luke 13.16). If the present age is thought of as under the dominion of Satan, then sin is easily ascribed to the activity of the devil, and oil as a vehicle of the Holy Spirit becomes an appropriate way of engaging in warfare against the ways in which the devil manifests his empire.

In and behind all this there is always the sense of oil – the oil of healing, not simply the oil of chrism – as signifying and effecting a union with the Anointed One, with the Jesus who is the health of mankind. When a person celebrates his return from the distance which is sin, he is asked to accept that all his sins have been laid on Jesus, that the Lamb of God has borne all his sins in his own body on the tree of the cross. The penitent is required to make an act of faith that Jesus with all the weight of the world's sins has been accepted by God, that he who has borne our sins is at one with God. Very much the same sort of thing is asked from the man who is anointed: an act of faith in the work of Jesus with regard to sickness. There is a Gospel text which is most important in this respect.

> When evening was come, they brought to him many that were possessed of devils, and he cast them out with his word and healed all that were sick, that it might be fulfilled what was spoken by the prophet Isaiah, saying, He himself took our weaknesses, our infirmities and bore our diseases. (Matt. 8.16–17)

The Hebrew text of Isaiah that is quoted here is quite striking. The Suffering Servant is said to be

> a man of sorrows and acquainted with sickness. Surely he has borne our sicknesses and carried our sorrows. It pleased Yahweh to bruise him; he has made him sick. He himself bore our sicknesses, and with his stripes we are healed. (Isa. 53.4)

One thinks of Ignatius of Antioch writing to Polycarp, 'Bear the sicknesses of all as a perfect athlete',[3] or of T. S. Eliot in modern times speaking of Jesus as the 'wounded surgeon'.[4] In that Jesus takes the sins of us all and takes them away, we call him the remission of our sins; in that he takes our sicknesses and takes them away, he is the health of mankind. And so for Jesus as the health of mankind, as for Jesus as the remission of human sin, there is a ritual way to enter into him, a sacrament of healing parallel to the sacrament of second repentance.

We have seen on a number of occasions that if we are thinking of a sacrament we should always envisage it as solemnly celebrated according to its full rite. In the case of the sacrament of healing there are two places where we can find what this would be. The first is the present practice in the Eastern rites, where there are seven anointings by seven different priests, accompanied by the reading of scriptural passages about healing, and long prayers asking for just such healing for this particular sick person. The other is in the Western practice, particularly as this has been recently restored, with its encouragement of making anointing a communal celebration with as many people present as possible. Part of the rite includes the blessing of the oil which normally happens at the bishop's Mass on Maundy Thursday morning, at the beginning of the celebration of Christ's victorious passion – the event from which the sacrament of healing derives its significance. Just as whenever there is a baptism we are brought back in memory to the Easter Vigil by the paschal candle that burns in the baptistery throughout the celebration, so whenever in the year a man celebrates the sacrament of healing, he is brought into immediate relationship with the triumphant death of Christ and with the whole Church by means of the oil blessed on Holy Thursday by the bishop. The form of blessing is as follows:

> O God, the Father of all consolation, through your Son you willed to heal the sicknesses of all. Listen to the prayer of faith, and send forth your Holy Spirit, the Paraclete, from heaven into this oil brought forth from the green olive tree for the restoration of our bodies. By your holy benediction, may all who are anoin-

---

[3] Ignatius, *To Polycarp*, I. 3.
[4] T. S. Eliot, 'East Coker', IV, in *Collected Poems 1909–1962* (London 1974; 1980), p. 201.

ted with it find in it a safeguard for their body, soul and spirit. May it dispel all their pain, all their weakness, all their sickness.

In the older rite, God was asked that the oil might be effective in strengthening the 'temple of the living God', that is, the body of the Christian man or woman. When the elders come to visit the sick man, there are readings and prayers about healing, and then the elders, the presbyters, lay their hands on the sick person. Although this is now done in silence, it used to be the case that an appeal was made to the promise of Jesus in the longer ending of Mark that believers would lay hands on the sick and they would recover; and there was an appeal, too, for the intercession of Peter and Paul, the healing apostles – and in the Dominican rite, for the prayers of St Vincent Ferrer, that great fourteenth-century thaumaturge. In any case the healing that Christ gives is primarily a gift to the whole Spirit-filled community rather than to specially endowed individuals. The office-bearer anoints in virtue of his office: it is not an extraordinary gift. When the ministers lay on their hands, it is as though the hands of the whole community were concentrated in this therapy of touch, the whole Church focussing their love and prayers on the person in need. Then there is the anointing itself with the words:

> through this holy anointing may the Lord in his love and mercy help you with the grace of the Holy Spirit. May the Lord who frees you from sin save you and raise you up.

This expression 'raise up' is polyvalent, and all its valencies lie somewhere around this sacrament. God raises up prophets, for example, and Christ raises up the sick; God raises up Christ from death and will raise up our mortal bodies. The prayer that follows asks that the man may indeed be healed and may resume his normal way of life. There is an implicit orientation here to the Eucharist. Like all the sacraments, healing is directed to fitting people for the Eucharist, in this case for celebrating the Eucharist in the full assembly of the people of God.

So this is the rite in its fulness, often celebrated in great assemblies nowadays, a real celebration of Christ as the health of the world, as the sacrament of man's total healing, his return from the far country, hag-ridden and disease-ridden, to the land where there is no more rain. So it can fairly be expected that the sick person will in fact be restored and make the return. The *Catechism of the Council of Trent* says:

> Pastors should teach that the sacred unction liberates the soul from the langour and infirmity which is contracted from sins and from all the other remains of sin. ... The recovery of health, if truly advantageous, is another effect of this sacrament. And if in our days the sick obtain this effect less frequently, this is to be attributed not to any defect of the sacrament but rather to the weaker faith of the greater part of those who are anointed with the sacred oil, or of those by whom it is administered. For the evangelist bears witness that the Lord did not effect many miracles amongst his own because of their unbelief. It may also be said that the Christian religion, now that it has struck its roots more deeply in the minds of men, stands in less need of the aid of such miracles than it did formerly, at the beginnings of the Church. Nevertheless, faith should be excited strongly in this respect.[5]

St Thomas too maintains that if bodily healing would be a help to spiritual healing then the sacrament always confers bodily healing, provided there is no impediment on the part of its recipient. Yet even if we may expect the sick man to recover since that is what the sacrament is chiefly for, he will not always recover. Sometimes it would require a miracle for him to recover, for he may be at the very doors of death. Sacraments are not meant to work miracles. But even if a man's sickness persists, it may come to have a different meaning for him. There can be a healing of hope as a result of celebrating the sacrament in the hope of a healing.[6] Ultimately, death itself comes to have a deeper significance since the death of Christ which has brought a definitive victory over death, robbing death of its sting, making it again merely biological, as before the Fall, and not what it has been ever since, a curse on humankind.[7]

---

[5] *Roman Catechism*, II. vi. 14, 16.
[6] For further thoughts, with less emphasis on the sheerly somatic side of healing, see *God's Way to be Man*, pp. 53–60.
[7] On the theology of death, see G. Preston, O.P., 'All Souls' Day', *Doctrine and Life* 31.9 (1981), pp. 576–580.

19

Models of Sacramentality

IN the preceding chapters we have been looking at sacraments as
discrete and iterative events in the life of the Church, articulations of the various facets of the Christian experience of Jesus
within the community which he founded and whose living centre
he is. We can now bring these threads together and see, more
deeply than at the outset of this section, what sense can be made
of the notion of sacramentality as such. If it makes any sense at all
to talk about sacraments, then there must be certain categories
into which we can place them, even though in the end we may
find ourselves saying that sacramental behaviour occupies a class
by itself. Yet even to speak of 'sacramental behaviour' is to give
expression to a conviction that sacraments are best understood in
terms of human activities rather than as objects in the natural
world or as human artefacts, finished works of art. 'Behaviour'
suggests that if we are to use the language of activity, it is the
activity itself we are concerned with rather than its results, the
end-product. This statement needs to be qualified in the case of
one of the sacraments, since, as we have seen, the difference
between the Eucharist and the other sacraments lies in the way in
which the other sacraments have reality only in their being
performed, whereas in the Eucharist the sacrament exists outside
the act of performance, even though it derives its significance
from the activity in whose course it is 'confected'; but otherwise
it may stand.

We might return first of all to what was said at the start of
this section about how sacramentality is rooted in human
nature, embedded in the fact that what makes us specifically
human is our peculiar bodiliness. One corollary of the pecu-
liarly human way of being bodily is our ability to project
ourselves onto the groundwork of external nature, or rather
to realise ourselves in and through external nature. We interpret ourselves to ourselves (and in this context it is hard

to distinguish between self-interpretation and self-creation) through our activities. We come to know who we are by what we do; and what we do makes us who we are. We respond to the given by organising it to create a new universe, by making it into our personal or collective history. We do this by dreams or by words, by symbols, by forms of art, by categories of thought. Take *dreams*, for example. There is an insight here which long antedates Freud and the rise of modern analytic or experimental psychology. The Old Testament is the most immediately familiar source of information about the significance of dreams in the ancient world. Both in antiquity (where dreams were often thought to come from an outside force) and in modern times (where we tend to ascribe them to the workings of the individual or collective unconscious), they are deemed to possess power over the future. They reduce the past and the present to an ordered and significant unity, and they permit the dreamer to take a new and often daring step into the future. It is for the sake of our dreams that we sleep. Deprive a man of his dreams by depriving him of his sleep, and in an astonishingly short time he goes mad, he becomes inhuman. In depth psychology healing is again and again accompanied by the interpretation of dreams, dreams which are themselves an interpretation of past and present experience and the creation of a new self. When a man is healthy in mind, then the dreams do not need to be interpreted, or even remembered; it is enough that they are dreamed. There are surely ways in which the sacraments function in much the same fashion, interpreting past and present and allowing a new future. Think, for instance, of the way in which in baptism the water of the font becomes the aboriginal water of chaos, the waters of Noah's flood, the waters of the Red Sea, the waters of Jordan, the water flowing from the side of Christ. In being plunged under this water, a person enters into the depths of all those waters and emerges a new man, a new creation. Or, in the case of the Eucharist, the bread and wine are interpreted by having a story told over them, a story which is both poetic symbol and historical account, and that story interprets the elements and changes them. Interpretation involves not only causing things to happen within a particular perspective ('I see it like this. ...') but causing them to be encountered within a particular state (I too am changed). Interpretation is a matter not only of imaging but also of creating in a particular way. Interpreting is a revealing representation of things. When we have seen a caricature of a person, for example, whether it be gentle, flattering or abusive, we can never see him in the same light again.

But perhaps the way in which dreams function most obviously is by creating a *story* for us. In dreaming there are seldom just images, no matter how archetypal. The images occur within a frame of reference which itself possesses sequence. This is true even though there may be no obvious first beginning in our dreams and no obvious last end. In the Judaeo-Christian tradition the story-telling that we meet with in dreams forms the most striking use of language in sacramental contexts. The Jewish term for this is *haggadah*, the word which has come to be the normal name for the telling of the story of the exodus at Passover. 'We should tell (*hagged*) our children the story of the exodus from Egypt.' But the *haggadah* of Passover tells not only the story of the escape from Egypt; it is the *haggadah* of the whole of Jewish history. It tells of how Abraham and his family worshipped other gods beyond the River; it includes details of a famous Passover in the early years of the Common Era; it tells of how in every generation men have risen up against the people of God to destroy them but how in every generation God has been with his people. And ancient as the words of the *haggadah* are, at Passover each year the participants know that in them they will hear something which has been prepared for them alone, that the ancient tale will interpret their existence to them, that they will find healing, salvation, liberation, in hearing the story of the whole people as addressed to themselves. This possibility of novelty depends on a certain refusal to be novel.

The word *seder* used for the *haggadah* means 'programme', 'order of ceremonies', because we all, like children, need to have a story read us which we know, a story in which familiarity is blended with suspense. Familiarity, in that we know how the story will end; suspense, in that we live through the story as it is being told, live through a succession of moments in which the end of the story is still future to its beginning and its middle. This can still be experienced vividly in the reading of the passion each Good Friday, a reading which stops short at the lifting up of the

Lord in death. We know the ending, but it is essential that we do not anticipate the ending as the story is in the telling. In a familiar story the world is safely predictable – we know the ending; and yet in a story the world is thrillingly incalculable – we have not yet come to the story's end. The story grants both security and the ability to surrender security in moving forward. In the story form, what is familiar is made to appear strange by being made sequential, and this produces insight.

If sequential stories are one way of realising ourselves, then *words* are another. I think here of the function of naming persons and objects, assigning them a rôle which creates their significance. It is here that contemporary linguistic analysis may be helpful. There are statements which have the grammatical form of being simply that but really *create* a situation rather than reflect it. Such 'performative utterances' are comparable to many sacramental affirmations: the recitation of the Lord's words at the Eucharist, the declaration of divine forgiveness in second repentance. Then again, there are *conceptual categories* which permit development of understanding about the natural world and allow us to make further bold use of its phenomena. The categories of thought employed in mathematics enable us to perform extraordinary feats of engineering when used as a grid on the material world. In 'primitive' societies it is not only scientific categories which make the world work for man, but wholly non-scientific ways of interpretation also. Jan Heinz Jahn says in his anthropological study of the cultures of Africa, *Muntu*:

> Sowing alone is not sufficient to make maize germinate and grow; speech and song must be added, for it is the word that makes the grasses germinate, the fruits grow, the cow go in calf and give milk. Even handicrafts need the word if they are to succeed. The prayer, or rather the poem, which the goldsmith recites, the hymn of praise sung by the sorcerer while the goldsmith is working the gold, the dance of the smith at the close of the operation, it is all this – poem, song, dance – which, in addition to the movement of the artisan, completes the work and makes it a masterpiece.[1]

[1] J. H. Jahn, *Muntu: An Outline of Neo-African Culture* (ET London 1961), p. 125.

The sacraments are also transformational takings up of the natural order by language working on the world.

But what then of this notion of artisanship and so of *art*? In artistic activity we transpose life into a significant whole. It is only in art that a man fully lives out his potentialities in a medium which he has created specially for his own self-realisation. We do not just take the things of the world around us and use them straight: we create things in order to use them. A person makes a violin and bow in order for them to be used to execute a piece of music; another writes music in order for it to be played. In this perspective we can speak of Jesus as he in whom God becomes God *for us*, as the man in whom God transposes life in all its dimensions into this single multiply significant person. He is God's symbol. In him God makes sense of the world for us, rendering nature and history intelligible as by his words (the parables, for example) and by his actions (with bread and wine, say), Jesus releases the iconic power of creation – its ability to serve as an image for man's self-realisation before God. So when the Word is made man, when, as Donne wrote, 'Immensity is cloystered in the deare womb of Mary', nature and history are humanised. In Christ the world finds its meaning, or rather, is transformed into meaning. We are close here to a grasp of what it means to call Jesus the primal sacrament, he who, as an early Cistercian writer put it, is *Dominus noster humanissimus*, 'our most human Lord'. Christ reveals a whole reality inaccessible to other means of knowledge because he is God's meaning for man, and man's meaning for God. In the light of his coming we realise that creation holds within it the possibility of becoming an epiphany or advent of God himself. In translating his own experience of the true meaning of the world into words and gestures Jesus actualises these iconic and epiphanic possibilities that lie dormant in the world. By doing so, he gives us the chance to enter into his own experience, which is itself creative of true humanity. Jesus takes the imaginative activities of man, which are always human and never merely brute, and he changes their significant value. For the theoretician of culture Lewis Mumford, in artistic creation what was merely useful becomes aesthetically significant. So in the sacraments human activities have bestowed upon them fresh power to signify beyond themselves. In any sacramental activity, to cite the Dominican tertiary and artist David Jones, we witness corporeal creatures doing certain manual things with material elements and proclaiming that these things are done for a signification of something.[2]

In performing a sacrament, either we celebrate some aspect of the significance of the world as revealed in Jesus, the poet of creation, or we celebrate simply his total significance. Either way, intrinsic to the notion of sacramentality is the idea of *celebration*. We may want to say that since the incarnation there are no specially holy times nor specially holy places; this is true to the extent that they are not there any more in the structure of the given world. But in order to create a sacramental happening, we have to carve out a special time and a special place. Or, rather, this time and this place become special, holy, epiphanic, by having the sacrament celebrated here and now. The fact is that man remains a being created for jubilation, desirous of celebrating in a specific and expressive way the chief events which mould his existence. He is a being *à la* Mozart, of a piece with him whose music Karl Barth called 'the chant of creation past and present in the peace of the future'.[3] Man is a festive being. The feast always has an exceptional character. It has to be begun and ended; it may not be allowed just to tail off. In a feast there is also an important element of gratuitousness or graciousness, of being unnecessitated and unnecessary. In a feast we ascribe to the object of our celebration (a birthday, for instance), a certain aesthetic exaltation by means of intensified words and probably music and dancing. In a feast we renounce ordinary functional time and space, the business (indeed, the busy-ness) of work and money-earning. In a feast there is an external, expressive, symbolic manifestation by which we make ourselves more deeply conscious of the importance of an event or a person or an idea which is already important to us. It is in festivity that we become most truly human, because in a feast, to quote David Jones on human craft,

There is making, there is added making, there is explicit sign, there is a showing forth, a re-presenting, a recalling, and there is gratuitousness, there is full intention to make this making thus.

[2] D. Jones, 'Art and Sacrament', in *Epoch and Artist* (London 1959), p. 163.
[3] K. Barth, *Church Dogmatics* III/3 para. 50.

Moreover, this particular making signifies a birth. It recalls a past event and looks back at some anniversaries and looks forward to some other anniversaries, it is essentially celebrative and festal; it would be gay.[4]

The goal is delight. In a feast we recognise how 'the body is not an infirmity but a unique benefit and splendour; a thing denied to angels and unconscious in animals'. In festivity is the condition for understanding. Martin Heidegger taught us how thinking and thanking go together, how we only think when we thank. In the magnifying of what we celebrate, there is the magnifying of the magnifying glass, the glass which focusses the rays of the sun to a point and gives those rays the possibility to set the world on fire.

If festivity is an indispensable category for making sense of sacramental activity, so is *play*. A hallmark of play is freedom of choice, not being constrained by other people or by circumstances. So in the sacraments we are not constrained in the ways we handle such artefacts as bread and wine, such objects as water and oil, in normal usage. Perhaps the best use of the word 'play' is as an adverb rather than as the name of a particular class of activities. 'Play' describes how an action is performed, under what conditions it happens. There is a paradoxical difference between play and the corresponding 'serious behaviour', even though play is deadly earnest for as long as we are engaged in it. Play is most typically seen in symbolic or 'make-believe' play, in which anything important that has happened is reproduced with significant variations. In such play, events are distorted, but not distorted out of true, just as in the sacrament of the Eucharist a death is represented, but in the breaking of bread and the pouring out of wine. No effort is made in such play to adapt to reality. And yet the play is quite literally 'make-believe': it makes us believe in the reality of what we are playing at. In play a child, but not only a child, explores his feelings and emotions, lessening his fears and increasing his excitement, trying to understand a puzzling event by graphic representation, seeking confirmation of a hazy memory, assimilating events in symbolic form. Play enables the child (and not only the child) to focus on what matters and eliminate what does not. Concrete objects are used symbolically

[4] D. Jones, 'Art and Sacrament', p. 164.

in play; impressions are translated into concrete actions. Play involves a realignment and reclassification of events and responses to events. It is the paradoxical behaviour of exploring what is familiar, practising what has been mastered, a form of pretence which is not intended to deceive or mislead. And so in the Eucharist the death of Christ is represented without the details of wood, nails and spear. We are brought into the presence of that event with our fears removed, and it is interpreted as being for us and for our salvation. In her book *The Psychology of Play*, Susanna Millar remarks that when play ceases, the individual has become more socially adapted, needing less and less to resort to symbolic substitutes and distortions of the real.[5] Yet for Christians it is what normally goes under the name of 'reality' that is distorted; it is the 'real' world that is askew. For Christians the possibility of getting better adapted to 'reality' is a threat, a danger to one's integrity. They know that it is only so long as they are able to become as little children and to play that they have any chance of entering the real world, the kingdom of God.

One of the interesting aspects of the word 'play' is its application to a particular sort of play, to what goes on in the theatre. Theatre too depends on a time and a place that are somehow special, different, set apart – set apart, above all, by the beginning of the play. The director Peter Brook has said:

> I can take any empty space and call it a bare stage. A man walks across this empty space while someone else is watching him, and this is all that is needed for an act of theatre to be engaged.[6]

In theatre as in liturgy there is the problem of the relationship between the script and the executing of the script, even though in Christian rites all that may represent the script will be a series of stage directions and general hints: 'do this for my *anamnēsis*'. In theatre as in the liturgy there is also the problem of the relationship between the director and the actors, and the question of whether the performance should be a unity in which all elements should blend, or whether, on the contrary, the jarring of externals is quite essential to the expression of the inner unity of a

[5] S. Millar, *The Psychology of Play* (Harmondsworth 1968).
[6] P. Brook, *The Empty Stage* (London 1968), p. 9.

complex work. In the theatre as in the liturgy, people look to the stage as to the sanctuary as the place where the invisible can be made visible, and can appear and take a deep hold on our thoughts. Each shares an uncertainty about the relationship between set and performance, wondering whether a new building calls out for a new ceremony, or whether the new style should come first. In our time each has experienced an inability to celebrate, unsure whether it is life or death it is contemplating, God or man. Brecht's insistence that theatre must include alienation effects raises an important question for the liturgy also, and especially for those groups that are close-knit and at ease together, and find it hard to see how the profound can reach past the everyday, how those aspects of life which the surface hides can be brought into prominence by a heightened language and ritualistic use of rhythm. The theatre, Brook says, consists of 'repetition with representation and assistance'. It is hard to think of a better formula for liturgical activity. *Repétition* in the French sense: what the English call 'rehearsal'. Liturgy involves drudgery, grind, discipline, dullness: the rehearsing of a story, the telling of it over again. And yet repetition eventually brings about change, as in the training of our bodies. Repetition becomes creative when it is harnessed to an aim and driven by a will. Then there is *représentation*, again in the French sense: what the English call 'performance', though in the liturgy repetition and representation are one. In representation something from the past is shown again, something that was once is now. Representation is not an imitation or description of a past event but rather abolishes time, the difference between yesterday and today, by taking yesterday's action and making it live again in every one of its significant aspects, including its immediacy. The Mass *is* Calvary. A representation, a performance, is what it claims to be, a making present, a renewal of the life that could so easily be lost if we thought only of repetition, of rehearsal. But for an event to be made present it needs help, *assistance* – again in the French sense, what the English less happily call an audience. The celebration of the action happens only within the context of the assistance, of those who 'assist' at Mass and so make the representation possible. Assistance is what turns repetition into representation, and representation abolishes the audience, takes us back into the mediaeval theatre before audiences were invented, back into the

189

young-time of Christian liturgy in which no one had any doubts on one score: in the sacramental activity of the Church there is but one celebrant, the whole company of earth and heaven in the one mystical person of Jesus Christ.[7]

---

[7] Cf. G. Preston, O.P., 'The Focusing of God', *New Blackfriars* 52. 618 (1971), pp. 495–500.

PART THREE

Living the Church: Some Privileged Moments

20

Eucharistic Assembly

IN addition to the range of metaphor, symbol and analogy for
the Church which we have just considered, there are also to be
found, embedded in the actual life of the Church, certain privileged moments from which we can gain a grasp of its inner
mystery. There are certain typical occasions when we may refer
ourselves experientially to what we mean when we say the words
'the Church'. These are punctual and predictable occasions when
the reality of the Church becomes manifested. At these moments
we can, as it were, 'see the Churching': we become aware of the
Church as an event, as a style of activity, as direction towards a
particular end. The supreme example of this is that moment
when the Church meets to make Eucharist. But there are other
occasions, too, when the Church realises itself in a plenary sense:
at one end of the scale any sacrament is such, at the other so is a
solemn session of a General Council. In such events is the Church
focussed. But what about when nothing is happening in any
particular way, when we cannot extract a privileged moment
from the total succession of moments? Is there nothing to be said
for these other times and seasons? In recent years it has become
fashionable to think of the Church in terms of event; people
speak of a preference for a 'dynamic' rather than 'static' or
'substantial' view of the Church. But a thoroughgoing ecclesiology will have to take account of static and substantial features of
the Church as well as dynamic ones. The Church is both happening and community, both creative of wider community and able
to celebrate the community it has. It is both event and institution,
and both must be allowed for. So there can be 'monuments' of the
Church, monuments of tradition. The Church is, for example,
baptisteries, altars and vestments; it is gestures of social conformity; it is texts which exist on the printed page even when they
are not being actualised. There is a deposit, a given pattern of
belief and life. The community may be most fully appreciated

when it is acting as a community, but that is not the only way in which it can be appreciated. We can engage in a different type of reflection on the Church which may be seen as *iconic* in character. People, places, objects may be iconic of the Church's deepest reality, focussing and expressing that reality both as event and as institution. With all these things, we are required to make an imaginative effort to submit ourselves to what is 'given' about the image. The best training we can have here to be a theologian is an education in literary or art criticism, for in these disciplines we learn to stand before a piece of writing or a painting and to appreciate it for what it is, to stand with it before the reality which it both expresses and gives access to.

We begin by looking at the way the Church comes together in eucharistic assembly. It does so in order to celebrate its own existence as the body of Christ. The Mass is, in Augustine's words, *celebratio corporis*, the celebration of the body. The Mass takes up the many senses of that word 'body' in Pauline usage. As expressive organ, the body expresses both our frailty and fragility, *and* the resurrection glory of Christ. The body, again, can be identified with one of its realisations, what Paul speaks of as 'our earthly body', or it can be transfigured (literally, 'meta-schematised') through the body of the glory of Jesus. The body can put a person over against other persons, or, as in the sexual body, it can provide a way of union. In the tenth chapter of his First Letter to the Corinthians, Paul passes on what he represents as already quite traditional language about the Eucharist: and this traditional language provokes him to enlarge his own understanding of what 'body' means. The fundamental meaning of the Eucharist is here presented in a context of loyalty and communion with the altar – or, rather, with what the altar signifies, what it points to. Fellowship and communion are concretised in the tangible facts of the body and blood of Christ. Intermediate between fellowship with God and the body and blood of Christ which came to be in Mary, there lies the mystery of the Eucharist. Body and blood are signs which typify and generate this fellowship.

> The blessing-cup that we bless is a communion with the blood of Christ, and the bread that we break is a communion with the body of Christ. (1 Cor. 10.16)

There is a unity to be found in common signs capable of representing multiplicity in unity. During the Mass, the celebration of the body, we are united as a community by repeating the signs that signify the very union between ourselves and God which they create and generate.

> The fact that there is only one loaf means that though there are many of us, we form a single body, because we all have a share in this one loaf. (1 Cor. 10.17)

Bread makes the people's unity a visible thing. And the mystery of the body, communicated in the sign of bread, creates a unity which is first and foremost that of our communion with Christ's glorified Body (a 'radial' communion, we might call it), and secondly and secondarily, a unit between all those engaged in the celebration (we might call that a 'circumferential unity'). The body expresses the oneness of Christ and his members, and the oneness of the members in Christ.

And so we come together to celebrate the body: we 'congregate', literally we 'flock together'. We do so in order to exhibit and further the reality of our being together. The whole situation of the Mass is iconic, an image of reality yet to be. We meet as one when in many ways we are not as one. And by placarding the death of the Lord until he comes, we engage in a prophetic sign. The special tense of the Eucharist is the 'prophetic perfect' according to which the Old Testament prophets spoke of future events as though they had happened already. Psalm 126 is a good example of this. Its author declares:

> When the Lord restored the fortunes of Zion,
> we were like those who dream.
> Then our mouth was filled with laughter,
> and our tongue with shouts of joy. . . . (Ps. 126.1–2)

yet follows up this apparent description of completed action with the cry:

> Restore our fortunes, Lord, like the wadis in the Negev! (v. 4)

This is how the Eucharist works also. In the reality of the present, in love ('his blood is incorruptible love', says Ignatius of Antioch) and in joy ('the blood of Christ is eternal and abiding joy', according to the same author), we behave as if the future had already come.[1] In the age to come there will be unity and brother-hood for all men in Christ. Indeed, his eschatological humanity is the only true humanity there is. Here in the Eucharist we try that out for size. We come together united by the one loaf and the common cup – not just any loaf, any cup, but the loaf and cup over which is told the story of God's activity in history, and especially of those three days around the Passover-time of the death of Jesus. This recounting of the story is what makes the celebration into sacrifice, something holy, set apart. The story enters into the elements in such a way that when we share them we share also the blessing, the *berakah*, of the divinity itself. The history of what God has done is made substantial in the elements as it was in the physical body of Jesus himself. In this mystery lies the unity of the people: they are constituted there as the body of Christ, just as in the glory of God's kingdom the unity of all mankind will be Christ, the Lamb standing as though slain in the vision of the seer of the Apocalypse. So the Eucharist is the expressive and constitutive sign of the Church's unity, a unity received from God himself. The celebration of the body is the sacrament of achieved reconciliation.

The Eucharist, therefore, is *convivium*, 'living together'; it makes us com-panions, those who share one *panis*, one loaf of bread. In the light of that hope for the future of all mankind which this experience brings, we try to understand the mystery hidden from all ages, and now made known to the Church in Christ Jesus. When the primitive Church sought for evidence of that mystery, it found it, most significantly, in the union of Jews and Gentiles in one body: the experienced overcoming of the profoundest cleavage of the ancient world. Adapting St Anselm, *Spero ut intelligam*: I hope in order that I may understand.

The Eucharist is the sacrament of peace. Typically, at a bishop's Mass, the celebration of the body begins with the words: *Pax vobiscum*, 'peace be with you', or, perhaps, 'peace with you', that peace which is the Lord himself. The kiss of peace, now restored to the whole assembly in the Roman liturgy, has always had an important place in the celebration of the body. It features in the New Testament itself where a number of letters (intended to be read out to people who had come together for the Lord's

---

[1] Ignatius, *To the Romans*, VII.

Supper) contain some such exhortation as 'Greet one another with the kiss of love' (1 Pet. 5.14). The kiss of peace, indeed, is as old as the Church itself. 'Peace' in Scripture means much more than the absence of war and conflict. It includes all that we would mean by well-being and justice. It means the victory of God's purposes, and so is associated with the proclaiming of a new order of things in the world. 'Peace on earth to men of good-will' (Luke 2.14) is the message of the angels at the birth of Jesus. The gospel is said to be 'good news of peace' (Rom. 10.15) just as Christ himself is called 'our peace' (Eph. 2.14). God shows himself to be a God of peace in that he calls us to live in peace together. Those who work for peace are called happy, blessed, the sons of God. Almost every letter in the New Testament begins and ends with the writer wishing his readers or hearers peace. In the Fourth Gospel this peace is closely associated both with the Last Supper and with the resurrection. 'Peace' there is the first word of the risen Jesus to the disciples who had broken their peace with him by their disloyalty (John 20.21). Peace is the end of tyranny, hostility, division, disquiet, alarm; peace is freedom, harmony, security and blessedness. At Mass the kiss of peace has come at various points, sometimes immediately after the penitential service, everyone forgiving his neighbour from his heart in order to be (or as a sign of having been) forgiven by God. In other rites, it occurs during the preparation of the gifts, a reconciliation of the hearts that will be lifted up to God in praise and thanksgiving during the eucharistic prayer. In the Roman liturgy it is traditionally associated with the Lord's Prayer and the fraction of the host to form the immediate preparation for communion. The first person plural of the Our Father reminds us that we come to God as members of one family, asking from him the daily bread of the Eucharist as the forgiveness of sin. Similarly, the kiss of peace dramatises the second part of the request:

> Forgive us our trespasses, as we forgive those who trespass against us. (Matt. 6.12)

It expresses our response to the words of Christ in the Sermon on the Mount:

> If you are about to offer your gift [in this case the gift of oneself by receiving the sacramental gift of God] at the altar, and there

remember that your brother has something against you, leave your gift there in front of the altar and go at once to make peace with your brother; then come back and offer your gift to God. (Matt. 5.24)

So too it is meant as a way of avoiding Paul's strictures on those who share the Eucharist when the congregation is divided, not discerning in it the body of Christ.

For the point of the Eucharist, the *res tantum* as the Thomists say, is the unity of the Church. Such unity of the body requires both the sharing of the one loaf to make us all one body, and the mutual reconciliation symbolised and effected by the kiss of peace. In the Roman rite, the Our Father is extended by a petition asking God to give us this peace in mind and body, to free us from that anxiety which is the most devastating of peace's enemies, as we wait in joyful hope for the coming of our Saviour, Jesus Christ. The peace we share is a foretaste of the peace which Christ will bring in his kingdom, and so there follows a prayer to Christ himself, asking him to give to his Church here and now that peace of the age to come, to make his present into ours. Then the person who is presiding says to the others, 'The peace of the Lord be with you always'. After they have answered him, he invites them to give each other a sign of peace. The form of this greeting naturally differs from place to place, though in some way it always expresses the Lord's own greeting, 'Peace be with you'. In the liturgy of St Basil, the form is 'Christ is in our midst!', to which the reply comes: 'He is and he will be always'. In the Dominican use, one says, 'Peace to you, and to the holy Church of God'. Then while the bread of life is being broken up for communion everyone sings the acclamation 'Lamb of God', which concludes with a further request for peace. So we prepare for communion with Christ and with each other. The kiss of peace and the communion go so closely together that for centuries anyone excluded from one was *ipso facto* excluded from the other. The kiss of peace, like any liturgical gesture, should never be purely formal: it must always be what Clement calls 'mystical'. (We should remember what the prophet Jeremiah had to say about those who said 'Peace, peace!' where there was no peace.) Like any liturgical gesture, it demands a consistency of one's intra-ecclesial and extra-ecclesial ministry. Ignatius of

Antioch points out that peace is one of the most important ways in which the gospel is preached:

By your concord and symphonic love,
Jesus Christ is being sung.[2]

The calling down of the Spirit, whose proper name is love, the Love between the Father and the Son, inevitably demands the naming of peace. In the *Sayings* of the Desert Fathers we read that an elder said:

Often at the moment when the deacon says, 'Give the peace one to another', I have seen the Holy Spirit on the mouths of the brethren.[3]

The kiss of peace most surely sums up a vital aspect of the celebration of the body, the Church's icon, the Eucharist.

The eucharistic assembly is an icon of the Church as event and as institution. It is a celebration of the body which is, and which makes, the unity of the people. It is a celebration of the blood-shedding of Jesus into which we ourselves can enter substantially. Perhaps this occurs even more potently in the cup than in the bread. Any meal, of course, should include food and drink. For the Jews (as for the British until recently), wine was not normally drunk at meals, and so, when it was, it produced a sense of occasion. Wine is what makes glad the heart of man, what cheers both man and God. The psalmist says that his cup is 'overflowing' and in the accounts of the Last Supper in the Roman canon these words are applied to the chalice there on the altar: *Calix meus inebrians*. The promised land was a land of vines, very different from the desert. At the Passover, in celebration of this gift of the land, everyone drinks four cups of wine and one of these Christ interpreted as the cup of his blood, the 'new covenant' in his blood. (The expression 'new and everlasting covenant' in all the official canons is a conflation of these words with some words from the Letter to the Hebrews.) In the Scriptures, blood is life, as it is for us – loss of blood leads to loss of life. And this life-blood can be shared, as in rituals of blood-brotherhood. The New Testament says that God 'made of one blood all

---

[2] Ignatius, *To the Ephesians*, IV.
[3] Cf. F. Cabrol, 'Baiser', *Dictionnaire d'archéologie chrétienne et de liturgie* 2 (1910), cols. 117–130.

nations of men for to dwell on the face of the earth' (Acts 17.26), and that his Son became blood-brother to all in taking the flesh and blood that all share. As the Suffering Servant foretold by Isaiah, Jesus poured out his life-blood for others. So he explains the cup as his life-blood 'poured out' (a sacrificial expression) for all. The 'cup' refers to his passion and death, the bitter liquid that the Father has given him to drink. During the pouring out of one of the cups at Passover, certain cursing verses from the psalms were recited against foreign nations who oppress Israel: 'Pour out your wrath on the heathens who know you not' (Ps. 79.6). Jesus' explanation that the pouring out of his cup is for the forgiveness of sins is probably in deliberate contrast to this custom. So the sharing of the cup situates the Eucharist in the context of violence. But it looks forward to the new age of peace, the time when the Lord will have come again. At Passover, one of the cups is drunk in anticipation of the coming reign of God. But at Jesus' own passing over to the Father he says that he 'will drink no more of the fruit of the vine' until he drinks it anew in the Father's kingdom (Luke 22.18). It is that kingdom of peace and justice which the Church in its Eucharist makes momentarily present on earth.

21

General Council

WHEN we looked at the root idea of the Christian people as Church, we saw the significance of the notion of assembly, of being called together. The very word 'Church' in its Greek form *ekklēsia* speaks etymologically of the calling of God. *Kalō*, the root of *ekklēsia*, means 'to call' in the everyday sense of that word, but in the Synoptic Gospels, and more intensely still in the Pauline writings, it bears the quite specific sense, often enough, of a call from God, a vocation. God calls people to salvation, to suffering, to that peace which is the peace of Christ, to freedom, to sanctification, to hope, to the inheritance of a blessing, to the promise of eternal life, to his marvellous light, to his eternal glory in Christ, to fellowship with his Son, Christ Jesus. He calls us also to the marriage supper of the Lamb, to the banquet of his kingdom already roughed out, symbolised and brought into the present, in the sacrament of the Eucharist. Christians can be identified as those who are called, called not as a motley conglomeration of individuals with no regard to the ties that must necessarily bind men together but called as a people, and called to be a people. The first Christians in Jerusalem at the time of Pentecost were conscious that they were what they were and where they were because of a call from God, and so they could speak of themselves as the *ekklēsia*. As we have seen, this primitive Church in Jerusalem, the church of Pentecost, had an altogether unique rôle in Christian history. This particular church was *the* Church: at first no distinction could be drawn between this church and the Church at large. The whole Church could and did assemble at one place.

> When the day of Pentecost had come, they were all together in one place. (Acts 2.1)

But it was only a very short time before there were Christians in other places, for the members of the Church, the Jerusalem church, fulfilled their commission to be witnesses of Christ in all Judaea and in Samaria and to the uttermost ends of the earth. The Christians in the Judaean and Galilean cities, the Christians in Samaria, were also then properly called 'the Church'. They were not simply *parts* of the Church: they *were* the Church in these places, the people called together to be there and then the people of God. Each individual church or assembly, called together by God, was the equivalent of the original church or assembly in Jerusalem. Yet inevitably there grew up in the Church the custom of speaking of the Church in one place and the Church in another in the plural – of speaking, in fact, of churches.

The odd way in which these church-words came to function reflected the odd reality they pointed to: each local church was as much Church (intensively) as the church of Jerusalem, the aboriginal church. And yet every other church was as much church as it was itself. These churches were there (as dots on a map) and yet the whole Church was there (so that before too long the map could have shaded areas), since the whole Church was not exhausted by any one local church. Nevertheless, whether it was a question of the church in a locality or the Church in the whole wide world, the primary sense of the church-word was that of a people called together by God in order to be his people in the whole wide world, the *oikoumenē*, the inhabited earth – for the Church is of its nature catholic, 'embracing the whole'. In principle, no human grouping was to be excluded from it; no nation or tribe or language or religious tradition was debarred from entering. Every human grouping was called by God, and those who heard the call were thereby called in turn to mission, to making the same call heard by others. This ecumenical, catholic quality of the Church (often spoken of as one of its 'marks' or 'notes') qualifies the Church both as local and as geographically universal. Among the early churches, each local church would have been conscious of itself as catholic or ecumenical, mainly because in it the supreme division, that between Jew and Gentile, had been overcome, but also because of the presence there of people from so many classes and races, of slaves and freemen, of Greeks and barbarians, all conscious of their oneness in Christ and calling each other brother and sister. The sense of the Church as catholic and ecumenical in terms of geographical extension came somewhat later. It took expression in the slow rise of the various rites within the Church, for the Church in the great provincial capitals of the old Roman Empire tended to acquire a dominance in the churches in the hinterland. Often enough such a metropolitan local church had founded these churches itself, their members hearing God's call in the voice of the missionaries from the regional capital and responding to it by accepting baptism at their hands. This is the origin of the patriarchal system in the Church. As in each local church there was a real experience of catholicity, so too in the Church extended throughout the world. The first is a catholicity of individual persons, the second of individual churches.

The Latin equivalent of *kalō*, the verb of calling, was also *calo*, to summon or announce. The people as summoned, the Greek *ekklēsia*, was the Latin *concalium* or *concilium*, an assembly or council. The primary and basic form of this council was the eucharistic assembly, the eucharistic council in which people heard and answered God's call to come together. The Church as local church was the council of believers, the assembly of those who believed in the Word of God which was Jesus, the Christ. In the eucharistic assembly, the motley collection of individuals became a council, in which one plus one equals one, the one Man Christ Jesus. In the Eucharist human beings ceased to be an agglomeration, forming instead a new whole, the body of Christ which communicated to its parts a pattern not written into their individual structures. We have already seen how this works in the case of the local church, where the one made up of the sum of all the individuals does not leave the individual untouched. May it not also be true of the Church universal, the Church as extensively catholic? How does the existence of other churches which are just as much Church as any one local church is Church, and form a catholic Church spread throughout the world, modify the existence of any and every local community?

In the first place, it modifies it by virtue of social mobility, in the ancient world just as now. People then, like people now, moved from city to city, and those people included Christians. When Christians moved, the church in the other city became their church: they belonged to it immediately. In the early ages of Christianity they were given letters of commendation from the bishop of the church from which they moved to the bishop of the church they moved into, and such letters sufficed to establish their claim to be Christians of equal standing with those resident in the city to which they went. Their equal standing was founded on the one baptism and one faith that all shared in allegiance to the one Lord. This was all very well in an ideal situation when all churches did hold the same faith. But a problem arose when some of the churches had a different way of expressing their faith from other churches, and this development was virtually inevitable when one considers how the faith took root among peoples with such very different ways of thinking. Might not these different expressions of the faith signify that the faith that was held was different, from one church to another? How was a church to ensure that its particular expression of the faith was orthodoxy, a genuine and valid response to the gospel? How was any church to be sure that the faith of a church to which some of its members moved was orthodox? How was a bishop to know whether he was doing right in commending one of his own people to another church, doing right by that other church's members? One possible way for a church unsure of its own understanding of the truth, or of the orthodoxy of a second church, to gain enlightenment was by way of appeal to a third church. An uncertain and worried church could come to the church in priority in its region so as to find itself, to find the reality of Church which should have been as much in itself as in the church in priority.

The church in priority amongst all the churches, from at least the time of Irenaeus, was the church in Rome – 'by reason of the more powerful authority of its foundation' as Irenaeus puts it.[1] The rôle of the church in Rome was not to initiate decisions in the realm of faith or doctrine, but rather to arbitrate, to witness as Church to the truth or falsehood of contentious issues of doctrine put before it. Its task and vocation was to say as Church what was the truth or falsehood with respect to some policy, position or practice prevailing in some other local church. One church, then, might listen to the faith of the Church incarnated in another local church.

But there were times when it was not any one local church that was troubled in its grasp of doctrine but all the Church: the one Church throughout the world was seriously concerned about some teaching gaining ground amongst the Christian people. In

[1] Irenaeus, *Against the Heresies*, III. 3, 4.

such a case it seemed inappropriate to appeal to one single local church and listen for the voice of God there. When all the churches were troubled, then all the churches had to be involved in sorting out the trouble – but they had to be involved *as churches*. There had to be some way in which they did not depart from orthodox behaviour as they attempted to establish the orthodox faith. At the first great crisis affecting all the churches, the answer was worked out (somewhat haphazardly to the historian's eye) in a form that has survived until the present. We call it a General Council. In celebrating (the word should be noted) a General Council, the people of God would be celebrating for the Church throughout the world the equivalent of the eucharistic assembly in a local church. What the eucharistic council is for the local church, the General Council is for the Church universal. This formula is not just in all respects, but it is illuminating. True, the Eucharist is not the object of the exercise in a General Council, although it may be celebrated during its course. Yet the object of both the eucharistic council and the General Council is to hear the word of God and to respond appropriately: in one case by way of the great prayer of thanksgiving, in the other by a way of a credal formulation. In each case the people of God is represented and endeavours to be faithfully itself.

How is it so represented there? Nowadays, there are rather strict rules as to what may, and may not, be called a 'General Council'. If we take the last such Council known to us, the Second Vatican, we find that its convocation was governed by the 1917 Code of Canons, whose regulations were meant to ensure that a General Council be a plausible representation of the universal Church. What, then, did that authoritative document require?

In the first place, the Code says that there can be no General Council which is not called by the Roman pontiff, and presided over by him in person or through a delegate. Only he can suspend, transfer or dissolve a General Council, and the decrees thereof want in binding force until they are confirmed and promulgated by him. If the Roman bishop dies during the course of such a Council it stands in abeyance until his successor decides to resume it. In all of this, the canons are trying to ensure the adequate representation in the Council of the Roman pontiff in the universal Church. The implication is that if this rôle be not adequately expressed then the Council will lack credibility as a representation of the universal Church. That Code also lays down rules for determining who should be summoned to a General Council with full rights to vote: the cardinals (whether they are bishops or not), patriarchs, primates, archbishops and residential bishops, and abbots or prelates *nullius*, those people who are equivalent to bishops in certain out-of-the-way territories. The aim here is to assure the representation of all local churches, those churches each of which is just as much church as the universal Church is. These churches are represented by the man who has the task of representing his church to the universal Church and vice versa in all matters not involving a General Council. Also summoned with plenary rights were the abbot primate of the Benedictines, the abbots superior of the various monastic congregations, the major superiors of exempt clerical religious orders such as the Dominicans and the Friars Minor, though not of other orders and congregations unless these are specifically mentioned in the decree convoking the Council. This recognises that there are theological traditions, ways of doing theology, in the Church which are peculiar not only to particular dioceses or 'national' churches but also to particular religious orders. (The obvious examples would be the Scotist and Thomist traditions represented classically by the Franciscans and the Dominicans. The Code implicitly recognised that there are many religious congregations which do not have a theological tradition in this sense.)

Theologians may be invited to the Council but they do not have a vote. The task of a Council is to listen to the word of God, often represented by an image of Christ or by a book of the Gospels enthroned in the council hall, to *witness* to the faith, not to argue about it. Theology, on the other hand, is all about arguing. The members of the Council may in fact argue, and perhaps argue acrimoniously, yet this disputing is only in virtue of listening. So credible a representation of the universal Church is a Council thus composed that the Code can continue by saying: 'an Ecumenical Council enjoys supreme power in the universal Church'. It is so much the Church, in other words, that local churches, or individual Christians, finding themselves out of tune with its decrees are required to bring themselves back into line on pain of finding themselves excommunicated, no longer members of the Church.

It must be conceded that the provisions of the Code for the summoning and constitution of a Council do not take the form of historical *reportage*. They are prescriptive, not rescriptive, laying down guidelines for the future, rather than delineating the history of General Councils in the past. For example, the first Ecumenical Council, Nicaea I, in 325, was summoned not by the pope of the time but by the emperor Constantine, as yet still unbaptised. It was Constantine who presided over the Council and promulgated its decrees, concerned as he was for the unity of the churches in the service of the unity of an empire. Again, the exclusion of certain of the laity from General Councils, for instance, only began at the Council of Trent. As late as the Council of Constance (1414–1418), the holy Roman emperor was in attendance as an *advocatus ecclesiae*. Throughout the Middle Ages there was oscillation between the idea that Councils depended for their authenticity on the adequacy of their representation of the Church and the notion that they were constituted as General Councils by the canonical legality of the way they were summoned. But neither of these criteria will work for all the Councils. Some that were properly summoned and reasonably representative of the whole Church have not subsequently been recognised as being General Councils. In the last resort, only the acceptance of a Council by the Church can be said to make it truly ecumenical and its decrees fully binding. Not that those decrees become true because they are subsequently accepted: that would be a logical fallacy. Rather, they are subsequently accepted by the whole Church, which body is guaranteed by God in Christ not to fail in faith, because they are true expressions of the faith of the Church (though always and inevitably inadequate expressions of that faith, open to subsequent refinement).

The recognition by the Church that a Council was genuinely ecumenical is a recognition that it was a Council 'assembled in the Holy Spirit'. It is one of the ways in which the whole Church exercises the charism of the discernment of spirits, for not every Council claiming to be assembled in the Holy Spirit has had its claim upheld. But a Council which is genuinely ecumenical will always make the claim that it is so assembled, in continuity with the astonishing expression of the 'Council of Jerusalem' in the

Acts of the Apostles which read 'It has seemed good to the Holy Spirit and to us' (Acts 15.28). Thereby it will be in continuity too with the claims of Constantine at Nicaea:

> The judgment of three hundred bishops is nothing other than the judgment of God, above all for the reason that the Holy Spirit, residing in the minds of these great men, has clearly revealed the will of God. There is no longer any reason for doubt.[2]

A General Council in its deliberations does not act like a modern boardroom and make decisions by majority vote. It attempts rather to do something of the sort that happens in the gatherings of Quakers, of the Friends. It tries to get the sense of the meeting, waiting until a clear consensus emerges, and seeing in that emergence of a consensus the activity of the Holy Spirit, who is the spirit of unity and concord. When a Council reaches moral unanimity, there is a sign of the presence of the Spirit. But the presence of the Spirit, the *esprit de corps* of the mystical body of Christ, is guaranteed only to the Church. Only insofar as a General Council really is general, standing in that relationship to the whole Church that the eucharistic council has to the local church, is the presence of the Holy Spirit promised to it. That presence, and the genuine representation of the whole Church, stands or falls together.

A General Council is an important way of focussing the Church. It is not that General Councils are essential to the Church in the way in which the eucharistic council is essential to it. A church without the Eucharist is no church, or at least, bearing in mind the curious history of Catholicism in Japan, never appears in its full reality as a church. It is conceivable that the history of the Church could have unfolded without General Councils. Nevertheless, *post factum* we can see that General Councils form part of God's will for his Church, in times of trial above all, and that in them the promise of the Holy Spirit to the community of Jesus is made concrete in history.

---

[2] Constantine, 'Letter to the Catholic Church of the Alexandrians', in Socrates, *Ecclesiastical History* I. 9, 24–25.

22

Church Buildings

THE eucharistic assembly is the primary focus of the Church, the point *par excellence* where the people of God comes together as Church to be made Church, the situation where the Church appears for what it is. But when it comes together, the act of congregating necessarily involves some sort of relationship with space and place. If it is right and fitting to give thanks *semper et ubique*, 'always and everywhere', yet the Church meets at a particular time and in a particular place. It does not matter absolutely where and when it so meets but it simply has to meet somewhere and sometimes.

The gospel is always tending to make the world more primitive. It sums up the history that preceded it, but it goes beyond it in going behind it and restores a primitive wholeness which was scattered in the course of human history. So the Christian community is always being urged to be Abrahamic rather than Mosaic and Adamic more than Abrahamic. This is not least true in matters of time and place. For the Mosaic system, certain times and places were specially sacred: the sabbath and the annual feasts, the tent of meeting in the desert centred on the ark of the covenant, and the temple in Jerusalem, represented mythologically in the Bible as a copy in stone and timber of the tent of skins. But for Abraham there were no times and places in which God waited to be met. Rather, it was when God was encountered that time became sacred, and place too. For Adam, God's dwelling was the whole inhabited earth, which God walked about in. The Apocalypse of John, resuming and reinterpreting all this, depicts the heavenly Jerusalem as having no temple nor setting sun, that is, no time. The presence of God is ubiquitous and constant. There is a new heaven and a new earth in which the original state is restored and raised up. This means that the Book of Revelation is a picture of the end, which is not yet. For the time being, the people of God are a pilgrim people, a people on the march, a people who move forward from one day to the next and set up camp at different places. They meet as a people at certain times and certain spots. For the Church of the New Testament and the early centuries, time and place were not indifferent. The time and the place when and where the Church met came to partake of the holiness, the set-apart nature, of the Church which met then and there. With time, the move came very quickly, for the Lord's Day had hallowed associations for the assembling of the Church which were as primitive as the Church itself. It was on the first day of the week that the Church was made Church from being a group of frightened and dispirited men, for it was then that Jesus came to meet them behind closed doors. As early as the Book of Revelation, the first day of each week was the day of resurrection, the 'Lord's Day'. As long as time goes on that association of the first day of the week with the resurrection of Jesus, and with the creation of the Church by the breathing of the Holy Spirit on a company of lonely disciples, will continue, in the same way that recurring times and seasons bring anniversaries of births and deaths and weddings. Only when there is one day, the 'first' or the 'eighth' as you will, shall anniversaries cease: on that day the sun's dominion will have its end. Such anniversaries are meant to give us new access to the original and originating experience they commemorate. On the first day of the week Christians do not only remember the appearances of the risen Jesus: they expect to encounter him afresh.

The Church took longer to re-experience space than it did to re-experience time. Early anti-Christian polemic accused the Christians of being atheists, partly at least because they had no temples. The New Testament, and the earliest generations of the Church, maintained that they did indeed have a temple – the body of the Lord Jesus, which had passed through death and was not in the glory of God. Alternatively, they claimed that their temple was the Christian community itself. To understand this argument, we have to remember that the basic meaning of 'temple' is a place where God, or a god, dwells. In Israel, we recall, there had always been a bifocal approach to the presence of God, the God who was not in any way circumscribed and yet who dwelt in the temple in Jerusalem. In the speech of Stephen in the Book of Acts, the proto-martyr declares that God does not dwell in temples made by human hands, implying, evidently, that he does not dwell there more than anywhere else. If God is in every place then he is in temples too, but not in temples in any particular way, not even in the temple in Jerusalem. The bifocal approach remains, but the second focus is now the glorified body of the man Jesus, the body which is the Church. Where the Church assembled, there the glory of God had its abode. 'Where two or three are gathered in my Name, there am I in the midst of them' (Matt. 18.20). And yet eventually a way had to be found for coming to terms with the pilgrim condition of the Church. God is where the Church assembles, but short of the city of the last day the Church must assemble somewhere. Could this 'somewhere' be called the place of God's presence? Clearly, it could, at those times when the assembly is actually in session. Could places take on holiness from the holiness of the holy people which assembled there? Strictly speaking, the answer to this must be no. No damage is done to the structure of Christian existence if a building in which the Church meets is demolished. There is no threat to faith in the destruction of a church by fire or earthquake. Nor is there any need for a Christian to go to one building in particular in order to worship God.

However, this does not entirely close the discussion. Assume that a group of Christians meets regularly for worship. It does not matter where: one week it may be in the house of one member, in the next of another. In a third week it may be at the grave of a member who has died, and in a fourth in some quiet place where it cannot be observed. On each Sunday God is as really present. But suppose the Christians in some locality are too numerous to meet in one another's homes, and that they fear divisions too much to split up into a lot of small sub-groups. Then they will have to find some one large place to meet, and it is unlikely that they will be able to find a different place each week, or even want to. What happens, almost inevitably, in such a situation is that the building where the Church regularly meets as Church in order to be made Church takes on pronounced Church-associations. Christians cannot pass it in the street or see it from a distance without thinking of all they have experienced within its walls. The four walls and roof that make a church can easily enough come to be called itself 'the church'. Once this linguistic usage established itself and a building ceased to be *domus ecclesiae*, 'the house of the Church', and became rather itself *ecclesia*, 'the church', then a number of other images came into play. The very building itself now became a fruitful locus for contemplating the mystery of the people, the people who are themselves 'Church' and 'temple'.

In the first instance, buildings were taken over for worship from secular or perhaps pagan-religious use. In Rome, and many great cities of the Empire besides, the original buildings so converted were the basilicas, a kind of market-hall-cum-law-court. With the victory of Christianity in the fourth century pagan temples like the Roman Pantheon were sequestrated. When such a pagan temple was taken over it was normal to bless it with exorcised water, in recognition of the reality of the false and demonic 'gods' (the evil angels) who had used it to pervert men's minds. Otherwise the only form of blessing was simply the celebration of Mass there. Originally, things were blessed just by being used. In time, however, Christians could not find lying about all the buildings they needed for worship, and the building of a church from scratch then became a step in the evangelisation of the world. A new church building was now a sign or sacramental of the Church as a missionary community, the *ecclesia congregans*. Just how the Church decides to construct an edifice in which to worship will always be a powerful indicator of how it thinks of itself. The structures of church buildings in different epochs are themselves monuments of tradition. When new buildings are erected, the assembly of believers creates its own worshipping space. Not that it has no place of its own: it has a most powerful sacred space already in that it is set apart for God. Just as before I am 'in' a place I am my own place through my own body, and yet go on to produce a place for myself, so the Church which is its own sacred space goes on to produce an ordered space from somewhere in the world. In my body I first experience the relationships of front/back, up/down and left/right, and then go on to order my world in series with this. So the organic body of the Church orders the world in which it meets in accordance with its experience of its own body. The anatomy of the body of the celebrating assembly is what produces a building that marks out a significant space in the world. What we have to do with in church buildings is not merely functionalism (to celebrate the Mass there must be some sort of table in some sort of room), but the expression of a mystery. In church architecture differences of style express differences of conceptual idiom in exploring this mystery.

The essense of the church building is the eucharistic room. To this room others may be attached, as in the oldest Christian building we know of, the church at Dura-Europos, and in many modern churches. The baptistery, indeed, may be a quite separate building as in a number of great Western cathedrals. The blessed sacrament may be reserved in a separate chapel, since it is irrelevant to the celebration of the Eucharist as such. Within the eucharistic room there is no one single centre of focus and attention but many: think only of the president, of the Book and of the altar-table. The way in which these three have been related in space at different times tells us much about their relative significance and inter-relationship at different epochs. We may distinguish five basic models. Where the altar is placed against the east wall of an elongated building, as in most mediaeval and post-mediaeval churches, the design represents a people *in via*, turned to the east in expectation of the Saviour's return, looking with the celebrant in the same direction. Such a design cannot do justice, however, to the element of realised eschatology in Christian faith, the way the Saviour is present here and now in the assembly whose feasting itself anticipates his glorious kingdom. Secondly, the altar may be placed somewhere in the middle of an oblong box with the worshippers arranged in two rows facing each other along the walls: the pattern of a typical monastic choir. This design images the heavenly assembly and clearly incorporates the element of realised eschatology lacking in the first. Unfortunately it has no way of expressing the sacramental ordering of the assembly, in that the celebrant's position *vis-à-vis* the faithful is lost sight of. Thirdly, there could be a circular space with the altar in the exact centre: this has been realised in the Templar churches of the Middle Ages as well as in such contemporary buildings as the Metropolitan Cathedral in Liverpool. The drawback of this scheme is that its eschatology is only too thoroughly realised. It expresses no future orientation at all. Fourthly, there may be an incomplete circle rather like an ancient amphitheatre with the altar placed centrally along the diameter, and ever-increasing semicircles of ministers and laity facing. This shape is perhaps rather too spectatorial, suggestive of attenders at a performance more than participators. Finally there is the basilica model which appears to be the most satisfactory expression we have of the mystery the building houses and reveals. Here the ministers sit in an arc behind the altar confronting the people who occupy a series of arcs beyond the holy table. In this scheme the president and ministers come forward on God's behalf to the people, they embody the apostolic ministry from Christ to humankind. On the other hand they are manifestly a part of the assembly as well, listeners as well as teachers.

What then is this mystery which the space of the church is to guard? No better entry can be found to it than the rite of dedicating a church in the Tridentine Pontifical. When that rite opens, the space to be consecrated is empty except for a single deacon. The bishop, priests and people are gathered in a place where the relics of the martyrs are preserved, the concrete expression of the community's radical witness to Christ, written in the blood of its members, and of the overshadowing presence of the heavenly Church of which the earthly Church is the outreach and colony. In this place the bishop invokes the presence of God: 'Be present, O God, one and almighty, Father, Son and Holy Spirit.' Then, while the Litany of the Saints is being sung, the bishop goes round the outside walls of the church, sprinkling it with holy water. He returns and knocks on the door with his pastoral staff, the symbol of his shepherdhood in the assembly. He strikes up a dialogue with the deacon inside, using the words of one of the 'psalms of ascent':

> Lift up your heads, O you gates, and be lifted up you everlasting doors,
> and the king of glory shall come in.
> Who is this king of glory?
> the Lord strong and mighty, the Lord mighty in battle.
> (Ps. 24.7–8)

This circumambulation is repeated three times, twice anti-clockwise and then clockwise. The circle is the most ancient form of the dance; ritually, to encircle an object is to incorporate it. (In the Hindu Scriptures, the creation of the universe is sometimes imaged as a magnificent circular dance of the gods.) At the end of the third circumambulation, the people call out 'Open up!', and the bishop with his attendant clergy and the masons responsible for the structure enter the building. A hymn is sung:

Peace eternal from the Eternal be to this house.
May endless peace, the Father's Word, be peace to this house.
May the loving Comforter bring peace to this house.

The bishop intones the *Veni Creator Spiritus*, and after prayers, the *Benedictus*, the Song of Zacharias, is chanted. During this the bishop takes his staff and using ashes scratches the letters of the Greek and Latin alphabets in the form of a cross across the entire floor of the church, so representing the catholicity of the body of Christ. He then mixes the principal sacramentals, wine, salt, ashes and water, into a mixture used for the sacring of the altar to which he now proceeds. The heart of this final, rather elaborate, ritual is the consecratory 'Preface'. The language of this prayer offers us a whole theology of the church building as a focus of the Church:

> Be present to the pious endeavours of your servants and to us who seek your mercy.
> May your Holy Spirit come down upon this your house, bestowing the fulness of his sevenfold grace
> on this house which we in our unworthiness are consecrating under the invocation of your holy name in honour of the holy cross on which your co-eternal Son suffered for the world's redemption, and in memory of St N.
> So whenever your holy name is invoked in this house, hear the prayers, loving Lord, of those who call on you.
> O blessed and holy Trinity, who purify, cleanse and adorn all things!
> O blessed majesty of God, who fill all things, contain all things, set all things in order!
> O blessed and holy hand of God, which hallows all things, blesses all things, enriches all things!
> O holy God, God of the holy ones,
> we pray to you for this your church:
> through our ministry, bless and consecrate it with your perpetual hallowing in honour of the holy and victorious cross and in memory of St N.
> Here may the priests offer you sacrifices of praise.
> Here may the faithful people pay their vows.
> Here may the burden of sins be loosed and the lapsed return to the faith.

In this place, by the grace of your Holy Spirit,
may the sick be healed, the weak recover their strength, the lame
  be cured, lepers be cleansed;
may the blind receive their sight and demons be cast out.
May all who are bowed down by any misfortune here be raised
  up and freed from the chains of all their sins.
May all who enter this temple to seek your blessings rejoice to
  have all they ask for,
that through your mercy they may glory in your gifts.

23

Pilgrims

THE foci of the Church we have looked at so far have in common a somewhat static quality. Although both the eucharistic assembly and the General Council are events, they are events at a particular time and in a particular place. They speak of the Church as assembled, even though the missionary function of the Church is not absent and the Eucharist at least is celebrated in hope: 'in joy and hope' says the Embolism of the Roman Mass, referring to the joy of the messianic era and the hope proper to a time of expectation.

These images miss out on a sense of going somewhere, of being 'on the way', of that dynamic quality summed up in the phrase 'the pilgrim Church'. Perhaps the pilgrim Church is nowhere more concisely and strikingly expressed than in the Epistle to Diognetus, an anonymous writing of uncertain date but no later than the third century of the Christian era.

The distinction between Christians and other men is neither in country nor language nor customs. For they do not dwell in cities in some place of their own, nor do they use any strange variety of dialect, nor practise an extraordinary kind of life. This teaching of theirs has not been discovered by the intellect or thought of busy men, nor are they the advocates of any human doctrine, as some men are. Yet while living in Greek and barbarian cities, according as each has obtained his lot, and following the local customs both in clothing and in food and in the rest of life, they show forth the wonderful and admittedly strange (*paradoxos*) character of their own citizenship. They dwell in their own father-lands, but as if sojourners (*paroikoi*) in them. They share all things as citizens, and suffer all things as strangers (*xenoi*). Every foreign country is their fatherland, and every fatherland is a foreign country. They marry as all men do, they have children, but they do not expose their offspring. They keep a common table but not a common bed. Their lot is cast in the flesh, but they do not live according to the flesh. They pass their time on earth, but they have their citizenship in heaven.[1]

And the author concludes:

> To put it shortly, what the soul is in the body, that the Christians are in the world. The soul is spread through the members of the body, but is not of the body, and Christians dwell in the world but are not of the world. The soul is indivisible but is guarded by a visible body, and Christians are recognised when they are in the world, but their religion remains invisible. The flesh hates the soul and wages war upon it even though it has suffered no evil, but just because it is prevented from gratifying its pleasures; and the world hates the Christians though it has suffered no evil but just because they are opposed to its pleasures. The soul loves the flesh which hates it, and Christians love those who hate them. The soul has been shut up in the body, but itself sustains the body, and Christians are confined in the world as in a prison, but themselves sustain the world. The soul dwells immortal in a mortal tent, and Christians sojourn (*paroichousin*) among corruptible things, waiting for the incorruptibility which is in heaven.[2]

In this description of Christians as sojourners, strangers and exiles the author of the Epistle to Diognetus is taking up a theme which runs through the New Testament and, indeed, was already present in the Hebrew Bible. The First Letter of Peter is addressed to 'the exiles, the sojourners, of the dispersion, of Pontus, of Galatia, of Cappadocia, of Asia and of Bithynia' (1 Pet. 1.1). It is as 'sojourners and aliens' that later in the same epistle they are exhorted to 'abstain from fleshly lusts which war against the soul' (2.11). Since they 'invoke the Father as one who is no respecter of persons', they are to 'pass the time of [their] sojourning here in fear' (1.17). In this, as the Letter to the Hebrews says, they are only living as the Old Testament patriarchs did, those who made it manifest that they were 'looking for a fatherland' and until they found it 'confessed that they were strangers and sojourners on the earth' (Heb. 11.14, 13). In particular, Christians share the lifestyle of Abraham who 'by faith sojourned in a

[1] Epistle to Diognetus, V.
[2] *Ibid.*, VI.

land of promise as a foreigner, dwelling in tents with Isaac and Jacob, fellow-heirs with him of the same promise' (Heb. 11.9).

It is scarcely surprising, therefore, that the earliest Christian communities should have called their faith 'the Way'. This sort of language was in any case in the air at the time, both in the synagogues and in the Greek schools. The Qumran community called itself 'the Way', those who joined it were 'those who chose the Way', and those who left it, 'those who turned aside from the Way'. The Jewish equivalent of what we should call 'moral theology' was *halakhah*, a noun derived from the verb 'to walk'. Behaviour is the way people walk in the Way. The Fourth Gospel actually goes so far as to identify Jesus himself with 'the Way': 'I am the Way' (John 14.6), the way that everyone was talking about. More specifically, he identifies himself with what Christians meant when they spoke about 'the Way', with the pattern of organisation and the total lifestyle in which Christians found their life with God. Christianity was not deified or made into an absolute. But Jesus was understood as claiming to be what the Church claimed to be: the Way. Ideally, the Church's pattern of life is that which Jesus is. Ideally, the Son of God and the sons of God have the same spiritual genetic code. The Fourth Gospel invites its readers to give the Church the same density as Jesus. Christians are to let it appear that they are the way which Jesus is, to let the community which Jesus founds and centres be genuinely revelatory of Jesus himself.

As 'the Way' Jesus assumes in himself the whole movement of Jewish nomadism and in particular the exodus from Egypt and the return from captivity in Babylon. In both cases the people had to pass to their own homes along a way. In the exodus from Egypt the way was already there, the 'King's Highway' so often seen by the Fathers of the Church as symbolising the central Catholic tradition. It was along this highway that the people travelled, turning aside neither to the right hand nor to the left until they had passed through the territory which separated them from the Land that God had given them. But the Way really entered deeply into the consciousness of the people of God only during the time of their exile in Babylon, their advent period. The function of the prophets who spoke for God during this period was to create hope by pointing to God as the hoping God, the distant God who is waiting for his people to make their way to him. Prophecy forces the future to be as simultaneous as possible with man's here and now. For Isaiah, for instance, the desert is the space, the emptiness, between Babylon and Jerusalem, where God is waiting for his people. Along that highway God's glory will be glimpsed, not because God himself will walk along it but because he will make his people do so. As Peter says in the New Testament, 'By holy living hasten the coming of the Day of God' (2 Pet. 3.12). This implies that hope is created when people are uprooted from their *status quo* and forced to march onwards. People learn to hope by being required to prepare a way along which they and others can catch up with Jesus of Nazareth, who is himself the Way. Proper waiting means being actively engaged in hastening God's kingdom, in bridging the gap between what is and what is to be, between Babylon and the new Jerusalem. This is the advent structure of faithful living in the Jewish and Christian traditions. The challenge is for us to match the work of Christ, to make Christ appear as the Way to the future and the Father, by ourselves walking along that way, building it as we go.

In Christ man's restless search for transcendence, for an ultimate purpose and destiny, is at last successful. In the personal history of the man Jesus is revealed to us the structure of every man's return to the Father, the pattern of God's plan for human history. People have always been fascinated by the quest: the quest for the Holy Grail, for the pearl of great price, the treasure hid in a field, in the wood at the world's end. All images of a way and a quest have held men entranced: the labyrinth, the tower, the ladder, the winding staircase, right through to the 'double helix' which is the basic structure of all living matter. For the Alexandrian Jew Philo, philosophy was the 'royal way'. Confucius called his system *Tao*, 'the way'. Men have always delighted in picturing their existence as a journey, a pilgrim's progress. All of this is brought to its climax in Jesus. As W. H. Auden says:

> He is the Way.
> Follow him through the Land of Unlikeliness;
> You will see rare beasts and have unique adventures.[3]

[3] W. H. Auden, 'The Flight into Egypt', IV, in *Collected Longer Poems* (London 1968), p. 196.

We know the Way only by walking along the way, as time and again in the New Testament people met him who is the Way as they walked along the way that led to Emmaus or to Damascus. *Solvitur ambulando*: find the answer by walking. There is a kind of knowledge which always escapes our verbalisation and can only be gained by walking. Along the Way we shall meet rare and probably dangerous beasts, for a living Way cannot be secure: only death brings security.

Thus it is that the Church is incarnated and imaged in the pilgrim, in the man who leaves where he is and goes somewhere else. The pilgrim's special grace is to set out for somewhere in such an attitude of mind that the journey on which he is engaged and what he does when he reaches journey's end form together one concrete activity. In the beginning, pilgrimages in the cultic sense did not enter into the life of the Church. Pilgrimage was apparently a pagan or Old Testament form of devotion. The ancient world knew pilgrimages to the shrines of the healing god Aesculapius, especially to his temple at Epidauros. And there were pilgrimages made to discover what the future had in store by going to the oracle at Delphi. Similarly, there were annual pilgrimages to the great festivals at the temple of Yahweh in Jerusalem. For Christians, on the other hand, the Lord was to be met with in every Eucharist, and his return was expected in the near future. So although the Christian life itself might be considered a pilgrimage, there were at first no pilgrimages as such, just as there were no Christian temples. Only when the sense of the imminent parousia faded did Christians begin to go on pilgrimage to the scenes of the earthly life of Jesus, above all to the tomb from which God raised him. Only later did people go from a distance to the tombs of the apostles and the great martyrs. In the Middle Ages, with the development of the penitential system perfected by the Irish monks, pilgrimages became increasingly important, and they have never lost their appeal since.

Reflection on pilgrimage and the experience of pilgrimage reveals a lot about the nature of the Church as a pilgrim people. Pilgrimage involves taking leave of home, a distancing of self from everyday life. The company of other pilgrims helps, increasing ardour, generating prayer in common that culminates in the sacrifice of the altar when Christ gives his body to strengthen the Christian on his way to God. A pilgrimage awakens the spirit of repentance, the sense of providence and of trust in God. It turns the pilgrim towards the final goal whose radiance already shines. Obviously enough, this can so easily be a form of escapism. Yet the fact that the *status quo* of the present age is so far from the kingdom of God – that new earth in which righteousness and justice dwell – should discourage us from using the word 'escapism' too pejoratively. If a pilgrimage includes the sick, it is particularly truly an image of the pilgrim Church. Here, in the modern Church, we might think of the significance of Lourdes. The Way which is Jesus, that Way which the Christian movement (itself 'the Way') must make appear, is a way for everyone. The exiles in Babylon learned to hope again by building a highway for all the people, not just for the mighty, the competent and strong, but for the weak too, the deprived and handicapped and underprivileged. If the underprivileged and the deprived, the little ones, did not get to Jerusalem (so said the prophets of the Return), then no one would get there. It could hardly have been otherwise, granted the prejudice of God in their favour all through the history of Israel, that prejudice which was given flesh and blood when in Jesus of Nazareth the Word of God chose to identify himself with them and called to himself those who were heavily burdened. The Christian movement itself, the way, must be a catholic way, available for everyone, in which everyone can walk. Even those who may not be very conscious of what it means to do the will of God, who may, perhaps, be incapable of doing God's will with full deliberation, but nevertheless have the will of God done for them by the rest of the Church.

It is when the experience of most Christians is mainly one of settled belonging that the figure of the pilgrim comes to be of the greatest importance. 'I beseech you as strangers and exiles' says Peter (1 Pet. 2.11). The word is *paroikoi*, a term which originally referred in Judaism to the colonies of Jews living in the Diaspora, people very conscious of all that divided them from the world around them, bound as they were to customs which made full social intercourse with their neighbours impossible. But the word *paroikoi* has come to be transliterated as 'parishioners', and the fate of a word is the fate of a culture. People who once thought of themselves as having their home elsewhere, as exiles, uprooted men, came to think of themselves as parishioners. The word remains the same, but the concept has altered radically. Yet every country today has in it groups of refugees and displaced persons, colonies of those whom we in Britain today speak of so expressively as 'non-patrials'. The figure of the pilgrim captures the meaning of the non-patrial, the stateless person, the man who belongs nowhere, who changes his country more often than he changes his shoes. The pilgrim enacts a protest against the settled quality of ordinary life and the settled nature of the Church. It is not a matter of how someone feels, necessarily, but of the sort of life that he observably lives. Just as there was among the monks of the early centuries a flight to the desert as the only way to keep alive real Christian faith in a world that had ceased to persecute Christians, so for some people there arose an urge to wander around the world, to act out their homelessness, to be true to what they had learned of Christ who had nowhere to lay his head and whose own did not receive him. The man called to this way of life would quite literally leave his own land and go to a place where nobody knew him. This was what the Greeks called *xeniteia*, in Latin *peregrinatio*, the root of our 'pilgrimage'.

The Greek and Latin concepts were slightly different. *Xeniteia* can only mean living in a strange land, being an exile, but the Latin *peregrinatio* can also connote travelling to a distant land for a definite purpose, and this has become the normal sense of the English 'pilgrimage'. You do not simply leave your home; you leave it in order to go somewhere else, and the end of the journey is implicit in every step you take. This is more like the way in which the Writer to the Hebrews thinks of the travels of Abraham and his descendants, 'those who live in tents'. And indeed Abraham and his tribe were 'ass-nomads': unlike the later camel-nomads, the Bedouin, they did not wish to wander for ever. They wanted to settle down in a land they could call their own. But they were not prepared to settle for a land that was not the land of promise. This is the true sense of the Church as a pilgrim people: not that Christians should regard being footloose as some sort of eternal ideal, but that given the present situation (which is obviously not the kingdom of God) the only way to be true to what they have been promised is not to settle down here. This involves sacrifice and renunciation, and like any Christian asceticism this should be not so much a rejection as a preference: the 'but' of 'yes, but', rather than a 'no'. As Hans von Campenhausen puts it,

It is the expression of the painful and strenuous effort to cut loose from the accepted way of life, domestic and traditional, an effort everyone must carry through if God is to be for him a real personal experience, so that it destroys the dulling inner attachment to house and country, to what is inherited and personal and therefore loved. 'The man whom God seeks is without a country.' He alone who is ready to abandon his last possession, his very self, can be given anew by God the incomparable good of the fatherland and of every other earthly good: in fact, we believe, we receive it in truth for the first time, and only so follow out to the end the way entered upon by the monastic *xeniteuontes* and *peregrini*.[4]

The renewal of the sense of the Church as a pilgrim people has come about at a time when the pilgrim nature of every man's existence has been forced again upon our consciousness. Hordes of refugees in all parts of the world, the crumbling of national boundaries, these things demonstrate how man is a pilgrim and sojourner on this earth. But there is a *goal* to man's journey, and only as a way to this goal is his pilgrimage Christian. The goal of the pilgrim in the Christian tradition is a Christian place, where he will be made at home and welcomed. Already in some sense he is at home, in the eucharistic assembly which meets *in via* and yet is a genuine experience, in anticipation, of the marriage supper of the Lamb, the feasting in the new Jerusalem.

---

[4] H. von Campenhausen, 'The Ascetic Ideal of Exile', in *Tradition and Life in the Church: Essays and Lectures in Church History* (ET London 1968), p. 251.

24

Saints

IN the Ecumenical Creed we profess the Church to be 'one, holy, catholic and apostolic'. This Church is the object of faith, something we believe 'into', according to the Latin. Yet this Church in which we are to believe is not meant to be something other than the Church of our experience. That the Church is one, holy, catholic and aspostolic is the gift of God, but it is a gift to be met with in time and space. The Church of the Creed is not a heavenly, a spiritual Church, purely and simply. Rather is it open, in part at least, to empirical observation. In the Creed we say of Christ that for us men and for our salvation he was crucified under Pontius Pilate, suffered death and was buried. There is the same combination here of what is in principle accessible to observation by anyone and everyone and what requires the eye of faith ('for our salvation'). The Church, too, is partly a reality of faith. It may appear to be divided, sinful, Latin and post-Tridentine; it requires faith to declare that it is really one, holy, catholic and apostolic. But as faith in the significance of the crucifixion of Jesus – that is, the resurrection – depends on observation of the crucifixion of Jesus (hence the indispensable rôle of the original eye-witnesses), so what we say about the Church depends on the visibility of the Church. It depends on the Church being visible in such a way that it is not nonsensical to talk about it in terms of these four notes or marks of the Church.

We have already seen that the Church makes itself present in a visible way in the eucharistic assembly and in General Councils. In both of these cases it is at least open to being experienced as one, holy, catholic and aspostolic. One: we can recall here that the whole point, the *res tantum*, of the Eucharist is the unity of the Church, the oneness of the Church body. In the case of a General Council its very character depends on a moral unity being established. *Holy*: the Church meets as the Church of God, precisely; in the Holy Spirit, separated, traditionally behind locked doors.

Catholic: in the eucharistic council and the General Council people of all sorts have a right to be present. *Apostolic:* eucharistic council and General Council meet to hear the apostolic word, to put themselves under that word, to be true to their origins. We all know that in practice a eucharistic assembly may not be one or holy or catholic or apostolic in the way in which those words suggest it should be; we can have a deep sense of the failure of a eucharistic council to be itself. And so for a General Council. But the very fact of the disappointment that councils of either sort so often produce demonstrates that in these instances the Church should be what we profess it to be in the Creed. We know that these councils are meant to focus the Church of the *Credo*.

But the Church is not only focussed in Councils; it can also be focussed in individual people. When we looked at ministries in the Church we saw how the president of the Eucharist is meant to focus the unity of the Church and to serve that unity. We shall see later, when we come to discuss the Church as communion, how the bishop of Rome has the task of serving and focussing the union of all the churches in the one Church. The bishop or the gospel-book bring to a point the apostolicity of the Church, though they are not the only apostolic element in the Church any more than the president of the Eucharist or the bishop of Rome are the only men of unity. The catholicity of the Church becomes more credible in a General Council, and of its nature cannot really be expressed by one sort of person. Nevertheless, the *holiness* of the Church does come to focussed expression in particular people: we call them 'holy' people, *sancti*, 'the saints'.

Holiness is God's proper nature. It is the same for God to be holy as for him to be God. Holiness is the way in which God is other than the world, the divine other than the created. The primary meaning of the word 'holy' denotes the otherness which makes God God. As Rudolf Otto puts it in *The Idea of the Holy*, he is so altogether other that his presence is dangerous, the mystery that makes people tremble.[1] To see God, in the Old Testament, is usually fatal; the divine is so different that nothing can come near it. It is suggested, interestingly, by creatures that

[1] R. Otto, *The Idea of the Holy* (ET London 1957).

do not fit into any normal category, as by the hippopotamus, the ostrich and the crocodile in the Book of Job. Yet God can and does demonstrate his holiness and he does this by his acts, and especially by delivering his people from slavery. Just because this exodus, or escape, of the Israelite slaves was so strange and unlooked for, it pointed to the way in which God is holy, outside normal categories. And yet though God is separate from all that is not God, he is separate for the people he freely chooses as his own. In Second Isaiah in particular he is not simply the Holy One but 'the Holy One of Israel' (e.g. Isa. 43.14). And so those elements of the world which he freely chooses to be holy for can themselves be called holy from their special association with him. At this stage of its development, the word 'holy' is equivalent to 'belonging to God', 'taken over by God', 'separated out by him who is altogether separate from the world'. People who worship the Holy One can, therefore, themselves be termed holy, as can the places where he manifests himself to them for their adoration, or the objects they use in their worship of him. The burning bush is holy, the land of promise is holy, the heavens are holy, Zion, the tent of meeting, the liturgical seasons, even the vestments of the priesthood of Yahweh: all can and do receive the description 'holy'. And above all, Israel is holy. It is 'a people that dwell apart, not reckoned among the nations'. As the Book of Deuteronomy puts it,

> For thou art a holy people unto the Lord thy God; the Lord thy God has chosen thee to be a peculiar people unto the Lord himself, out of all peoples that are upon the face of the earth. (Deut. 7.6)

(Notice that in all this, the antonym of 'holy' is not 'sinful' but 'profane'.)

By and large the same usage continues in the New Testament. The holiness of God is rarely mentioned, always assumed. Jesus is 'the Holy One of God' (Mark 1.24), the one in whom what it is to be God is translated into human terms, in his being made holy as man by God. In the so-called 'high-priestly prayer' of John 17 Jesus prays to his Father to consecrate him, to make him altogether set apart for God, and to consecrate his followers in the truth of God's word. The holiness of anyone else, it seems, involves a participation in the holiness of Jesus, who is therefore spoken of liturgically as 'the only Holy One', the *solus sanctus* of the *Gloria*. But he communicates his own holiness to others, to the Church, through the Holy Spirit. Thus Christians are described as 'those who have been sanctified' or simply as 'saints', a word which in the New Testament describes not the morally perfect but those who participate in the mystery of the Last Day. To the question, 'Who is God?' the Jewish-Christian tradition answers 'God is he who ...'. That is to say, God is the subject of a story. He shows himself as he who is, as holy, through being involved in a narrative. The holiness of his people cannot simply be ethical holiness. It must be the kind of holiness that befits participators in a particular kind of history. They are required to become holy by entering into the motivating forces of the God who writes the story, by sharing his prejudices. What is given in the unfolding of the story is experienced as a summons to correspond to the story's meaning: 'You shall be holy, for I the Lord your God am holy' (Lev. 11.44). History here has imperative force.

There is no avoiding the profession of the Church as *holy* Church: it is part of the gospel of the given. However obvious at times the corruption of the Church, Christians are not at liberty to deny the Church's holiness. For the Church to declare that it is holy is for it to engage in what is only a matter of duty. It is part of the business of 'declaring the mighty works of God who has called us out of darkness into his marvellous light' (Col. 1.13). The profession of these mighty works, made above all in the Eucharist, is not a profession of what God has done in theory but of what he has done in fact, and done for his Church which is composed of weak and sinful people, conceived in sin, born into a sinful world and often enough ratifying the form of that world by their own sinful choices. But the experience of sin is not the only experience of Christians: there is also an experience of the transforming grace of God – not simply of what God has done in Jesus of Nazareth but what he has done in, say, Mary, and in people at every period of Church history. And so there is a duty to acknowledge the transforming and transfiguring grace of God in the Church as a historical reality. That God makes his people holy is not simply something one knows in faith. It is also a matter of constant experience for every one of us in our own lives but also for the Church at large in certain particular people in whom the transfiguring grace of God has been particularly evident. Our sense of the grace that heals and raises up needs to be made concrete in specific instances. To reflect on God's ways with all Christians and the ways of all of us with God, we could do worse than reflect on his ways with particular individuals, those whom God has chosen in a particular way for the sake of each and all of us. In theory, we could do this by reflecting on the life of absolutely *any* person, even among those who never understood that God did have any dealings with them, or even that there was a God at all. In principle, any reflection on the life of any man can give us insight into the ways of God: the reading of any biography or autobiography, or any piece of historical writing. We are all bound together in one bundle of life and no man is an island. But there are certain individuals whose lives have an altogether exceptional value in this regard, certain people, each with his own temperament and time in history, each with his own place on the earth's surface, who yet have an exemplary value for all men everywhere. These are the people we call 'saints' in the modern sense. Reading their lives, their 'legends', we find light for our living before God. With their lives coincided an acceptable time, a day of salvation which can become living and actual for us. The treatment of the grace of God in theological writing and the discussion of Christian living in the works of moral theologians can very easily become dry and dessicated. Reflection on these mysteries is better aided by hagiography, by the reading of the lives of the saints. Delehaye's study *The Legends of the Saints* is probably the best accessible work on hagiography, and provides the necessary critical tools for reading at least the more ancient lives of the saints.[2] But, granted the care with which one should approach them, it remains true that hagiographical accounts are among the most important forms of the Church's self-presentation in literature.

The veneration of the saints began very early in the history of the Church. Some of the most primitive Christian texts outside the New Testament testify to it. Even within the New Testament, there is the account of the martyrdom of Stephen in Acts 7, which sets the pattern for the earliest Acts of the Martyrs. The development of the cult of the saints began with the veneration of

---

[2] H. Delehaye, *The Legends of the Saints* (ET London 1962).

martyrs; from there it moved on to the venerating of people who had been imprisoned for the faith though without actually suffering violent death (the confessors), and finally to the veneration of people whose lives witnessed in some outstanding way to the truth of the faith, even though their witness was not in blood. The earliest non-martyr to be venerated was Martin of Tours, whose most ancient liturgical office is still extant. In it there is a constant apology for the fact that he was not a martyr, combined with continual insistence that even so he bore a witness not inferior to that of the martyrs themselves. (Veneration of Mary seems to have come into use from a different motive, and became widespread at the time when the Arian heresy was disturbing the Church's life.) The mere fact that a person had suffered martyrdom was enough to single him or her out for veneration, and this would consist in, first, an appeal for their intercession, and second, a commemoration of them in Mass, especially on the anniversary of their triumphant sufferings, when Mass would normally be celebrated over their tombs or at the place where they suffered. From the sixth century of the Christian era onwards, for a period of some four hundred years, there was a massive increase in devotion to the saints, particularly in connection with their relics. The tendency was to look on the saint as a heavenly patron, one who would work on behalf of his client. This factor rather won the day over seeing the saints as examples of the victorious grace of God, or as a pattern for the rest of the Church to imitate. One wonders to what extent people preserved in practice the careful theological distinction between God as the giver of all good gifts and the saints as intercessors with God in Christ. During these centuries, although popular opinion was still the springboard for a recognition of individual Christians as saints, it became more and more the case that the bishop had to authorise popular devotions, to give them the seal of his approval. When the Western Church entered its age of centralised government at the end of the first millenium, the bishop of Rome acquired increasing authority over the cultus of the servants of God until finally in 1234 it was laid down that *only* the pope could speak authoritatively on whether a person was to be venerated as a saint or no. That remains the present *status quaestionis* in the Catholic Church, although the various stages of the canonisation process were not worked out in detail until the time of Benedict XIV in the eighteenth century, and have been modified in various minor ways since.

The procedures of the canonisation process are not especially significant, apart from the attempt they represent to exclude from veneration people in whom it seems at the least rather queer to believe that the grace of God was truly active. More important is a lively sense of the reality of the saints in the Church, for it is in them that the Church makes that necessary confession of faith in its own holiness. As Karl Rahner has put it, the Church

> proclaims the fulfilment of the law which has been accomplished in us by the grace of God. Hence, she must be able to state her holiness in the concrete. She must have a 'cloud of witnesses' whom she can indicate by name. ... The mission to praise the grace of God as something which has come and conquered contains the obligation of the Church to call herself the one who is holy throughout the ages, and to make this statement about herself in a concrete way as seen in the prize of the saints given by name.[3]

In acknowledging that in some of its members the grace of God gained an obvious and tangible victory, the Church is saying too that what we hope for is not just an object of hope. The last day, the day of God, is not simply future but already happens in the midst of human history: as Paul expressed it, 'on us the ends of the ages have overlapped' (1 Cor. 10.11).

There are various ways of distinguishing between the saints. The traditional way is based either on the outcome of their lives (the martyrs) or the rôle they played in the Church in their own time (bishops, doctors) or on the state of life in which they lived out their Christian faith, especially at the time of their deaths (confessors, virgins, widows and so on). This is the normal style of sub-dividing the Church's 'cloud of witnesses', and recent changes in the liturgical books of the Latin rite have done little to dislodge it. But there is a more profound way of identifying significant differences among the saints. First of all, we can single out those saints who had a unique office at a particular time in the history of salvation. These are mainly the saints of the Old Testament, such as Abraham and Moses, but they include also

[3] K. Rahner, S.J., *Theological Investigations* (ET London 1967), p. 96.

Mary, John the Baptist and Joseph. Secondly, there is what might be called 'charismatic' holiness, the holiness of great individualists among the saints, people scarcely to be imitated literally but in whom nevertheless the holiness of God himself shines through. Joan of Arc or Benedict Joseph Labré are examples that spring to mind. Thirdly, there are those whose holiness is representative or typological, saints who have created a style of Christian living that is accessible to many others also. By their lives they witness to the fact that a certain kind of life or activity is a genuine Christian possibility, and their personal project opens up this possibility to others. Karl Rahner calls saints of this type 'creative models'. Their most obvious instances are the founders of the great religious orders, for their lives are the paradigm cases of the kind of holiness to which their followers aspire. The desire of religious orders to have their founders canonised is therefore not an ecclesiastical attempt to 'keep up with the Joneses' but a desire to have some sort of guarantee that the rule of life they follow is truly Christian and evangelical. With such representative or typological saints it seems to be the case that their style of Christian life never ceases to be a possibility for others, and never fails in its power to attract others to itself. Not that religious orders in the narrower sense do not come and go; nevertheless, it seems highly unlikely that, for instance, Benedictine monasticism – or, for that matter, the hermit life, or the life of total dedication to teaching or preaching or the nursing of the sick – will cease to be lifestyles in the Church.

In this way the veneration of the saints testifies not only to the Church's holiness but also to its catholicity, the way in which holiness is within reach of a whole variety of personality types as wide as humanity itself. The confession of the saving humanity of the Word of God, of Jesus as the New Man for all men, is earthed in a confession of the well-nigh infinite variety of men and women who have shown forth the humanity of Jesus in a multitude of ways in a vast variety of cultures and at very different epochs. Deprived of the sense that the Church is never without its saints in any age, it would be easy to regard Christian living as an increasingly problematic enterprise. But as long as there is a lively sense of the gift of God which is holiness being totally accepted by nameable individuals in every age, then there is no chance that the Church will ever be given over to despair.

25

Martyrs

WHEN we looked at the sacraments and their place in the life of the Church we had occasion to notice more than once that the deepest reality of the sacraments is to be found in martyrdom: in that form of witness which consists in a man's shedding his blood for Christ. The reality of baptism is to be found in the baptism of blood; the reality of confirmation is to be found in Christians who remain true to their commission to be witnesses of Jesus 'to the uttermost ends of the earth' – to the extent that they prefer nothing, not even life itself, to fidelity to that commission. The reality of the Eucharist consists in a Christian becoming himself the bread that is broken and the wine that is poured out for the salvation of the world. The reality of ministering within the Church finds its reality in that utter consistency of *diakonia*, of service, which serves one's fellow-men even when they so little value that service that they would have the servant put out of the way. The most thoroughgoing way to be a Christian is to lay down your life for the Lord and for your friends, for those whom you choose to make your friends even while they insist on treating you as their enemy.

The best place in the New Testament to locate the primitive understanding of martyrdom in this sense is the Apocalypse, the book which, according to Jerome of Bethlehem, contains as many riddles as it does words. And yet the opening chapters read easily enough, Christ the universal king writing to his churches. One letter each to each of the seven churches of Asia, the seven (like the seven of the sacraments) that is the seven of fulness rather than of quantity. The seven churches are *all* of the churches as well as being these particular seven. Before a person was baptised in one of these churches they were examined as to their suitability. They underwent a 'scrutiny' to see whether they were ready to be baptised into Christ, to enter sacramentally into the death of the Lord. But the author of the Apocalypse sees that the

whole Church is about to be baptised in fire, with the fire (sometimes quite literally so) of persecution. And so Christ himself
begins to scrutinise the churches. He tries to ensure that everything about them is as it should be, so that they will be able to
pass through the fire of persecution without losing themselves.
The first church he examines is the church in Ephesus, in that city
which was called 'the supreme metropolis of Asia', the city of
Diana, her temple one of the wonders of the ancient world, her
citizens reputed throughout Asia as fickle, superstitious and
immoral. But the church there comes out well enough from its
scrutiny: its faith is orthodox, it is full of energy, it keeps faith in
a city where compromise was all too easy. And yet Christ does
have something to say against this church: it has departed somewhat from the love it had at first. The suggestion is that its
concern for orthodoxy, wholly laudable in itself, has led it to
weaken its concern for love. Though it has discerned the spirits
correctly it has allowed its love for those to whom the spirits
came to cool. If it is to come alive from the baptism of fire it must
be as loving as it is orthodox. Of its nature martyrdom is a
witness not only to the truth as it is in Jesus but also to the love of
Jesus for the persecutors themselves. Rejection of false ideas must
not entail the rejection of those who hold those ideas.

Next there comes a scrutiny of the church in Sardis, the city of
Croesus, the town where money was invented, self-assured on its
acropolis but notoriously decadent and loose-living. Laodicea
also has to undergo scrutiny: a city endowed with a fine medical
school and enormously wealthy from its flourishing clothing
industry. Neither of these churches turns out to be ready for the
baptism of fire. The church of Sardis is at peace, but its peace is
the peace of death. It is lethargic, tolerant of the intolerable. Like
the city itself it believes its future to be assured. Of the church in
Laodicea Christ has nothing good to say at all. It is dreadfully
decent and respectable, 'neither hot nor cold', and the Lord will
'spew it out of [his] mouth' (Apoc. 3.16). The metaphor is taken,
it seems, from the warm medicinal springs around the city, their
taste comparable presumably to those of Bath which Dickens'
Sam Weller likened to that of warm flat-irons! There must be
something of a boiling quality, a certain craziness, about any
church that can measure up to the Lord's scrutiny, that can pass
through the fire of persecution to reach the Lord. If a church does

234

not find itself in a certain posture of 'contestation' with regard to the society in which it lives, something will be amiss in its interior life. To live the gospel is inevitably to challenge the surrounding milieu. Not that one should set out to find ways to rock the ship of State; yet by an inner necessity that will occur, by the simple fact of the Church's constant memory of the death of Christ at the hands of a circumambient society. There is a connection here between our modern use of the word 'contestation' and the older usage in the Church's linguistic tradition whereby it referred to the great prayer of the Mass, the *contestatio missae*.

When the Book of the Apocalypse, of the 'unveiling', has come to the end of the initial scrutiny of the churches by Christ, a new section of the work begins. In his first vision, John of Patmos was told that he was to be shown 'the things that are and the things that are to be hereafter' (Apoc. 1.19). In the seven letters he unveiled what was really staring Christians in the face all the time, though they were too blind to see it. These constitute, evidently, 'the things that are'. Only now does he go on to reveal 'the things that must be hereafter', the outcome of the events in which they were all engaged. The future will be unveiled in the context of the liturgy of heaven, which in its turn is the context of the worship of the Church on earth. It is on the Lord's Day, the day of the Eucharist, that John is 'in the Spirit' (Apoc. 1.10), and sees a door opening from the worshipping Church on earth to the worshipping Church in heaven. The description he gives of the heavenly assembly is all of a piece with the accounts we have of the lay-out of Christian assemblies very shortly afterwards: the bishop presiding, surrounded by the elders (presbyters) and deacons, and everyone singing hymns. These hymns are the 'canticles' that formed part of the worship of the primitive Church and in the modern Roman liturgy are sung daily at Vespers. The *Sanctus*, the hymn to the holiness of God known to all the later great Mass-rites of the Church, is also sung. This worship is itself presented as a contestation – a challenge thrown down to the world around the churches, and especially to the world of the Roman Empire. It is the One who sits on the throne (the One never described by John) who is addressed by the hosts of heaven as 'Lord and God', the title the Roman emperors were claiming for themselves. It is before the One who sits on the throne that the elders (who are themselves kings) throw down their crowns, in a gesture of submission that the Caesars were demanding from the vassal rulers. The worship of the Church, heavenly and earthly, is to be directed to God alone. Just by being so exclusively directed to God, worship is an implicit rejection of any other claim to divinity, or any demand that men should treat something or someone other than God as God. John uses only psychedelic imagery about the One, so great is his sense of God's ineffability: he is, he says, like a jasper or a carnelian. Who and what he is can only be inferred from the behaviour of those who worship him, who worship the One whom no image can capture, not even (perhaps especially not) the image of an earthly emperor. The early Christians, by their refusal to throw away their royal freedom at the feet of anyone other than this God who is so very other, were thereby striking a blow for the freedom of all mankind. They were offering an alternative to the all-pervasive emperor-cult, an alternative that could not be contained within its own terms of reference and so ineluctably led to that baptism of fire which the churches would soon endure.

The Church's worship, therefore, is the setting from which the great drama of subsequent world history will be unrolled. It is the operations-room from which each new episode of the story will be set in motion. Each new movement in the liturgy of that Church releases the spring of a new chapter in the struggle of the people of God with the world. A scroll appears, ready for someone to open it and to read. The scroll of the Hebrew prophets is here presented as sealed with seven seals, for in Roman law a man's last will and testament had to be so sealed, and could not be executed until each of seven witnesses had broken a seal. When John complains that no one is able to undo the seals, he is told that the Messiah, the Root of David, will do it. Jesus, that is, will make sense of the past of God's people, that history which is itself a testament, a promise of future blessings. The last chapter of the last book of the Hebrew Bible (2 Chronicles) says that Israel 'mocked the messengers of God and despised his words and scoffed at his prophets' (2 Chron. 36.16); Jesus took over this way of thinking. In the Gospels he quotes a now lost martyrology wherein the Wisdom of God was made to recite a list of the persecuted servants and messengers of God from Abel down to Zechariah. The story of the wicked husbandman in Mark 12 is another such interpretation of the history of God's people in terms of the martyrdom of the messengers whom God sent, a story heading directly towards Jesus and his fate. The sufferings of the great men of the Old Testament form the prologue to the passion of Christ. Told that the Lion of Judah will unseal the scroll, the seer turns to look at this lion and finds a lamb with its throat gashed open. It is this Lamb who manages to break the seals, and from each unsealing a new stage unfolds for the life of the people of God. It is the sacrificed Lamb who produces the continuing life of the Church and thus interprets the martyrdom of the prophets from the past. Although he is the Lion of Judah, the power of God (with his seven horns) and the wisdom of God (with his seven eyes), he is the Lamb that stands (as the Lord) with the marks of slaughter still upon him, the risen Jesus with the wounds that did not heal. The Jesus whose confrontation with the world led to his death, and who in that death continued to love the world that killed him, is he who unfolds the book of world history and makes sense of it all. The only way of *making*, producing, sense of it is the way of the person who is a Lion by means of being a Lamb. The pattern of his life is reproduced in the Apocalypse, and its victorious outcome creates in turn the downfall of the Roman Empire, Babylon the Great. The system of pagan Rome is defeated, therefore, in the martyrdom of Christians (their conformation to the cross of Jesus), not in their taking up arms against it. They are able to break that system because they take their inspiration from the slaughtered Lamb whose life is poured out sacrificially into the chalice, the Lamb addressed as such in the Eucharist of the Church.

The Book of Revelation now goes on to reveal yet another aspect of what is involved in martyrdom. Between the sixth and seventh trumpets, after the plagues sent upon the earth and before the people of God pass through the Red Sea of blood and fire, there is a pause. In this pause John is prepared for the next step, that of bearing witness, of martyrdom. As so often in the imagery of biblical prophecy he is given a little book to eat. This book, however, is not sealed; rather, it is an open secret. John is now, if you like, Christian, the Christian Everyman of Bunyan's allegory. He is no longer concerned with deep mysteries and arcane sayings. He no longer has to be clever and to interpret. He simply has to witness: to make the gospel his own, inwardly to digest it and then act upon it. The message is a joy, sweet to the taste, for it is good news, the law of liberty. But it turns his stomach, for the witnessing has to be given not only in words but in deeds. By undergoing martyrdom the Christians will bear their witness to the Lamb when at last their exodus gets under way. The New Testament is conscious that while it may be a mad thing to be a Christian it is not a stupid thing. It insists that Christians be able to give a reason for the hope that is in them, an *apologia* for the *logos* they bear. They must be able to hold their own in debate. At the same time, the early Christians knew well enough that this by itself would not suffice. They needed not only John's original vocation as an interpreter, someone who can reveal the mysteries of Jesus and make sense of the life of the Church, but also his other mission, that of someone who can simply say it and suffer it 'the way it is'. There would be times for all of them when all they could do was to bear witness, when it would not avail, even were it possible, to give as good as they got in argumentation.

Central to the biblical notion of witnessing is an image derived from a court of law. The witnessing even to blood normally took place, in point of fact, in the context of a trial before judges who stood for the world at large. So the story of the passion of Jesus himself is predominantly a story of judicial proceedings, his death the carrying out of a judicial sentence. The Fourth Gospel, playing (as so often) on words, draws out the ambiguities in any law-court by saying that at the trial of Jesus 'Pilate sat him in the judgment-seat', implying that, in a sense, the real judge was Jesus himself (John 19.13). As with the Master, so with the disciple. Martyrdom embodies and typifies the conflict between sacred and secular history: it is the official proclamation of the gospel to the accredited representatives of the earthly city. The primary task of a witness in a court of law was to attest to a fact, to say what he had seen and heard. In the Lucan writings, indeed, this is the principal meaning of witnessing-words. But soon enough the term comes to include also witnessing to a truth, to an interpretation of facts as well as to facts themselves. As early as other parts of the New Testament itself, the balance begins to shift from the witness which a man gives to facts he has himself observed to the witness he gives to a truth he has received from others. The martyr witnesses to the truth 'as it is in Jesus'. In the Fourth Gospel, Jesus, who is the martyr *par excellence*, says that

238

he has come in order to bear witness to 'the truth' (John 18.37).

In Christian martyrdom, this bearing witness to one's conviction is only secondarily a matter of convincing someone else of the truth one believes. True, 'the blood of [the martyrs] is the seed [of the Church]', according to an ancient formula.[1] Nevertheless, this is always regarded as a by-product. The primary concern of the martyr is to witness to Christ for Christ's own sake, to be true to Christ. If other people are convinced, well and good, but the witness is not to be weighed in terms of the likelihood that others will be converted. The essential act of the martyr is the surrender of what is most dear, life itself. No matter how convinced of the resurrection he may be, no matter how sure that Christ has drawn the sting of death, there is still nothing higher than his life for him to give. To give up his earthly existence for the sake of Christ is the highest act of love of which a man is capable, and it is a dying into the death of Jesus.

Perhaps even more important, however, is the sense that the martyr in dying enters into a total conformity with *the* Martyr, the Christ. The New Testament is full of references to people carrying about in their bodies the dying of Jesus in order that the life of Jesus might be made manifest in them. It is in a man's martyrdom that the presence of Christ is most effectively experienced. The primitive *Acta* of the martyrs make it clear that at the moment of their martyrdom Christ is present in his witnesses and suffers in them. It was not just that at the moment of their sufferings the martyrs saw a vision of the glory of Christ. More than this, there is a real presence of Christ in the midst of their agonies, this Christ who has entered his glory along the path they were treading. So the death of a martyr comes to be conceived of as a sacrifice within the one sacrifice of Christ: in the martyrs Christ continues the sacrifice which he completed once and for all on the cross. The cross, represented in the Eucharist, is the sacrifice from which all martyrdom takes its origin. Because of this sacrificial character of martyrdom, rather than through its exemplary value, the blood of the martyrs turns out to be the seed of the Church. The martyr calls down blessings on the world and the Church which nourished and sustained him. He makes up

[1] Tertullian, *Apology* 50.

what is lacking in the birth-pangs of the Messiah. He fills up the measure of the sufferings which accompany the full formation of the body of Christ. As Bishop Ignatius wrote to the Ephesians: 'I sacrifice myself for you, Ephesians, the ever famous church'.[2]

And so from earliest times there has been a custom of offering the Mass on the graves of the martyrs. Here one must certainly speak of 'offering' the Mass, as well as of 'celebrating' it. The Mass is experienced as, above all, a sacrifice when it is offered on the tombs of the martyrs. It was this primitive custom that led to the later Christian practice of keeping relics of martyrs under the altar. Once the liturgical cult had established itself, people looked back to the text of the Apocalypse which speaks of the souls of the martyrs being under the heavenly altar, and crying out in supplication.

> Holy, faithful master, how much longer will you wait before you pass sentence and take vengeance for our deaths on the inhabitants of the earth? (Apoc. 6.10)

This was to link another aspect of the Eucharist with one of the important themes of martyrdom: that of expectation of the parousia. If the martyr's death was explicitly connected with the death of Christ, then the death of Christ, as an appeal for God's ultimate intervention in this world's affairs, quickly came to be seen as continued in the deaths of the martyrs. The prayer *Maranatha*, 'Come, Lord Jesus', of the eucharist was the prayer of the martyrs for resurrection, for their individual resurrection and for the resurrection of the whole body of Christ. We recall this today when we place relics of the martyrs under the altar of the eucharistic sacrifice, for they are there precisely as relics in expectation of the second coming of the Lord. The relics long to stop being relics: they focus the prayer for the raising of the dead. As such they intensify the prayer which the Mass itself is: 'Come, Lord Jesus'.

---

[2] Ignatius of Antioch, *To the Ephesians* VIII.1.

26

John the Baptist

WHEN we looked at sanctity, at the figure of the saint as one in whom the holiness of the Church comes to particularly pointed expression, we made a distinction between charismatic and representative holiness. Some of the saints celebrated in the course of the year should be seen as typical representatives of one way in which the people of God experiences the holiness of God working within it. So, for example, St Francis Xavier may stand for the missionary work of the Church, while St Dominic is the preacher *par excellence*. These should be contrasted with those saints who are celebrated because they are unusual and interesting instances of the way in which God makes his people holy: St Thérèse of Lisieux is a case in point. But both of these categories are to be separated from yet another: that of saints celebrated because they had and have a wholly unique rôle in the working out of God's purposes for us men and for our salvation, a rôle played by no one before or since. They were made use of by God at a particular time and in a particular place for the furthering of that plan of his for all peoples, at all times and in all places. And so it is right and fitting, our duty and our salvation, at all times and in all places to give thanks to God for them.

One such person was Mary of Nazareth, the mother of Jesus, the one person (and in the nature of things there could only have been one) who was chosen to be the mother of the Word of God made man. She it was who, as St Thomas points out, said 'Yes' for us all. Other such people were Peter and the rest of the Twelve, the twelve gates of the Jerusalem which is the city of God, the twelve to whom no one could succeed in every respect. The apostolic ministry as such is uniquely theirs and cannot be shared in, even theoretically, by other people. Amongst such people, once again, are John the Baptist and Joseph, the foster-father of the Lord. For both of these we are told by the Church's liturgy that it is right and fitting always and everywhere to give thanks for them: in other words, in telling the story, the *narratio plena*, of God's dealings with men they have an inalienable and indispensable place. For each of them it can be said that only secondarily do we see in them a typical example of fidelity to rôle or personal holiness. Primarily they are honoured because each of them had an essential job to do and did it. Indeed, we do not have much in the way of data to go on when it comes to their personal holiness: all that we have is a handful of stories about how they did what they did. Joseph in particular has been the subject of a great deal of sheer fancy with no basis whatever in the extremely limited sources we have at our disposal. Over the past four centuries in particular there has been a sentimental devotion to Joseph which has made him, for instance, the patron of workers and of a happy death – although we have no way of knowing what his attitude to work was, nor anything about his death apart from the (presumable) fact that he did die. Yet for Joseph as for John the Baptist it is surely conceivable that he could have done the job he was given to do and not have been holy in himself. If one looks at the ancestors of Jesus in the two family trees contained in the Gospels, for instance, it is not too much to say that they can be summed up in the words 'sex and violence'. Conceivably God could have used John the Baptist and Joseph in a similar fashion to the way he used these dubious forebears of the Lord: as an instrument purely and simply. Even in the case of Mary it is conceivable that she could have had no other rôle in the plan of God than the provision of a female body. It is easy enough, after all, to get a woman with child without her consent. Like the woman in the science-fiction story *The Midwich Cuckoos*[1] she might have been a mere host for the growing body of Jesus. But the nearer people get to Jesus, the less is that the way God works. As the humanity of God increases, so does his concern for the humanity of those who have to do with the working out of his plan. So Mary is the mother of Jesus in the fullest human sense, the most human way we can imagine. And similarly, the sources tell us, for John the Baptist. His mission did not leave him untouched; he was no puppet with a cloth finger outstretched towards Jesus and a voice other than his own. His witness engaged all his powers, the witness of a whole life. In this

[1] J. Wyndham, *The Midwich Cuckoos* (London 1957).

sense, John was a martyr, a witness. He demonstrated this in
martyrdom in that word's modern sense, the shedding of his
blood. Nevertheless, although he died because he refused to say
anything other than the truth of God's word, his martyrdom lies
outside the public plan of God. In theory, he could have died of
old age without any lessening of his indispensable rôle in God's
plan. This was Joseph's situation, also. How and when he died is
of no possible theological interest. The death of John the Baptist,
like the death of Joseph, was not the form of his unique work in
the plan of God. And yet, just because John did die a martyr's
death, privately and obscurely, we can see that in him public
mission and personal holiness went side by side.

His public mission, not his private death, is what characterises
John and focusses the Church in his person. What he had to do
and did he had to do and did for us all, just as at the annunciation
Mary had to and did say 'yes' for us all. What precisely he had to
do and did was to witness: to see and then to declare what he saw.
John sees Jesus of Nazareth come to the fords of the Jordan to be
baptised in the baptising of all the nation. He sees Jesus take on
the condition of us all, freely, of his own choice, by opting to be
baptised at the hands of John. And then John says what he has
seen in words and gestures. He is a finger and a voice enunciating
the proclamation, 'Behold, the Lamb of God!' (John 1.29), like
the image of him in Grünewald's painting of the Crucifixion at
Isenheim where John stands pointing at the Crucified with a great
elongated finger. In this sense John is the first of the apostles, an
apostle to the apostles, just as he is the last of the prophets, the
prophet who speaks for all the prophets. As Ethelbert Stauffer
puts it:

> He is the man who in his own person sums up the pre-Christian
> era, because he brings it to an end. He sums it up in himself so as
> to bring it to an end, and in order to make way for the new age –
> in which there is no room for himself. Just as Moses could only
> see the promised land from afar, so the Baptist could only behold
> the kingdom from afar off. This makes plain not simply the
> greatness and the tragedy of one human being, but the greatness
> and the tragedy of the whole Old Testament dispensation. The
> last and greatest representative of the Old Testament stands and
> greets the promise from afar off – and dies. For the new Elijah is

Christ's forerunner in more than his appearance and his message.[2]

John's message, once he has seen Jesus and given his witness to what he has seen, is that Jesus must increase while he himself must decrease. He perfectly fulfils the rôle of the forerunner in a way that Judaism and all the rest of the religious traditions of mankind have not fulfilled it. The rôle of the forerunner is to make way for the one who is to come: John does this, as the apostle of apostles. As apostle he says to Andrew, 'Behold, the Lamb of God' and Andrew immediately leaves off following John and starts to follow Jesus. He finds his brother Peter and leads him also to Jesus. From this point on, John began to decrease and Jesus to increase, and John was content that it be so. He had fulfilled his rôle.

And yet John goes on fulfilling his rôle in the Church: he continues to point away from himself and towards the Lamb of God. He still stands in the Church, as he stands in the church at Isenheim, as a finger and a voice. His words go on resounding in the Church, 'Behold the Lamb of God', and they become the words of the Church itself, giving the Church as institution its significance and its rôle. His are the words in which the minister of the Eucharist in the Western Mass points away from himself and towards the real presence of the Lord in the sacrament. The minister, who stands in the place of John the Baptist, has to grow less so that the Lord may grow greater among his people. But had not John the Baptist first pointed him out, at that critical juncture in human history when the Word made flesh came to the fords of the Jordan to commence his work, then the Church itself would never have heard the news that God was giving it. And so it is right and fitting that at all times and in all places Christians should give thanks to God for John the Baptist who at a particular time and place did the job which he had been given to do. In his pointing towards Christ he focusses in his own person the very being of the Church, which exists not for itself but for its Lord. Appropriately, therefore, in the icons of the *Deēsis* he stands opposite Mary and points to Jesus, standing in the place of the Church before Christ. His was a unique witness to Jesus, a founding witness, but the whole Church has to bear in itself the

[2] E. Stauffer, *New Testament Theology* (ET London 1955), p. 100.

witness that John bore and bears. The institutions and work of the Church are to be judged by the extent to which they point away from the Church and towards the Lord of the Church.

It is hard to be the witness of a voice. There is a problem of *language*, of finding words in which to communicate the witness, words which make enough sense to the hearer and are true enough about Christ to refer the hearer to him. It is always difficult enough to speak about Jesus, the Word of God as word of man, in such a way that the words are mediatorial and not an end in themselves. In an increasingly pluralistic and de-Christianised world, the problem is likely to intensify. The Church today knows the force of all the arguments against the existence of any reality that can be called 'God'; knows too how hard it is to establish a case for Christian values in a non-Christian society. But in John the Baptist as a figure of the Church we see that our primary obligation is not to argue but to witness. Witnesses do have a duty, it is true, to equip themselves to give a reason for the hope that is in them, an apologia for the *logos* they carry. But in the final analysis all that they are required to do is to bear testimony: to say what they believe, what they have seen and heard. The fact that we shall not be able to argue convincingly in favour of what we say is no reason for not saying it, for suppressing our witness to the truth as it is in Jesus. Often enough that may be all we can do, but it will always be what we have to do, what the Baptist did and does. The witness, after all, is the witness of the finger as well as of the voice, the witness of the *body* – of how we live and behave, letting people see our good works so that they can glorify our Father who is in heaven. It is here that the private martyrdom of John fits in with his public ministry. If in the Catholic tradition we have always distinguished between office and holiness, nevertheless it has been equally strongly maintained that there is every reason for concern about the personal holiness of the man with the mission. The Catholic Church has ever rejected the view of those sects which denied that sacraments are valid means of grace when celebrated by people not themselves holy. And indeed we know how we may at times bring someone nearer to God, in ordinary life, though we are at a distance from God ourselves. And yet John the Baptist is not only a finger and a voice; he is called by Jesus a 'burning and a shining light' (John 5.35), he is 'the friend of the Bridegroom'

(John 3.29). In his own life he enters into the fulness of Trinitarian life, though in his mission he stands archetypally as the representative of the human space in the encounter of man with God. He is the witness to the whole kenotic economy in his testimony to how Jesus freely accepted the ministry of John by accepting baptism at his hands. In John all men say Yes to the encounter with God, to the friendship which God offers, to the economy of salvation that runs by way of the humiliation of Jesus. The Yes that we give in faith to the offer of God's friendship, the Yes to the way God has done all things well in the death and resurrection of Christ, the Yes in which Christian faith consists, is a Yes that has always to enter into the primordial Yes of John the Baptist. It is a Yes that enables the life of the Trinity to be expressed in the life of every believer, standing before the Father in the place of the Son and in the space and atmosphere which is the Holy Spirit. John the Baptist in his public mission is conformed to the Son insofar as he is simply the word of the Father; he is conformed to the Holy Spirit in that he has nothing to say about himself and everything to say about Jesus.

27

Joseph

IT is one of the oddities of Church history that the figure of John the Baptist has dropped almost entirely out of Western consciousness, though he retains his full significance in the Liturgy itself and remains a highly significant figure in the popular attitudes of the Christian East. In the West his place in general consciousness has been taken over very largely by Joseph, the foster-father of Jesus. This is probably the result in good measure of sentiment rather than theology. Joseph has become the patron of a happy death, or of those who have to work and eat bread in the sweat of their brow. In the devotion to the Holy Family there has been an attempt to sacralise one sphere of human life as public institutions fall increasingly outside the control of the official Church. It is difficult to find an appropriate patristic reading for the feast of St Joseph, because in point of fact Joseph attained his present popularity as the patron of various things and people almost entirely after the Reformation. Teresa of Avila was perhaps the first person of influence to make much of St Joseph. And yet in modern times, biblical scholarship has provided the grounds for a reassessment of the position of Joseph in the whole economy of salvation, and shown him to have a rôle which in its uniqueness and importance is comparable to that of John the Baptist himself.

'Redaction' criticism of the Gospels has shown us the special position occupied by Joseph in the working out of God's plan. For Luke, Joseph has no particular significance, except that he can be used as a proof of the poverty of Jesus, a theme dear to the writer of the Third Gospel. Like Matthew, Luke traces the family tree of Jesus through Joseph, but this seems to be because his genealogy concentrates exclusively on fathers, not mothers. But for Matthew, Joseph is extremely important. Matthew shows practically no interest, by way of contrast with Luke, in the figure of Mary. Once again, as with the Baptist, Joseph stands for the

Old Testament – but in a more precise way than he. If John is the human space in the encounter of God with man, if his Jewishness and his place in the prophetic tradition are really rather incidental to his more primary rôle which is one of bearing witness for all men and saying Yes for all men to the divine encounter, then Joseph represents, by comparison, the profound Jewishness of the actual and particular space which was the medium of God's coming. The first two chapters of Matthew's Gospel show us a Joseph whose distinct identity is frequently in danger of merging with the figure of the patriarch Joseph of the Book of Genesis: the one whom God sent before his people to save them. Joseph the husband of Mary, like Joseph the son of Jacob-Israel, is a dreamer; and like him he is obedient to the instructions he receives from heaven. Through Joseph the husband of Mary, the new Israel – which is personally Jesus – goes down to Egypt so that he can recapitulate the exodus from Egypt of the first Israel which had travelled there through Joseph, the son of Jacob.

But the Joseph of the New Testament has a still more significant rôle than this. He is primarily 'Son of David': this is his mode of address.

> Joseph, Son of David, do not fear to take to you Mary your wife because what is conceived in her is of the Holy Spirit. She will bear a son, and you will call his name Jesus. (Matt. 1.20–21)

'*You* will call his name Jesus.' The primary task of Joseph is to give Jesus a name, in the modern sense of a man marrying a woman in order to give her child a name, as well as in the sense of his giving him the name 'Jesus' as such. Joseph's rôle is to legitimise Jesus as the Son of David, which in the Jewish perspective of Matthew's Gospel meant to legitimise him as having any claim at all to be the Messiah. Only if he were son of David could he be Messiah. In the person of Joseph, the line of David accepted Jesus as one of its own, a legitimate successor to the great David himself, 'great David's greater Son'.[1] The continued presence of Joseph in the Church is the continued presence of

---

[1] From James Montgomery's Advent hymn, based on Psalm 72, 'Hail to the Lord's Anointed'.

Israel and the line of David. This is not simply because Joseph is a Jew. All the apostles are Jewish; Mary is Jewish; John the Baptist is Jewish; most of the early bishops of Rome were Jewish. Rather, it is because the public mission of Joseph is to be Judaism recognising Jesus of Nazareth as the legitimate Son of David, with all the weight that the word 'legitimate' must carry for a people of the law. Joseph, as the continued presence of Israel officially and publicly in the Church, keeps alive the notion and the reality of the Church as a 'third people', the Church of Jews and Gentiles whom God has made into one new race. This unity of Jews and Gentiles in the one Church is for Paul *the* mystery *par excellence*, kept hidden from all ages and generations but now, in the Christian era, at last made known. Joseph, in legitimising Jesus as Son of David, legitimises him as the one who makes both Jews and Gentiles one. He stands in the Church as Israel recognisant of its Saviour, the prototype of that future Israel which according to the Paul of the Letter to the Romans, will one day accept Jesus as Messianic Son of David.

It is at this point that we may find useful one mediaeval meditation on Joseph, the treatise *On Jesus at Twelve Years Old* by the English Cistercian abbot Aelred of Rievaulx.[2] All modern scholarship would agree that the story of the finding in the temple as Luke presents it has considerable elements of allegory about it. It is like the first occurrence of the theme-song of the entire Gospel. At Passover time Jesus is lost in Jerusalem by those nearest to him and found again on the third day in his Father's house: surely a pointer to that Passover twenty years later when again those closest to him would lose him in Jerusalem and find him again on the third day in his Father's house, with his Father, where his Father was. Granted this, Aelred's suggestion that the three days' loss also has reference to the time of all subsequent human history may not be too much of an act of 'eisegesis'. As Aelred reads the story (and he does not pretend that this is the only or even the primary meaning it carries), the father and mother of Jesus are the synagogue and the Jewish people who lost Jesus for the two days of history subsequent to the crucifixion, those two days which Aelred thought were coming to an end in his own historical period. On the third day, the last Day, Aelred

[2] Aelred of Rievaulx, *On Jesus at Twelve Years Old* (ET London 1956).

looked to a time when the father and mother of Jesus, the synagogue and the Jewish people, would come to identify Jesus in the crowd, would find him again after having sought him sorrowing for so long, even though they should have known where to look. Within this perspective of the hope of the eventual reconciliation of Israel and the nations in one body, St Joseph stands in the Church as the first-fruits, the pledge, of the whole people that will one day come in. A Church without Joseph would be an unbalanced Church, a Church that had forgotten its Jewish origins and its Jewish hopes.

But there is one other way in which Joseph focusses the Church, one other public mission which only he could have fulfilled. The story of the Annunciation to Joseph can easily be misread. But there is in fact nothing in it to suggest that Joseph was unaware that Mary's child was conceived by the Holy Spirit. The story as told by Matthew does not compel us to think that Joseph suspected Mary of unchastity; his fear was the result of his very awareness that her coming child was the work of the Holy Spirit. Faced with this, his immediate reaction was to ebb, to back away gracefully. This was no place for the likes of him, here where such mysteries were being wrought. The angel's task is to inform him that this is not so. He must not withdraw from the mission he has been given, the mission of making the son of Mary the Son of David. His rôle it is to serve the beginning of the mystery of man's salvation. It is the same problematic that Paul faced so often: the tremendousness of the task laid on the Church, the unworthiness of the Church to carry it out, the whole business of treasure in earthen pots. Joseph, as the man called on to serve the mystery of God's dealings with men in their final and definitive form, stands as the one who epitomises the Church in its rôle of serving the plan of God. If we see the Church as focussed in Mary alone, we shall be in danger of having too triumphalist a sense of the Church. The glory of the Church will be to act as Mother to Christ, to bring him forth into the world. But if we hold together a number of images and include there by Mary's side that of Joseph, we shall see that an equally significant task of the Church is to step perpetually back into the background. Joseph served the plan of God and then disappeared before it, leaving hardly a trace of his intervention. Yet that intervention was as crucial as the intervention of John the Baptist, as the intervention of Mary. Joseph is not such a bad choice for celebration as patron of the universal Church.[3]

[3] See also G. Preston, O.P., 'The Significance of Saint Joseph', *Doctrine and Life* 31. 2 (1981), pp. 73–76.

28

Mary

A great sign appeared in heaven, a woman clothed with the sun, and with the moon under her feet, and on her head a crown of twelve stars ... (Apoc. 12.1)

A woman with child, a woman giving birth. Whatever arguments there may be about how precisely this 'great sign' is to be understood, Christians would agree that Mary belongs with it somewhere. If the sign is not a description of Mary, then Mary is the highest personification of the sign. And certainly Mary in the Church is herself just such a sign, there to be contemplated, thoughtfully and lovingly. Mary holds the action in the one moment of her own person: Mary in whom all has been fulfilled, all that was promised by the Lord to anyone who believes. Appropriately, in the Latin Church's custom of commemorating the Blessed Virgin Mary on *Saturdays*, we have associated the sabbath with Mary, the day on which God finished his work and rested, the day amongst days which he 'blessed'. The sabbath does not deny the work of the six days but completes it. It crystallises and holds the whole of creation, all the work of God. It is a sign, as Mary, to whom we dedicate the sabbath, is a sign.

'Sign' is perhaps the oldest title of Mary. 'Our Lady of the Sign' is one of the commonest types of icon among Eastern Christians who understand these things so well – Our Lady *of* the Sign or simply Our Lady the Sign. She belongs with that sign which Ahaz refused to ask from the Lord, but was given: the girl conceiving and bearing a son and calling his name Immanuel. Mary at prayer with Immanuel on her breast, our Lady of the Sign, is a way of depicting this mystery which goes back at least to the fourth century. Mary the Sign is to be contemplated rather than used; she summarises in a single image, her own person, so much that we otherwise know of only in the flux of action. So the *Akathistos* hymn addresses her as the 'summary of Christ's truths', 'the epitome of his dogmas', as well as 'the beginning of his wonders'. She is an icon of salvation history, of the story of man's relationship with God and God's with man, God in three persons. And the icon, in modern Eastern Christian thinking, is the real presence of what it symbolises, of the energetic process which it depicts. It is a presence that is not enclosed in the painting itself but radiates around it. The icon is the condensation point of the person or event shown there. The defence of images by the Seventh General Council is much more restrained than this contemporary Eastern Orthodox theology which ascribes such power to icons. But if this modern approach is not implicit in the conciliar definitions, it is none the less true about those icons which are persons, and in particular about the icon of God which is Mary of Nazareth. Whatever may be the case with icons made with paint on wood, there is a real presence of ultimate mysteries in the icon which is a fulfilled person. Life, indeed, is an art, the art of arts, the creation of oneself from prior existent materials. The image which is Mary opens out into what goes far beyond one particular woman who lived at one particular time in one particular place; and yet the whole of human history would have been different without this particularity. She is not simply one example of how God works, but the supreme paradigm of his working: in Paul Claudel's words, a 'living Bible'.[1] She is the fixed goal of God's eternal plan, *termine fisso d'eterno consiglio* as Dante says, 'the consummation, planned by God's decree'.[2] She is the best part and chosen portion of the first Church, Israel, and the exemplary model of the young Church, the Christian people, the third race composed of Jews and Gentiles. As the great sign offered us by God she invites thought – as any symbol invites thought – because the meaning of this sign is so rich and varied. This is a simple sign but it is not a bland statement. In true simplicity there can be genuine complexity, tensions, variety, ambiguity, paradox; and they have to be acknowledged and exploited. In true simplicity there is much that is implicit, and can only with difficulty, if at all, be made explicit. For St Basil, the word of truth in the economy of the

[1] Cf. Soeur Paul-Emile, S.G.C., *Le Renouveau marial dans la littérature française depuis Chateaubriand jusqu'à nos jours* (Paris 1936), pp. 165–194.
[2] *Paradiso*, Canto XXXIII. 3.

Spirit is so concise that little means much. So it is with this sign, which in its content is so deep and complex, a ganglion of all God's ways with us and ours with him.

It is the sign of a woman with sun and moon and twelve stars, the woman who is Israel, the Lord's bride who, according to the Song of Songs,

> looks forth as the morning, fair as the moon, pure and clear as the sun, and terrible as an army with banners ... (Song of Sol. 6.10)

terrible, that is, as the angelic host of heaven. The women of the royal court called her blessed, all the generations before the coming of the Lord in our flesh as well as all the generations after. Here is the Israel, too, of Joseph's dream, the Israel which Joseph saw as sun and moon and twelve stars. Joseph's brothers envied him we are told, but his father Jacob 'kept the saying in mind' (Gen. 37.11), doing exactly what Mary did when she lost her child and found her boy, when he went down with Joseph and herself to Nazareth and there was subject to them. Mary is Israel, forever a Jewess, the true Judith, blessed of the Most High God above all women upon earth, the glory of Jerusalem, the joy of Israel, the great rejoicing of our people.

The great sign invites our contemplation. The whole vocabulary of this passage invites it. When God's temple in heaven is opened, how could we not contemplate? Originally, to contemplate is to mark out a space, preferably a circle, and to fix one's attention on what is within that space. A temple is any enclosure marked out for the purpose of coming into contact with things divine. Here we are in the world of that form of contemplative Marian praying we call the rosary. Within the circle of the rosary lies the temple, the space in which we see and ponder things divine. Here is the enclosed garden which is the image behind our word 'rosary', the walled rose garden, the small area in which great things happen. That is the usual Christian pattern, and the pattern of the Incarnation. In the grotto at Nazareth, the inscription reads: *Verbum caro hic factum est*: 'The Word was made flesh at this spot'. Whether that particular spot or not does not matter: but certainly the Word was made flesh at some particular spot, some 'here'. The world's Creator, the uncontainable One, was contained in

Mary's womb, the *claustrum* of Mary, as the hymn puts it, her 'cloister'. Did not Jerome of Bethlehem write of that place to which his name remains forever conjoined that in this small spot of earth, heaven's Maker was born? And the mediaeval English carol echoes this:

> There is no rose of such virtue,
> as the rose that bare Jesu.
> For in that rose enclosed was
> heaven and earth in little space.[3]

In the rosary we muse over all heaven and earth contained in the little space which is Mary. The 'quiet rhythm' and 'lingering pace' that Pope Paul VI recommends in his letter on Marian devotion give us time to waste. They claim time for us to loiter in watching. We 'loiter with intent', with the intention of watching until the rose reveals its heart to us, that heart which has healing properties for our hearts and minds, health in person, Jesus the Saviour. When in the litany of Loreto we call Mary 'health of the sick' we hail her as the rose of great 'virtue', that is healing power. She is the flower whose fruit is himself the healing of the nations. In greeting Mary, again and again, as the blessed mother of the blessed fruit of her womb, we are putting ourselves in the presence of the fundamental mystery of Christianity: God made man so that we could live in God. Mary is the place of the incarnation of the Word, where in the name of the whole human race – as St Thomas says – there was spoken that perfect Yes which makes possible all our relationship with God.

The great sign we are given is the sign of the Incarnation. The woman is clothed in the fulness of time, with that sun and moon and those stars which were made to mark time, to tell us when the appropriate time had come. 'Let there be lights in the firmament of heaven', says the creating God, 'and let them be for signs and for seasons and for days and years' (Gen. 1.14). When the fulness of time had come, God sent forth his Son, born of a woman. *God* sent him forth; and this great sign is in *heaven*. God sent him forth born under the law; and this woman is Israel, the people to whom the law came through Moses. God sent him forth to redeem those who were under the law, that we might receive the

---

[3] 'Rosa mystica', in M. G. Segar (ed.), *A Mediaeval Anthology* (London 1915), p. 65.

adoption of sons, of those many brethren of whom Jesus is the first-born, the 'rest of the woman's children who keep the commandments of God and hold the testimony of Jesus' (Apoc. 12.17). So the great sign of the incarnation is shown to us for our contemplation, that incarnation which was not finished at the moment of Mary's acceptance of God's will but was fulfilled only when the man-child was caught up to God and to his throne. God's temple is opened in heaven: so it is appropriate for us to *contemplate*. We are shown a woman crowned with stars: so it is fitting that we should *consider*. The woman means Mary, the spotless mirror of the Church (as the last Council of Catholicism called her): so we do well to *reflect*. God's wonders are shown in her; and so we *wonder* at all his mighty works epitomised in her. 'And I looked,' says the visionary John again and again in the Apocalypse. And again and again we look at this mighty sign we are offered in Mary, circling round and round it, spiralling inwards and upwards. In our contemplation of Mary we are not trying to prove anything. We are trying to discover what is at the heart of the sign, at the heart of the rose, in the heart of Mary.

Naturally enough, we already have some idea of what is to be discovered in that pure heart, in the heart of her who – like all the pure of heart – sees God. What lies in the heart of Mary now? At the birth of Jesus, when the shepherds had been and gone, Mary, so Luke tells us, 'kept all these things, pondering them in her heart' (Luke 2.57). At the return of her family to Nazareth she did the same. Like Jacob keeping Joseph's vision, that vision which was his own mystery as Israel, Mary keeps these things which are her own mystery as 'filled with grace'. Like Daniel, too, keeping in his heart those things which were the night visions of the Son of Man, the man-child, surely, of John's vision, on whom the great red dragon made war. She ponders these things and brings them together so that she can understand the things which Luke does not hesitate to say she did not understand. 'She confers silently in her heart', says Claudel, 'and reunites in a single focus all lines of contradiction'.

When we look at Mary we are looking at our own mystery, looking at a mirror in which we see ourselves, different and distinct from each of us as she is. We see the Church in Mary and Mary in the Church. When we call her the Immaculate, for instance, we use of her, personally, individually, the language used in the Letter to the Ephesians for all Christians, personally, collectively.

> The God and Father of our Lord Jesus Christ ... chose us in Christ before the foundation of the world, so that we should be holy and without blemish [immaculate] before him in love. (Eph. 1.3, 4)

The purpose of the plan of God, of the coming of God in the flesh of Jesus, the life and the death and the rising, and the coming of the Holy Spirit, is that we, the people of God, the one person of the Church, should be immaculate. We look for the full effect of the sacrificial Death of Christ in a people that is perfect and complete, without lie or deceit, undefiled, integrated, whole, a worthy offering to God. In looking for the new heavens and the new earth, we look for an immaculate Church, immaculate like its Lord who redeemed it with precious blood as of an immaculate Lamb. But we believe that there is already an immaculate Church of God, a bride without spot or wrinkle. That Church is Mary. 'Filled with grace' is Mary's true name, the name God first gave her and by which he still knows her. It is possible to contemplate the immaculate Church in faith, not just in hope. What is said in hope of the universal Church as virgin and mother is said in faith, and in an individual and unique way, of Mary. She is herself with her own unrepeatable life history. But in her there has been a fulfilment of what was promised by the Lord to those who have believed. All the mysteries of Jesus have now been embodied in her flesh. Nothing had to be foresworn; nothing had to be denied. And so the fulness of time is about her. That is what we mean by the assumption: Mary is adorned with all time. She is, as Mother Julian of Norwich saw her, 'little waxen above a child',[4] the sixteen- or seventeen-year-old girl of Bernadette's vision; but she is also the old woman Church that Hermas saw, old because 'she was created the first of all things, and for her sake was the world established',[5] the seventy-two-year-old woman of Franciscan tradition. In Mary assumed into heaven, caught up by the Jesus who is the first and the last, there is a great sign for

[4] Julian of Norwich, *Revelations of Divine Love*, 4.
[5] *The Shepherd*, Visions II. 4.

us to see and wonder at and love, and as we do so, be filled with hope for ourselves. 'Wilt thou see in her', said the Lord to Julian, 'how *thou* art loved?'[6]

[6] Julian of Norwich, *Revelations of Divine Love*, 25. For Fr Geoffrey's Mariology, see further: *God's Way to be Man*, pp. 99–103; 'The Annunciation', *Doctrine and Life* 31. 3 (1981), pp. 143–147; 'The Visitation', *ibid.* 31. 5 (1981), pp. 277–281; *Hallowing The Time*, pp. 10–13, 25–26.

PART FOUR

The Mystery of the Church

29

Koinōnia

In the old Roman baptismal Creed, the so-called 'Apostles'
Creed', we confess that we believe in the Holy Spirit, the holy
catholic Church, the communion of saints, the forgiveness of sins
and life everlasting. Notice here the phrase 'the communion of
saints', *communio sanctorum*, a phrase which has aroused considerable controversy in its time. Grammatically, *sanctorum* is a
genitive plural, but it may be either masculine or neuter. Is the
phrase to be translated as 'the communion of saints', *sancti*, 'holy
people', or as 'the communion of holy things', *sancta*, that is
(taken in the round) 'the sacraments'? In the one case it would
stand in apposition to 'The holy catholic Church'; in the other to
'the forgiveness of sins'.

In his study *The Meaning of 'Sanctorum Communio'*, Stephen
Benko argues learnedly that originally we are dealing here with a
neuter form.[1] The clause does not simply restate our belief in the
Church from a new angle, but is a new start, an independent
article introducing the clause about the forgiveness of sins. Its
basic meaning, therefore, will be 'participation in the holy things'
(the sacraments) which effect the forgiveness of sins, namely
Baptism and the Eucharist. From the time of Nicetas of Remesi-
ana around the beginning of the fifth century, so Benko maintains, the expression came to be understood more and more as
referring to the social character of the Church itself. It was taken
to stand for the communion of the members of the Church with
one another rather than simply the communion of each of them
in holy things. And it is this latter view which has predominated
from then until now, even though the sacramental meaning
recurs time and again in the intervening centuries. St Thomas, for
instance, in his *Commentary on the Creed*, relates the *sanctorum
communio* to the forgiveness of sins rather than to the Church as
such:

[1] S. Benko, *The Meaning of 'Sanctorum Communio'* (London 1964).

Among the things that the apostles believed and handed on is the fact that in the Church there is a communion of good things: this is what we call *sanctorum communio*. Thus the good of Christ is being communicated to all Christians, just as the excellence of the Head is communicated to all the members. This communication takes place through the sacraments of the Church, in which the virtue of the passion of Christ is at work in conferring grace for remission of sins. Through the seven sacraments we obtain forgiveness of sins, and that is why at once there is added the words *remissionem peccatorum*[2].

But it is clear from elsewhere in the same commentary that St Thomas interprets the *'communio'* article of the creed in *both* a personal and a neuter sense:

Through this communion we obtain two things: first, that the merit of Christ is communicated to everyone (i.e. in the sacraments), and second, that the good of each one is communicated to the other.[3]

But though the overwhelming weight of interpretation has favoured a personalist view of this article, Benko insists that it can be definitely established that the original meaning was neuter and not personal. And he believes that we would do well to restore this meaning to the popular understanding of the article in the Church now.

A more widespread and prominent consideration of the sacramental interpretation of this clause would be of distinct advantage to the Church. It would be not only a return to the original meaning of the clause, but also a means of drawing the denominations more closely together. A confession of our common participation in Baptism and the Eucharist would be a declaration of our oneness through our sharing in the benefits of Christ's death and resurrection. Lack of unanimity concerning Baptism and the Eucharist is a major stumbling-block in the way of Christian unity. Properly understood, *sanctorum communio* may help to remove this block.[4]

[2] Thomas, 'Exposition of the Creed' in *Opuscula Omnia* IV (Paris 1927), p. 381.
[3] *Ibid.*, p. 383.
[4] S. Benko, *The Meaning of 'Sanctorum Communio'*, p. 141.

Whatever may be the practical advantages of the neuter interpretation of this article for contemporary Christians, J. N. D.
Kelly in his *Early Christian Creeds* insists that, on the contrary,
the original meaning was personal. He points out that the work
of Nicetas, which Benko regards as the decisive move away from
the clause's original sense, is in fact the first comment on it that
we have. As Kelly writes,

> It would be foolhardy to work on the assumption that the cri-
> terion of what ought to have been embodied in the Creed (e.g. a
> reference to the sacraments of the Church) supplies the key to
> what was actually embodied in it.[5]

Kelly admits that the question is probably insoluble, yet comes
down in favour of the personalist interpretation of the words.
Even here however, there are two possible interpretations available, although they are certainly not incompatible with each
other. It may be a question of fellowship with holy people, with
the saints understood as either martyrs and saints in the narrower
sense, or as all believers, the whole people, of God. Or again it
may be that *communio* has a concrete meaning and refers to the
Catholic Church of the Creed's preceding article as that fellowship or community which consists of holy people. Either way,
according to Kelly, the personal reading is the better established.
Let us take two examples of its sources. Here, for instance, is
Nicetas speaking:

> What is the Church other than the congregation of all the saints?
> From the beginning of the world, patriarchs, prophets, martyrs
> and all other righteous men who have lived or are now alive or
> who shall live in time to come make up the Church, since they
> have been sanctified by one faith and one way of life, and sealed
> by one Spirit, and so made one body, of which Christ is said to be
> the Head, as Scripture puts it. Moreover, the angels and the
> heavenly virtues and the powers too are banded together in this
> Church. So you believe that in this Church you will attain to the
> communion of saints.[6]

Some fifty years later Faustus of Riez offers the same inter-

---

[5] J. N. D. Kelly, *Early Christian Creeds* (London 1950; 1952), p. 395.
[6] Nicetas, *Explanation of the Creed*, sub. loc.

pretation, although for him the saints are those whose moral goodness was outstanding.

> Let us believe in the communion of saints, but let us venerate the saints more for God's honour and glory than in the place of God. Let us worship in the saints the fear and love of God, not God's divinity. Let us worship the merits of the saints, merits which they do not have from themselves but which they have earned for their devotion. Thus they deserve to be venerated worthily, in that through their contempt for death they pour into us the worship of God and a longing for the life to come.[7]

But whatever may be the correct understanding of the original meaning of this article in the Roman baptismal Creed, there can be no doubt that it carries an appeal to a fundamental element of the Christian experience in the Church, that of communion, fellowship, in the Greek *koinōnia*. In ordinary secular Greek the word *koinos* has about the same range of meanings as the English 'common' which can carry a pejorative sense yet equally can simply mean what is available to a group of people without distinction (as in 'The Book of Common Prayer'). In the New Testament these two meanings, 'profane' or 'what is held in common', recur. Some of Jesus' disciples are said to have 'eaten their bread with common (that is, unwashed) hands' (Mark 7.2). On the other hand, some of the most valuable possessions of the Christian community are regarded as common to all. Paul addresses Titus as his 'true child, according to a common faith' (Titus 1.4); Jude writes to other Christians about their 'common salvation' (Jude v. 3); in the idealised Jerusalem church of the Acts of the Apostles 'all who believed were together and had all things common, and they sold their possessions and goods and parted them to all, according as any man had need' (Acts 2.44–45); or again, 'the multitude of those who believed were of one heart and soul, and not one said that anything of the things he possessed was his own, but they had all things in common' (Acts 4.32). This holding of all goods in common, this economic *koinōnia*, communion, fellowship, is represented as a continuation of the style of life Jesus shared with his disciples in the Gospels (they kept a common purse), and a realisation of what

---

[7] Faustus, *Homily* II *on the Creed*, sub. loc.

the Old Testament had promised 'in the last days'. Just as Deuteronomy 15.4 had prophesied 'There shall be no poor with you', so the Acts of the Apostles declares 'There was not a needy man amongst them' (4.34).

But this ideal of having all things in common in the New Testament Church was but the translation into economic terms of a reality experienced at more profound levels. *Koinōnia* is a word that occurs but rarely in the Septuagint of the Old Testament and where it is met with it means normally the fellowship between man and man, in something of a Friendly Society sort of way, or the fellowship between worshippers of God. Occasionally we find it used for the fellowship between those who worship a god and the god himself, but never for any sort of relationship between Yahweh and *his* worshippers. This kind of close relationship was unimaginable, or if imaginable then unthinkably offensive, in the case of the Lord God of Israel. In the Old Testament a just man always remains at a certain distance from God. He is dependent on God, related to him by love and service, trusting him, but never his fellow, never in this sense enjoying a communion, a *koinōnia* with God. Even though the sharing of a sacrificial meal had an important part in Israel's worship, and was conceived as the worshippers' sharing the feast with God himself, it still never happened that the relationship between God and his people came to be called a fellowship. This is true even of those places where one would most expect to find it, say in the account of the covenant meal with the elders on Mount Sinai. Here there is every indication that the meal is taken with Yahweh himself, but the story never states this and ends up awkwardly:

> Then went up Moses and Aaron, Nadab and Abihu and seventy of the elders of Israel; and they saw the God of Israel, and there was under his feet as it were a paved work of bright sapphire and as it were the very heaven for clearness. And upon the nobles of the children of Israel he laid not his hand; and they beheld God and did eat and drink (Exod. 24.9–11).

Perhaps the most striking change in the New Testament is the ease with which the group of words that cluster around *koinōnia* are used of the relationship between God and man in Christ and not just for what men share between themselves. *Koinōnia* with

God in Christ is the basis for *koinōnia* between Christians. Take, for example, the First Letter of John:

> What we have seen and heard we declare to you, that you also may have fellowship with us; yes, and our fellowship is with the Father and with his Son Jesus Christ; and these things we write that our joy may be fulfilled. And this is the message which we have heard from him and announce unto you, that God is light and in him there is no darkness at all. If we say that we have fellowship with him and walk in the darkness, we lie, and do not live the truth; but if we walk in the light, as he is in the light, we have fellowship one with another, and the blood of Jesus his Son cleanses us from all sin. (1 John 1.3–7)

So fellowship with God and fellowship between Christians is here spoken of in the same breath. John is careful to situate the fellowship which should obtain between Christians within the context of the fellowship that does obtain between them and God, always provided that the Christians do not break the fellowship (with the light) by walking in darkness. Just as in this letter our love for God and each other is grounded in God's love for us, so our fellowship with each other is grounded in the *koinōnia* we enjoy with God. Though the *koinōnia* between Christians takes on visible forms and must be translated into deeds, especially in the economic realm, it is truly *koinōnia* only because of the *koinōnia* of all the faithful with the Father and the Son – that communion of God with man in Christ, which can also be called the fellowship of the Son (as in 1 Corinthians), and the fellowship of the Spirit (as in Philippians), a fellowship which Paul prays may be with the Christians at Corinth together with the grace of our Lord Jesus Christ and the love of God. Nevertheless, the *koinōnia* between Christians *does* indeed take on visible forms, so much so that the collection of money taken for the poor Christians in Jerusalem by the better-off Christians in Macedonia and Achaia can be referred to as their *koinōnia* and Paul can praise in another of his letters the liberality of the *koinōnia* of the Corinthian church.

The focal point of the communion of Christians with Christ and in Christ with the Father comes in the Eucharist which right from New Testament times has been talked about as a *koinōnia*, a fellowship, of the body and blood of Christ.

The cup of blessing which we bless, is it not a *koinōnia* of the blood of Christ? The loaf which we break, is it not a *koinōnia* of the body of Christ? Seeing that there is one loaf, we who are many are one body, for we all partake from the one loaf. Behold Israel after the flesh: do those who eat the sacrifices not have *koinōnia* with the altar? (1 Cor. 10.16–18)

This passage, which occurs in the context of an argument against the advisability of eating meat which had been sacrificed to idols, is highly instructive. Paul points out that sharing a meal involving this meat runs the risk of entering into communion with the demons in question, and so of provoking the Lord to jealousy. *Koinōnia* is not only a word of fellowship: it is a word with boundaries. To belong to one *koinōnia* may necessitate not belonging to another. Fundamental loyalties are involved. A person must choose which *koinōnia* he is going to belong to, even though if he chooses to belong to the *koinōnia* of the body and blood of Christ it is only possible because God has called him into the *koinōnia* of his Son. Belonging to the *koinōnia* of the Father and the Son and the Holy Spirit involves continually opting to remain within that *koinōnia*, that fellowship of light, choosing not to have fellowship instead with darkness and the powers of darkness. The development of this vocabulary of *koinōnia* in the Church tends to lay ever-increasing emphasis on the *koinōnia* focussed in the celebration of the Eucharist. This is so much so that from the early fourth century at the latest it was common-place to talk about sharing in the eucharistic gifts simply as communion, as *koinōnia*, without it being necessary to add the specifying words 'in the body and blood of the Lord'. From this, the word could come to mean the consecrated elements themselves, as in the way we speak of 'receiving communion'. And so at this last stage we are very close to the Thomist teaching that the reality of the Eucharist, 'the thing itself', the whole point and purpose of the elements, is the unity of the mystical body, the *koinōnia* between all the members of the Church, rooted as it is in the *koinōnia* of the Trinity. *Communio* can speak of the Church and of the Eucharist alike. The wheel has come full circle, and we are back with the ambiguity of the credal phrase: *sanctorum communio*, the communion of holy people or of holy things. Whatever the original meaning may have been, not long after this article first found its way into Western creeds, *communio* could be used to refer either to the eucharistic gifts or to the fellowship between Christians that is rooted and grounded in their fellowship with the Trinity. Père de Lubac maintains that *sanctorum communio* can only refer to communion in the sacraments since a creed has to do only with God's initiative in regard to man and man's salvation – and not with the way men subjectively appropriate that divine initiative.[8] That being so, he argues, just as the Creed says nothing about faith or hope or charity, but only about what we believe in, hope for and love, so too the Creed should not be expected to say anything about the relationships obtaining between Christians. *Sanctorum communio* must refer to the source from which Christians receive their personal holiness and their brotherly fellowship with one another. But this in fact solves nothing. Christians do indeed receive their holiness and their fellowship with their brethren from the sacraments, but they also receive them as a result of the *communio* they have been given with the Father and the Son and the Holy Spirit.

The double meaning of *sanctorum*, interpersonal or sacramental, ecclesial or eucharistic, continues throughout the later centuries of the Church. When Augustine, for instance, speaks of 'the *communio*', he simply means the Church. In many of the Fathers, the *sanctorum communio* means the visible Church. The phrase ceased to have to do primarily with the attitude of mind appropriate to people who had been called by God to live in fellowship with each other, and came to refer to the fellowship itself, to the very community which was visible and self-evident. Then it could also be a term for the link which formed the social unity of the Christian churches throughout the world. And here too the eucharistic communion was close to the heart of it all. Christians were in communion with each other if they were in eucharistic communion with each other. If they broke eucharistic communion between them then one or another group was outside the *communio*, outside the *koinōnia*, outside the fellowship, literally ex-communicated. Hertling in his study 'Communio und Primat' remarks how the same shift occurred with other words, words like *eirenē*, 'peace', *agapē*, 'charity', and *concordia*, 'con-

[8] Cf. H. de Lubac, *The Christian Faith: An Essay on the Structure of the Apostles' Creed* (ET San Francisco 1986), p. 218.

cord'.[9] These words became ways of designating the Catholic Church throughout the world, the Church in which all the members and all the local churches were indeed in peace and love and concord with each other. When Christians moved from church to church they took with them letters of introduction for the bishop of the place to which they were going from the bishop of the place they had come from, letters known usually as *litterae communicatoriae* or *litterae pacis*. Hertling has an interesting passage on this custom.

> Every bishop or at least every Church of any importance, later on chiefly the metropolitans, drew up a list of the principal Churches of the world with which they were in communion. Such lists served as directories when it became necessary to issue passports. Then again, the documents of travellers were checks with the aid of the same lists. A passport was accepted when it came from a bishop mentioned in the list. Outside Africa, the Donatist bishop with whom Augustine was at loggerheads did not of course appear on any list. Augustine was thus able to tell him: 'Make out a passport for Alexandria or Antioch, then, and we shall soon see whether you are on the list of orthodox bishops there'.[10]

Similarly, excommunication, deprivation of the Eucharist, was the way the Church carried out its penitential discipline. To deprive a man of the communion of the Eucharist was to say that he was outside the communion of the Church. To readmit a man to the communion of the Eucharist was to readmit him to the communion of the Church. Communion (eucharistic) is communion (ecclesial). People could be outside the communion (in both senses) either because of going wrong about the faith or because of sin. In the case of sin it seems obvious enough that it would be the local church which would deal with the matter of penitential discipline, even though other churches might become interested if they thought that some particular church was being either over-lax or over-rigorous. After all, even in the ancient world news travelled and what was happening to the church in

[9] L. Hertling, S. J., 'Communio und Primat', *Miscellanea Historiae Pontificiae* VII (Rome 1943), pp. 1–148. (There is an English translation: *Communio: Church and Papacy in Early Christianity*, Chicago 1972.)
[10] *Ibid.*, p. 12; cited in J. Hamer, O.P., *The Church is a Communion* (ET London 1964), p. 166.

Antioch would soon be known by the church in Alexandria. But it was not quite so obvious what should be done in the case of a doubt about the orthodoxy of someone's faith, especially the faith of a bishop of another church. How did you know whether a bishop really did belong to the *koinōnia*, the *communio*? One way was by testing the links he had with the episcopate as a whole, often a difficult enough business. The other was by seeing how he was regarded by the oldest churches, by those churches which later became patriarchal sees. Of these the church of Rome has always held the first place. If some bishop is in communion with Rome that fact alone means that he is in communion with all other churches in the *communio*, in the *pax*, the *agapē*, the *catholica*. Archbishop Jerome Hamer quotes a letter from Ambrose in 381 to the emperors Gratian and Valentinus in which he asks them to

> make sure that the Roman church, head of the whole Roman world, is not destroyed, for from it there spreads to all the other churches the rights of communion which must be reverenced.[11]

It is on the basis of this kind of thinking that amongst Catholic churches of whatever rite the bishop of Rome is mentioned in the eucharistic prayer. By praying for named individuals you say who you are in communion with, you declare the *communio*. Simply praying by name for another bishop will do, but most probably in the Roman Canon the *una cum* that precedes the name of the pope and the local bishop and the reference to all (the bishops) who are right-believing and right-teaching in the catholic and apostolic faith should be translated not as though it were a prayer *for* these people but as a statement that the Eucharist is being offered together *with* them, in their *pax* and their *communio*.

The Church, then, is *communio*, *koinōnia*. The Church *is* a fellowship, a communion. Communion is a concept that covers the way the individual Christian experiences his life within the Church, his sharing the sacraments with other people, his being sustained by the faith and hope and love of other people and his ability to sustain them by his. To this we must add his sense that the bodily death of others does not interrupt the communion he

---

[11] Ambrose, *Letter* 11, cited in *ibid.*, p. 167.

has with them, but that he can pray for them and that they can and do pray for him. Communion also covers the relationships that obtain between local churches and those relationships between individual members of a local church that can be earthed in concrete activities of sharing goods, whether spiritual or material, whether locally or universally. This whole nexus of relationships is expressed and celebrated in the sacraments, especially in *the* sacrament that expresses *communio* so intensely that it can itself be called *communio*. As Ivo of Chartres says, 'the communion of saints is the truth of the sacraments of the Church'.[12] And *communio, koinōnia*, roots this experience of the Christian man and the Christian body in the ultimate mystery of God. The *communio* that Christians experience is the translation into human terms of the *communio* that exists between the persons of the Trinity, a *communio* into which men have been admitted by the Father in making his Son share the *communio* of our flesh and blood. In the last three chapters of this book we shall look at the trinitarian shape of this communion.

---

[12] Ivo of Chartres, *Sermon XXIII on the Apostles' Creed*.

30

The Church of the Spirit

THE Church is a communion, a fellowship, a togetherness in life and liturgy. And this togetherness, this *sobornost*, is rooted and grounded in the togetherness, the *koinōnia*, of the three-personed God. To this communion we have all been given access through the incarnation of the Word of God, by his own entering into *koinōnia* – or, as the Russians say, *sobornost* – with us. Those who share in this togetherness of *koinōnia* are in the Greek termed *koinōnoi*, a name that cannot be translated by a word which preserves the same linguistic form as 'fellowship' or 'communion', and so will have to be translated 'partakers'. Christians partake with one another of goods both material and spiritual, and this is based on their common partaking in the life of the Godhead itself.

> God's divine power has granted you all things which pertain to life and holiness, through the knowledge of him who called us by his own glory and virtue, by which he has granted us his precious and exceedingly great promises, so that through these you may be *partakers (koinōnoi)* of the divine nature, having escaped from the corruption that is in the world. (2 Pet. 1.3–4)

Christians, then, according to this Second Letter of Peter, are said to have a fellowship with God which is a real sharing in the life of God as he is in himself, in his holiness, the way in which God is God. 'God chastens us for our profit', writes the Author to the Hebrews, 'so that we may be partakers of his holiness' (Heb. 11. 10). So the fellowship is with the Father, with the Son made man, and with the Holy Spirit; in this fellowship lies the deepest nature of the Church.

'The grace of our Lord Jesus Christ, and the love of God and the fellowship of the Holy Spirit be with you all' (2 Cor. 13.14) are Paul's closing words to his Corinthian converts. This fellowship of the Holy Spirit, the *koinōnia* of the Paraclete, can be appealed to by Paul, writing this time to the Christians at Philippi, as an unassailable datum, a given:

> So if there is any comfort in Christ, if any consolation of love, if any fellowship of the Spirit, if any tender mercies and compassions, fulfil my joy, that you be of the same mind, having the same love, being of one accord, of one mind, doing nothing through faction or vain glory, but in lowliness of mind each counting the other better than himself, not looking each of you to his own things but each of you also to the things of others. (Phil. 2.1–4)

Then follows the famous hymn about Christ who was in the form of God but humbled himself, emptying himself so as to be highly exalted. Christ here is put forward by Paul as a model for the Philippian fellowship: 'Let this mind be in you which was also in Christ Jesus, who ...' (Phil. 2.5). We have here, therefore, on the one hand an assumption about the fellowship of the Spirit as a datum of Christian experience, and on the other a demand that this fellowship be expressed in the way people live together in a style of life based on that of Jesus himself. The Letter to the Hebrews also speaks of this same fellowship, describing Christians as those who

> once enlightened and tasted of the heavenly gift ... were made partakers (*koinōnoi*) of the Holy Spirit and tasted the good word of God and the powers of the age to come. (Heb. 6.4–5)

But what exactly is this 'fellowship of the Spirit'? Is it perhaps the fellowship produced by the Holy Spirit? Or again is it rather an actual fellowship or partaking in the Spirit himself?

The text from Hebrews I have cited clearly bears the latter meaning, but then it does not speak explicitly of 'the fellowship of the Holy Spirit'. If we look at that phrase's grammatical form it is quite possible that the fellowship in question is a fellowship between men and women produced by the Holy Spirit in his activity among Christians. It would then be another name for the Church, the Church seen under the aspect of the fellowship of members with one another. There could be no objection of principle to this understanding, even if it were not (as indeed seems likely) the strict meaning of these particular texts. There are those who argue strongly, for example, that the phrase *unitas*

Spiritus Sancti, 'the unity of the Holy Spirit' in the doxology at the close of the Roman Canon refers precisely to this: the unity, produced by the Holy Spirit, which we call the Church. Equally, however, from a grammatical point of view, the 'fellowship of the Spirit' could also suggest that the Spirit himself is what all Christians possess in common, in *koinōnia.* This would make better sense in the context of the Pauline greeting formula 'The grace of our Lord Jesus Christ and the love of God and the fellowship of the Holy Spirit be with you all' already cited. The grace in question is surely a gift of Jesus, something that Jesus produces outside himself as an effect. (The love of God, similarly, is the love which God shows towards us.) Would it not follow, then, that the communion of the Holy Spirit should refer to the Spirit's work, to what he was looked to for amongst those to whom Paul was writing? The people are to share in the Holy Spirit as the living source whence flows that *koinōnia* they have amongst themselves. The *koinōnia* produced by the Holy Spirit was and is a result of the *koinōnia* in the Holy Spirit. So, for example, in Acts, the *koinōnia* to which the Whitsun converts commit themselves flows from the Spirit which has been poured out on the Church, the Spirit promised in Peter's Pentecost sermon to anyone who would be baptised in the name of Jesus. This gift of the Holy Spirit, for the author of Acts, was the most significant *koinōnia* of those who repented and were baptised. It was a gift whose presence was ascertainable by a number of signs, mainly charismatic; and if it appeared not to have been given at baptism then steps had to be taken to remedy the deficiency. When people had received the Holy Spirit and become partakers of him then the Spirit produced a unity between them and their fellow-Christians. The unity, however, did not produce the Holy Spirit.

The Spirit in the Church is the gift of the Father. Paul speaks in the Letter to the Romans of 'the love of God which has been poured abroad in our hearts through the Holy Spirit which was given to us' (Rom. 5.5). The love is 'poured abroad' just as the Holy Spirit was 'poured out' on the disciples in the upper room on the day of Pentecost. Every time a man repents and is baptised, what happened for the whole Church on that occasion happens for him as an individual. He enters into the communion of the Holy Spirit which the whole Church already enjoys, and through that communion in the Holy Spirit comes into communion with all his fellow Christians. The Church is the result of that communion of each person with the Holy Spirit, even though the communion may be enjoyed only provided that the person does not close himself off against communion with all those other men and women who share the Spirit's fellowship. As Paul tells the Corinthians, it is 'in one Spirit that we are all baptised into one body' (1 Cor. 12.13). The Spirit produces the body of Christ, not the other way round, even if it is through the body that God pours out the Spirit of Pentecost. As we shall see in the next chapter, this means that the doctrine of the Church runs parallel to the doctrine of the Incarnation: as the physical body of Jesus is produced by the Holy Spirit from Mary the Virgin, so the Church-body of Jesus is also produced by the Holy Spirit in whom all believers share when they themselves enter into the experience of Pentecost. In the Lucan writings that experience is compared to the annunciation to Mary. The Holy Spirit comes down on the Church as on Mary – that Holy Spirit who is the 'power of the Most High', the 'power from on high' which Jesus promised the apostles at his last appearance to them after the resurrection (Luke 1.35; 24.49). This Pentecost experience sets the tone for the rest of the time of the Church, the time between Pentecost and the parousia when, in Lucan terminology, 'this Jesus who was received up from you into heaven shall so come in like manner as you beheld him going into heaven' (Acts 1.11). The Church between Pentecost and the parousia is the Church of the Spirit.

As we have seen already, God gives the Spirit to all who believe and are baptised, and this gift is expected in the New Testament to have observable effects. Paul can tell the Thessalonians not to quench the Spirit; he can assume that the Galatians knew they had received the Spirit through the hearing of faith; he can make the experience of the varied gifts of the Spirit in the Roman Church the basis for an appeal for unity and holiness. Rudolf Schnackenburg points out how the phrase 'God has given us the Spirit' in the Johannine Letters has all the appearance of being a fixed formula from the early Christian catechism.[1] The early Church understood that it was through this Spirit that its work

[1] R. Schnackenburg, *Die Johannisbriefe* (Freiburg 1965), pp. 209–215.

was undertaken, through the Spirit that its own internal life was founded and its task of spreading the gospel carried forward. In the Acts of the Apostles, time and again it is the Spirit who inspires the missionary activity of the Church. It is the Spirit who tells Philip to go and run alongside the Ethiopian's coach; it is the Spirit who catches Philip away after the Ethiopian has been baptised; when the persecution that Saul launched comes to its end with his conversion it is in the comfort of the Spirit that the Church throughout all Judaea and Galilee and Samaria is built up and multiplied; it is the Spirit who tells Peter that three men are looking for him after he has seen the vision of the sheet let down from the sky, the beginning of the story of Cornelius, the Gentile Pentecost; it is the Spirit who tells the church at Antioch 'Separate me Barnabas and Saul for the work to which I have called them' (Acts 13.2). Similarly, it is in the Spirit that John sees the visions of the Apocalypse, and the Spirit who speaks words of support or judgment to the churches mentioned in that book.

From the experience of the activity of the Spirit of God, from what the Spirit does and says to the Church at particular times and particular places, the move is made to an understanding of the abiding presence of the Spirit in the Church and in each believer. The Church can now be seen as the very sphere of the Holy Spirit. The most obvious image for the Church as the locus of the continuous presence of the Spirit is that of the temple. So Paul can ask the Corinthians:

> Do you not know that you are a temple of God and the Spirit of God dwells in you? If any man destroys the temple of God, God will destroy him, for the temple of God is holy, which temple you are (1 Cor. 3.16–11)

Or again he tells the Ephesians that the Gentiles

> are no longer strangers and sojourners, but they are fellow-citizens with the saints, and of the household of God, being built upon the foundation of the apostles and prophets, Christ Jesus himself being the chief corner-stone, in whom every building, fitly framed together, grows into a holy temple in the Lord, in whom you also are built together into a habitation of God in the Spirit. (Eph. 2.19–22)

The temple is constructed 'in the Lord' as well as 'in the Spirit'.

The work of building is the work of the Spirit, but the building has the pattern and plan of Jesus. What the Spirit does is to make one temple, the one temple which is the flesh-body and the Church-body of Jesus, just as he makes one new Man, the whole Christ. It is not as though the Church is simply some institution with its basic charter or constitution laid down by its founder at some point in the past. The Church is a reality in the Spirit. The Spirit of God, who can only be spoken of in terms of wind and fire and water, is the agent for the building up of the Church. As such he is as important a pole of the mystery of the Church as is the Son himself. Not that he is free-floating or altogether unpredictable as a fluid element beside the fixed point of Jesus of Nazareth. We do not discern the working of the Holy Spirit on the basis of our own distorted psyches, by some sixth sense or hunch or whatever – even though it may feel like that at times. The pattern for the Spirit's activity is already set in the historical life of Jesus. Any activity which would run counter to the life of Christ cannot be proposed by the Spirit of God, the Spirit whom God pours out on the crucified Jesus and through him on all who repent and are baptised into the death of Christ.

The implication of this is that there must be no radical cleavage between Spirit and institution. If an institution really does snuff out the Spirit then it is not a Christian institution in the form in which it is presenting itself, although even then it may need radical reform rather than suppression. The work of the Spirit may be expected to produce institutions, to be structuring activity. It may be expected that the Spirit's work will be of a piece with the creation of the fleshly body of Jesus of Nazareth, an incarnating activity, a love seeking to express itself in forms. This is the pattern we meet with in the Acts of the Apostles and in the Pauline Letters. The Spirit produces not only the charisms to be found in the churches but also their ministries and offices, their institutions. Thus in Paul's farewell speech at Ephesus he tells the elders of the church: 'The Holy Spirit has made you *episkopoi* to feed the Church of the Lord which he purchased with his own blood' (Acts 20. 28). Likewise, the Council of Jerusalem believed that it had seemed good to the Holy Spirit as well as to them to lay upon Gentile Christians no greater burden than certain necessary things, precise requirements of a highly formal kind. Whatever tension Christians may experience between the work of the

277

Spirit and the work of the Son, it must be said that there can be no ultimate incompatibility between Spirit and institution, Spirit and embodiment. The trinitarian form of the Church's *koinōnia* rules this out.

This trinitarian form of *koinōnia* is expressed liturgically in a number of ways. The greeting with which we began this discussion fits into a liturgical context, following as it does on Paul's invitation to the brethren to 'salute one another with a holy kiss' (1 Thess. 5.26). It is the Spirit who makes all Christian liturgy possible. As Paul remarks in the Letter to the Romans:

> As many as are led by the Spirit of God, these are sons of God. For you did not receive the Spirit of bondage again unto fear, but you received the Spirit of adoption by which we cry *Abba* (Father). The Spirit himself bears witness with our spirit that we are children of God, and if children then heirs. (Rom. 8.14–17).

And again, in the Letter to the Galatians:

> When the fulness of time came, God sent forth his Son, born of a woman, born under the law, that he might redeem those which were under the law, that we might receive the adoption of sons. And because you are sons, God sent forth the Spirit of his Son into our hearts crying *Abba* (Father), so that you are no longer a slave but a son; and if a son then an heir through God. (Gal. 4.4–7).

The work of the Holy Spirit in making us one new Man, the whole Christ, involves putting us in the position of Jesus vis-à-vis the Father, the position of those who come with frank openness before God and address him as *Abba*. In the liturgies of the Christian Church this is clearly recognised. So, for example, the Holy Spirit is called down on the waters of the font to make them capable of bringing into being people who will be sons of God, sons in the Son, born anew from water and the Holy Spirit. At Confirmation, the Holy Spirit is called down on people to conform them still more closely to the Jesus who is filled with the Holy Spirit and gives the Holy Spirit. And according to a very significant eucharistic tradition, the Holy Spirit is called down on the bread and wine to make them the body and blood of the Lord, to incarnate Jesus in the place of these elements so that we may be made into the body of Christ, living with his life. And whether or not a specific eucharistic prayer contains an explicit epiclesis of the Holy Spirit on the gifts, in every case the Father *does* consecrate the gifts by the action of the Spirit. It is immaterial how that action is understood to be linked with the 'words of institution', the words used by Jesus at the Last Supper and normally appealed to in the course of any eucharistic prayer. Again, in the sacrament of the forgiveness of post-baptismal sins, many rites make a particular appeal to the Church as the sphere of the activity and indwelling of the Spirit. In the Syrian rite, for example, much is made of a text in Genesis: 'My Spirit shall not abide in man forever, for in their going astray they are flesh' (Gen. 6.3). Pentecost is understood as the reversal of this sentence, just as the miracle of tongues reverses the judgment of God at the Tower of Babel. As the sin of man brought on the Flood, the reversal of creation, the return of the primaeval chaos, the taking away of the Spirit, so Pentecost is the new creation, foreshadowed by the dove, an image of the Holy Spirit, in its flight home with the olive branch in its beak, the branch that produces the oil of the Holy Spirit. So when a man by sinning reverses the new creation which is his remaking at baptism the Spirit leaves him, just as he leaves the sphere of the indwelling of the Spirit which is the Church. Restoration to the Church is parallel to the restoration of *koinōnia* in the Holy Spirit, and so the rite of reconciliation has to do with expressing this return of the Holy Spirit. As an ancient Syrian text, the *Didascalia Apostolorum*, puts it:

> The laying on of hands takes the place of baptism for the sinner, for we receive the communication of the Holy Spirit both through the laying on of hands and through baptism.[2]

In the sacrament of healing in the modern Roman rite, the prayer is that

> through this holy anointing and his loving mercy God may help [the sick] by the grace of the Holy Spirit, so that [he] may be set free from his sins, healed and raised up.

In being thus the moving force behind the Church's prayer, and the means whereby God answers that prayer, the Spirit already puts the Church within the age to come, within the present of Jesus which is the future of the world. The Spirit of

---

[2] *Didascalia Apostolorum* X.

God is the Spirit of the last times, of the *eschaton*, of the reign of God. The Spirit, after all, was the promised Spirit. As Peter puts it in his Pentecost sermon (slightly adapting here the original text of the prophet Joel),

> And it shall be in the last days, says God, I will pour forth of my Spirit upon all flesh. On my servants and on my handmaids in those days will I pour forth of my Spirit, and they will prophesy. The sun shall be turned into darkness and the moon into blood before the day of the Lord comes, that great and notable day. (Acts 2.17, 18, 20)

The Holy Spirit already puts Christians in some way into the last days, and yet the last day has not finally come in such a way that there is nothing left to hope for. The New Testament preserves this tension by talking about the Holy Spirit as 'first-fruits' or 'earnest'. The first metaphor is taken from Jewish ritual practice whereby at harvest time the first of the crop was dedicated to God; in accepting it, God accepted the harvest as a whole and assured it of his blessing. The Holy Spirit as presently experienced is a foretaste and a guarantee of the full outpouring of the Holy Spirit at the end, of the complete realisation of the reign of God. In experiencing the working of the Holy Spirit here and now (in charisms, in institutional ministries, in prayer and liturgical celebration) the Christian community is experiencing the reality of the age to come. At the same time they were not definitively there, not yet wholly and entirely in that age. 'Earnest' refers to the down-payment on money promised. In giving this earnest God has bound himself to give his kingdom in full. The Spirit already works in Christian lives, for the coming of the kingdom in power. He produces in those lives his own fruit which Paul identifies as love, joy, peace, long-suffering, kindness, goodness, faithfulness, meekness, temperance. It is in just such as these, he tells us, that the kingdom of God consists. 'For the kingdom of God is not eating and drinking but righteousness and peace and joy in the Holy Spirit' (Rom. 14.17). The Spirit who is the first-fruits and earnest of the age to come also works and prays for that age to come. 'The Spirit and the Bride say, "Come!" ' (Apoc. 22.17). It is the Spirit who will at the last raise up our mortal bodies.

The Church which is the body of Christ is also, then, an epiphany of the Holy Spirit under the conditions appropriate to the in-between time, to the 'eschatological pause'. This is an epiphany of flesh, in the realm of the concrete and particular, of the given and historical of what can be seen and heard. Peter says at Pentecost,

> Being exalted at the right hand of God and having received from the Father the promise of the Holy Spirit, Jesus has poured forth this which you see and hear. (Acts 2.33)

The Spirit is not of his nature hidden and inaccessible. Rather, consistently with the action of God by his Spirit in the whole biblical tradition, he epiphanises in flesh and blood. He does so by his transforming activity, whether that be of a spectacular sort, as in some of the charisms, or of a less spectacular, as in such fruits of the Spirit as gentleness and faithfulness. He will epiphanise most typically (which does not mean in a timeworn way) in the difference he produces in the whole of the life of the community, institutions and all, in the increasing intensity of the one life we live with all men. It is on all flesh that the Spirit of God is poured out. All living things, insofar as they are alive, are manifestations of the Spirit of God. The Spirit poured out in the end-times is meant to make them what they were made to be, to incorporate them in the re-creation of the world which was created in the Word of God. The Spirit always goes with life. The resurrection life which has appeared in Jesus of Nazareth is a life which Christians share already, and also a life to which they look forward at the last day. That life they share now by their *koinōnia* in the Holy Spirit, through whom God raised Jesus from the dead. That Spirit is now revealed as the Spirit of the Father and the Son, the source of new life which the Father gives to the Son. It is only possible to speak justly of the Spirit if we acknowledge him as the Spirit of the Father and the Son, the go-between God, the God who joins Father and Son in love, and makes us sons in the Son, and thereby one flesh, one body.

The Spirit, then, is given by God when men repent and believe. He is the divine response to faith in the story of Jesus, the real presence of that story within us and amongst us.[3] How this *koinōnia* of the Spirit is also a *koinōnia* with the Jesus whose story we have heard and believe we shall see in the remaining chapters.

---

[3] Cf. the meditations on Pentecost in *Hallowing the Time*, pp. 144–154.

The Church of the Son

'IN one Spirit we were all baptised into one body' (1 Cor. 12.13). Repentance and faith give a man *koinōnia* with the Holy Spirit and by virtue of that partaking he also has *koinōnia* with all his fellow-Christians who are partakers with him of the same Spirit. He belongs to and within the communion of holy people, of the holy people who share holy things, the sacraments and mysteries of the Church. But the body into which we were all baptised by the one Spirit is itself the body of the Son, the body of Jesus of Nazareth, the Word of God made man. The Church, the body of the Messiah, the messianic community, is *koinōnia* with Jesus Christ as well as *koinōnia* with the Holy Spirit. True, it is through the *koinōnia* of the Spirit that the Church becomes the *koinōnia* of the Son, but nevertheless it does really become that. Paul writes to Corinth:

> God is faithful, through whom you were called into the *koinōnia* of his Son, Jesus Christ our Lord. (2 Cor. 1.9)

The writer of the Letter to the Hebrews writes that 'we have become *koinōnoi* of Christ' (Heb. 3.14), and St John affirms, 'Our *koinōnia* is with the Father and with his Son, Jesus Christ' (1 John 1.3). But there is a typical difference between the *koinōnia* we have with the Spirit and that we enjoy with the Son. The fellowship is structured, it is truly trinitarian in form and not at all unitary, unitarian. The rôle of the Holy Spirit is a unifying rôle; according to the Christian understanding, in the Godhead the Holy Spirit unites in his person the Father and the Son. The Father is distinct from the Son but they are two who become one in a third 'person', the Holy Spirit, and not just in the divine essence which they share. The Holy Spirit is the personal love of the Father for the Son, and the Son for the Father, the One in whom Father and Son each finds himself again in a total manner. As Jesus prays that Christians may be one as he and the Father are one, he prays for them to enjoy the fellowship of the Holy Spirit, the fellowship which *is* the Holy Spirit and the fellowship which the Spirit will produce amongst them. The Spirit, then, is the unifying force in the Godhead, and the Church as a unifying force is itself the epiphany of the Holy Spirit. The *koinōnia* of the Son, on the other hand, is the Church precisely as unified, the Church as the body of Christ, the Church as the revelation of the Father's love for us.

In the Letter to the Romans Paul speaks of the 'mystery' which has been

> kept in silence through times eternal but now is manifested and through the Scriptures of the prophets, according to the commandment of the eternal God, is made known to all the nations unto obedience to the faith. (Rom. 16.25–26)

Elsewhere he specifies the content of the mystery: it is 'the mystery of God's will' which was

> to be put into effect when the time was ripe: namely, that the universe, all in heaven and all on earth, might be brought into a unity in Christ. (Eph. 1.10)

This is somewhat more explicit, but later on in the same Letter to the Ephesians he has more to say about

> the mystery of Christ, which in other generations was not made known to the sons of men as it has now been revealed to God's holy apostles and prophets through the Spirit: namely that the Gentiles are fellow-heirs and fellow-members of the body and fellow-partakers of the promise in Christ Jesus through the Gospel. (Eph. 3.4–6)

Paul claims for himself the task to

> make all men see what is the dispensation of the mystery which from all ages has been hid in God who created all things, to the intent that now to the principalities and powers in the heavenly places there might be known through the Church the manifold wisdom of God, according to the eternal purpose which he purposed in Christ Jesus our Lord. (Eph. 3.4–11)

283

So the mystery is a mystery of unity, visible in the Church as the *koinōnia* of Christ. The mystery hidden from all ages is manifested in the unity that was experienced in the New Testament Church as the barrier between Jew and Gentile came tumbling down. The Church-body of Jesus is the epiphany of the mystery by virtue of overcoming divisions, of reconciling what would otherwise be at variance. Its distinctive mark is that

> if one member suffers, all the members suffer with it; or if one member is honoured, all the members rejoice with it. (1 Cor. 12.26)

The *koinōnia* of the body of Christ is not simply a matter of faith: it is possible to point to ways in which that fellowship is realised. There are ways in which Christians stand together, share a common experience and a common hope, and so mutually sustain each other. So it is that Paul wants the Christians in Rome to strive together with him in their prayers to God for him, that he may find rest together with them (cf. Rom. 15.30–32). He wants to be comforted in them, each of them by the other's faith, theirs and his. Likewise, he desires the Christians at Colossae to be

> knit together in love, to all riches of the fulness of understanding, that they may know the mystery of God, Christ, in whom are all the treasures of wisdom and knowledge hidden. (Col. 2.2–3)

All of these texts are concerned with *koinōnia* in terms of the body and its unity. But the overcoming of oppositions and divergences in the *koinōnia* of the Son is rooted in a *koinōnia* with the Son himself, the Word Incarnate who is Jesus of Nazareth. Just as when we talked about the *koinōnia* of the Holy Spirit we saw that the fellowship between Christians was subsequent to the fellowship which each enjoys with the Holy Spirit, so now the fellowship between Christians understood in terms of the body is a fellowship subsequent to that which the members of that body enjoy with its Head.

> Doing the truth in love, may we grow up in all things unto him who is the Head, Christ, from whom all the body, fitly framed and knit together through that which every joint supplies, according to the working in due measure of each several part, makes the

increase of the body unto the building up of itself in love. (Eph. 4.15–16)

We have seen already how words like these ('joints', 'ligaments') are borrowed from the medical science of Hippocrates and Galen, who had maintained that the sensitive and motor nerves of the entire body derived from the head. The head was thought to hold the whole body in unity, and all the body to tend towards the head. So the head would be the standard of existence and life for the body, whose growth would take place according to the structures centred and held together in the head. Thus there is only one work of the Holy Spirit, namely the whole Christ, a work that was first enfleshed in the individual human existent Jesus of Nazareth and then continues to take flesh through Jesus as Head in terms of the pattern found in him, 'the mind which was his'. Christians share in the pattern of the historical Jesus who is not other than the glorified Christ.

They share more particularly in what we have come to call the 'paschal mystery' of Jesus, his death and glorification. The New Testament letters speak so often of our dying with Christ, suffering with him and being crucified with him. They talk not only of our being conformed with his death but even of our being buried with him. And finally they tell us of our being quickened together with him, being raised up with him and being seated with him in the heavenly places. From this there issues a language about how we may expect that we will also reign with him, being manifested together with him in glory, when the body of our humiliation will be conformed to the body of his glory so that we may be with him for ever. As we sing in the liturgy, 'Christ has died. Christ is risen. Christ will come again.' In this way we are conformed to him and enter into a common history and destiny. So Paul writes to Corinth:

> As the sufferings of the Christ overflow to us, even so our consolation overflows through the Christ. If we are afflicted, it is for your consolation, which works in the patient endurance of the same sufferings which we also suffer. And our hope for you is firmly grounded, for we know that as you are partakers (*koinō-noi*) of the sufferings, so you are also of the consolation. (2 Cor. 1.5–7)

The sufferings of the Messiah overflow to Paul, as does the consolation that comes from the Messiah's victory. And through Paul's work of preaching all the Christians to whom he is writing may share in that victory as they also share those sufferings. Not by some sort of masochistic adding to the sum total of the world's pain by inflicting pain on oneself, but because there is simply no way to separate the Messiah from the messianic community. Though the Messiah is indeed Jesus of Nazareth he is in such solidarity with his community that his brethren will inevitably share his fate and his destiny. And as the historical career of Jesus shows, this will involve suffering, the kind of suffering that follows on a collision-course with the principalities and powers, the present world order. It is for this reason that the sufferings of the martyrs are traditionally described in terms of the passion of Jesus. As Pascal puts it, 'Jesus will be in agony until the end of the world'.[1] These words do no more than echo a homily of Pope Leo the Great centuries before:

> The passion of the Lord is prolonged until the end of the world. He it is who suffers in and with all who bear adversity for the sake of justice.[2]

This too is part of the mystery, the divine plan. Jesus says to the travellers on the road to Emmaus:

> 'O foolish men and slow of heart to believe in all that the prophets have spoken! Was it not necessary for the Messiah to suffer these things and to enter into his glory?' And beginning from Moses and from all the prophets he interpreted to them in all the Scriptures and things concerning himself. (Luke 24.25–27)

So too in the synagogue at Thessalonica Paul

> as his custom was, went in unto them, and for three sabbath days reasoned with them from the Scriptures, opining and alleging that it was necessary for the Messiah to suffer and to rise again from the dead, and that 'This Jesus whom I proclaim to you is the Messiah'. (Acts 17.2–3)

But it is not simply that the passion of the Lord is prolonged until

---

[1] *Pensées*, No. 919 (Lafuma enumeration).
[2] Cf. M. B. de Soos, *Le Mystère liturgique d'après S. Léon le Grand* (Münster 1958), pp. 59–60.

the end of time in all who bear adversity for the sake of justice. There is a specifically ecclesial dimension in all this.

> I rejoice in my sufferings for your sake, and fill up on my part what is lacking in the birth-pangs of the Messiah in my flesh, for the sake of his body, which is the Church. (Col. 1.24)

Paul suffers in his apostolic work in a way consistent with the ending of that work in martyrdom. He will bear witness by his death to what he has borne witness to in his life. This suffering is a necessary part of the coming to be of the Church-body of the Messiah. Paul in his own body, his whole existence, shares in the life-pattern of the Messiah; and this pattern, given the world as it is, entails suffering, for there is a vast distance between the structures of this world and the kingdom of God which the Messiah both inaugurates and is. The sufferings and death of the Messiah are the sufferings and death of his community:

> For the love which the Messiah has for us controls us, convinced as we are that as one died for all, therefore all died; and he died for all, so that those who live should no longer live to themselves but to him who for their sakes died and rose again. (2 Cor. 4.14–15)

In some way, everyone who would believe in Jesus, being prepared to accept a common destiny with his, was identified with him on the cross. He and they formed one single organism which has died already, once and for all. As we express this ritually in baptism, when we become members of the body, the funeral is over.

> All we who were baptised into Christ Jesus were baptised into his death. We were baptised with him through baptism into death. We have become united with him by the likeness of his death. Our old nature was crucified with him, that the body of sin might be done away, that we should not longer be in bondage to sin for he who has died is justified from sin. The death that he died, he died to sin once and for all. Even so reckon yourselves to be dead to sin. (cf. Rom. 6.3–11)

It is by a ritual expression of the identity of the death of Jesus under Pontius Pilate with what is now happening to the convert that a man becomes a Christian. And the subsequent sufferings that come his way as a member of the messianic community belong intrinsically *both* to the death of Jesus under Pontius Pilate *and* to the ritual enactment of that death in the convert's baptism.

But the Christ who has died is also the Christ who is risen. The resurrection is God's reversal of the Crucifixion as man's attempt to put an end to the Messiah, to close mankind off from the intervention of God, to keep things as they were. But the resurrection is also the acceptance of the crucifixion as a death which the Messiah freely accepted. It is God's affirmation of the way of life of the Messiah, which brought him to his death at the hands of other people. The resurrection is not to be understood as a somewhat belated succumbing to the temptation to come down from the cross. Contrarywise, the New Testament, regarding the resurrection as the divine affirmation of the permanent validity of the cross, expresses this in those appearance narratives where the focus of attention is the wounds of Jesus, wounds which were not healed but glorified. And so the believer shares sacramentally and morally in the dying of Jesus. He bears about in his body the dying of Jesus just as Jesus still bears about in *his* body the marks of the nails. *Koinōnia* with the Messiah means that we participate now both in the humility and suffering of Jesus and also in his resurrection and glorification.

Our share in the resurrection of the Messiah is also meant to be a matter of experience in the Church. It is found in the common life of the Christian people and in their freedom, *vis-à-vis* God and *vis-à-vis* the world. Resurrection life is life together, a life in *koinōnia* which needs to be expressed visibly and tangibly. In the Acts of the Apostles the Jerusalem church expressed its *koinōnia* in the resurrection of Christ by sharing their material goods, declaring that they already shared in the victory of Christ because they no longer needed to establish their individual identities by way of private possessions. So too martyrdom is a way of sharing in that resurrection, or rather of making visible the fact that Christians do already share its triumph. Again, virginity, living without the hope of children, is another traditional way of demonstrating *koinōnia* in the Resurrection of the Lord. Some of these ways of expressing resurrection are less accessible to us, perhaps, for they have been institutionalised so often and lost something of their 'bite'. H. A.

Williams can even speak of 'our evident immunity to the threatening glory of resurrection'.[3]

Nevertheless, the Church can never altogether lose its hope. 'Christ will come again!' we proclaim in the great prayer of the Mass. There is a future for the body of Jesus, the messianic community, the *koinōnia* of the Son. It is true that, very often, New Testament passages which speak of our being raised up with Jesus and seated with him in glory in the heavenly places are not particularly future-orientated: instead, they are meant as statement of present fact. Where Jesus is, there are his people – already in 'heaven', already sharing the life of God. But despite this, there is always a hope for the final epiphany, the resurrection of the body, the definitive appearing of a reality which now genuinely *is*, but only under the conditions appropriate to this present age. As Paul tells the Philippians:

> Our citizenship is in heaven, from where also we await for a Saviour, the Lord Jesus Christ, who shall fashion anew the body of our humiliation, conformed to the body of his glory according to the working by which he is able even to subject all things to himself. (Phil. 3.20–21)

What is expected is the abolition of the final distance between the Messiah and the messianic community, between the present of Jesus and our present. The Church of the parousia will remain the Church of the Son. Indeed, it will be more truly the Church of the Son than it is now.[4]

And all this *koinōnia* in him is expressed and effected sacramentally in the Eucharist; the *koinōnia* is Christ's body and blood. The one loaf and the one cup, at the deepest level of their reality, the *res tantum*, is the unity of the Church, the unity which is Christ's body, Christ's life. It was in one Spirit that we were baptised into that one body. It is a community that has been baptised, that already has *koinōnia* in the Spirit, which celebrates the *koinōnia* of the Lord's body and enters into that fellowship.

---

[3] H. A. Williams, *True Resurrection* (London 1972), p. 7.

[4] Cf. the meditations on Christology in *God's Way to be Man*, pp. 22–26 (Birth and Infancy); 35–39, 48–52, 61–67 (Baptism, Temptations and Ministry); 76–81, 92–98 (Death and Resurrection); 'The Sacred Heart of Jesus', *Doctrine and Life* 30. 6 (1980), pp. 279–283; 'Holy Week and the God of Fear and Love', *ibid.* 31. 4 (1981), pp. 206–208; *Hallowing the Time*, pp. 27–55 (Advent and Incarnation); 61–65 (Epiphany); 95–131 (Passion and Resurrection); 140–143 (Ascension).

We see this in the order of Christian initiation, wherein the celebration and sharing of the sacrament of the body and blood follows on the being baptised and confirmed in the one Spirit. Even so, the *koinōnia* of the body and blood is not the last word in the process. Christianity is not a Jesus religion any more than it is a Spirit religion. Christianity is the religion of the holy and undivided Trinity. We have *koinōnia* not only with the Spirit but also, in a different mode, with the Son, and we have *koinōnia*, in a different mode again, with the Father. It is to that we must turn in our last chapter.

32

The Church of the Father

IN the Johannine Letters we learn that 'Our fellowship is with the Father and with his Son Jesus Christ' (1 John 1.3). In a second Johannine idiom, we 'abide in' the Father and he 'abides' (or 'indwells', 'remains' or 'makes his home') in us.[1] As we have seen, it was in the Spirit that we were baptised into the *koinōnia* of the Son: yet the origin and goal of the process is neither Son nor Spirit but the Father himself. We have fellowship with the Father because 'God's seed abides in whomever is begotten of God' (I Jn 3.9 [variant text]). That is, we have fellowship with the Father precisely *as* Father, to the degree that we are made one New Man with the Son, conformed to the Son's image, being members of the Son's body. We stand where the Son stands, and have that same filial relationship with the Father which the Son himself enjoys. We form one body with the Son, living by the same Spirit or vital principle as he, and living before the same Father, the ultimate mystery of existence. This mystery, the Ground of Being and the Granite of it, we learn to perceive as personal and to address as 'Father'. The disciples of Jesus once asked him to teach them to pray as he does; in response they received the Our Father. The Lord's Prayer is the prayer of those who stand where Jesus stands. It is the sign of the *koinōnia* with the Father of those who have been baptised in one Spirit into one body. This is why traditionally people say the Our Father for the first time as Christians immediately after they have been initiated into Christ by baptism and confirmation. The Lord's Prayer is the setting in which the revelation of the mystery of God as Father is first experienced.

The New Testament often speaks of God as Father, although in the Old Testament this is a rare designation for him and an unknown form of address. In the Synoptic Gospels we hear the

[1] See R. C. Brown, *The Gospel according to John*, I (New York 1966), pp. 510–512.

expression 'the Father' twice only and both times on the lips of Jesus. The German exegete Ernst Lohmeyer suggested that we may infer from this that the expression 'the Father' was understood to be not so much a name for God as a way of speaking to him and with him.[2] In Matthew and Luke Jesus addresses God five times as 'Father' or 'my Father': there can be little doubt that this was a distinctive mode of address of Jesus for God, and that he encouraged his disciples to speak in the same way. Straightaway, we hear of this God as the Father who is 'in heaven' (Matt. 6.9). This addendum may give us a moment's pause. What precisely is contributed by the phrase referring to 'heaven'? Heaven, we can say, is the creation as inconceivable to man, just as earth is the creation he can conceive. But heaven, the things invisible and inconceivable, is not God. To use the language of Scripture we might say that heaven is the 'throne' of God; but, strictly speaking, we have no right to deify the reality we cannot conceive any more than that we can. Heaven, as where God is, witnesses to the infinite distance between the Creator and his creatures. When Jesus tells his disciples to speak to him who is in heaven, he is pointing them away from the God who dwells in Zion, or the God who makes his voice heard on Sinai, or the God about whose mountain (Jerusalem or Gerizim?) there was such fierce debate between Jews and Samaritans. Jesus points people away from any limitation on the nature of God by any particular place or any particular tradition. The God who is in heaven, but is not heaven, is the God who is *altogether* inconceivable and yet not thereby God. He is not simply what we cannot conceive, but he is the Creator and Lord of what we cannot conceive. 'Heaven' breaks down any attempt to confine God. But, says Jesus, this God who is in heaven is to be addressed as 'Father', a mode of address which makes this God who is infinitely distant and mysterious and altogether other at the same time very near.

Speaking of God as Father, and even speaking to him in some form of address which included the name 'Father', was not altogether unknown outside of Christianity. Homer talks about 'the Father of men and gods', 'Father Zeus, who rules over the gods and mortal men'.[3] But it would seem that this conception of

---

[2] E. Lohmeyer, *The Lord's Prayer* (ET London 1965).
[3] *Odyssey* I, 28.

fatherhood always involves that of lordship, not just as a correlative but as the dominant idea in what it means to be a father. As Aristotle says:

> The rule of a father over his children is like that of a king over his subjects. The male parent is in a position of authority both in virtue of the affection to which he is entitled and by right of his seniority, and his position is thus in the nature of royal authority. So Homer was right and proper in using the invocation 'Father of gods and of men' to address Zeus, who is king of them all.[4]

In other words, when in ancient Greece people spoke of Zeus as 'father' they had in mind principally his lordship, the relationship of power and authority to obedience and submission. In the Old Testament God is called Father of Israel, and Israel is called the firstborn son of God. God is 'the Father of Israel, who created him, who made him and established him' (Deut. 32.6). But here too the fatherhood of God is inseparable from his lordship, and in speaking of God in this way the intention is always to refer to his right of dominion as father over his sons, or his son, Israel. As a synagogue prayer repeats time and again, 'Our Father, our King'. There is, however, one exceptionally interesting text which suggests that in not calling God 'Father' the people have thwarted his plan for relationship with them.

> I said, How gladly would I treat you as a son, giving you a pleasant land, a patrimony fairer than that of any nation. I said, you shall call me 'my Father', and never cease to follow me. But like a woman who is unfaithful to her lover, so you, Israel, were unfaithful to me. Come back to me, wayward sons! (Jer. 3.19–20, 22)

In contrast, the word 'Father' appears as the central term in Christian praying from the very beginnings. To cry out 'Abba, Father' is said by Paul to be the way in which the Holy Spirit prays in those who are Christ's.

> As many as are led by the Spirit of God, these are sons of God. For you did not receive the spirit of bondage again unto fear, but you received the Spirit of adoption, by which we cry Abba, Father. The Spirit himself bears witness without our Spirit that we are

[4] *Politics* I, 12.

children of God, and if children, then heirs, heirs of God and joint-heirs with Christ. (Rom. 8.14–17)

The New Testament certainly regards this ability to call on God as Father as based on the revelation of God in Jesus of Nazareth and on the outpouring of the Holy Spirit. Its authors think of it as distinctive of Christians, because distinctive of Christ. God is revealed as Father because Jesus is revealed as Son. Since the Son has been revealed, and admits disciples into his relationship with God, they too can have fellowship with the Father. *Koinōnia* with the Father is only possible on the basis of the human life and work of Jesus of Nazareth, the Messiah, the Son of God.

This communion was historically realised in those incidents which must be acknowledged as incontrovertibly true of the life of Jesus, incidents which the Gospels understand as the irruption of the reign of God into history. For example, there would be the meals which Jesus took with crooks and whores, meals in which he welcomed them with a welcome they experienced as the welcome of God. Then there were the miracles, the works of re-creation of humanity, wherein the natural world is submitted to man once again. Or again, there were the parables of the kingdom, in which in the words of Jesus the Word of God comes to expression as promise and threat, offering and judgment. In all his life and work, in fact, Jesus speaks for God. He does so in such a way that men may stand with him before the face of God as God's own children. For Jesus as the only-begotten Son is already in *koinōnia* with the Father: he is in the Father and the Father in him. In Jesus God and man are reconciled and share a common life. Jesus is God turned towards man and man turned towards God. If we are in the Son, then we are in the One whom the Son reveals.

This *koinōnia* with the Father is something which has to be lived, and expressed in our behaviour; for it may be lost unless it becomes the subject of a reiterated option. Just as *koinōnia* with the Spirit and the Son have their modes of visibility, so does *koinōnia* with the Father.

God is light, and in him is no darkness at all. If we say that we have fellowship with him and walk in the darkness, we lie and do not the truth. But if we walk in the light as he is in the light, we have fellowship one with another, and the blood of Jesus his Son cleanses us from all sin. (1 John 1.5–7)

An evil way of life, the kind of life that prevents communion and openness with other people, is a sign that a person does not enjoy *koinōnia* with the Father. This is not to say that a man must be morally blameless if he is to have such fellowship with the Father, but simply that he must want to have the fellowship. He will find it through perseverance in the fellowship of the body of Christ, the body of the accepted sacrifice. Faith in the sense of intellectual assent to God in the way he has revealed himself is necessary, but it is not sufficient. We must also abide in the teaching of Christ, walking as he walked in the life of *agapē*.

He who says, 'I know him', and does not keep his commandments, is a liar and the truth is not in him. This is how we know that we are in him: he who says that he abides in him ought himself also to walk as he walked. (1 John 2.4, 5–6)

Such agapeistic, loving fellowship is already eternal life:

We know we have passed out of death into life because we love the brethren. (1 John 3.14)

Such a loving lifestyle expresses and advances the reign of God in the world: it demonstrates its power and increases its area of influence.

So the *koinōnia* we have with the Father is not merely a matter of standing before the Father with the Son. It also entails acting and speaking *in persona Christi* in the Father's name. There can be no fellowship with the Father unless there is an active realisation of what it is to be a son in communion with the Father. As the First Letter of St John puts it:

Beloved, now we are children of God, and it is not yet made manifest what we shall be. We know that when he shall be manifested we shall be like him, for we shall see him even as he is. And everyone who has this hope set on him purifies himself even as he is pure. (1 John 3.2–3)

For the ultimate goal of Christian ethics is nothing less than this: seeing God as he is. Not that our fellowship with the Father will one day be all, and our fellowship with the Son and Spirit cease. The *koinōnia* is always trinitarian, as God is always trinitarian.

Indeed, the experience of the threefold form of the *koinōnia* with God in the Christian fellowship underlies all the dogmatic endeavours which issued in the Catholic understanding of the Trinity. Like so many of the teachings of the Church, that dogma is not meant to be the solution of a problem, but rather a stating of the problem in all its starkness.

It is not to be expected that in the end there will be no mystery about the innermost being of God. Even in his revelation in the Son through the Holy Spirit, the Father remains hidden. He may be spoken to as Father and spoken for as Father by the Son and by those who in the Son are themselves sons, but he does not become unconcealed. The life we live with Christ in God is a life hidden with Christ in God: it cannot be traced to that ultimate source where God remains the God who hides himself, though in truth he is the God of Israel, the Saviour. What is required of us is obedience and acceptance of the sonship God chose to give us through the incarnation, death and resurrection of the eternal Son. Our sonship in the Son is founded on the reality of God's eternal Fatherhood. Yet that Fatherhood remains ever beyond us, the source of the divine nature of which he has made us partakers.

Perhaps here we stand most in need, not so much of words as of images and icons, verbal or plastic representations that contain what they represent, and give the grace of which they speak. In the New Testament we are offered many verbal icons of the Church, many ways of representing the Son who speaks for and to the Father. We can finish by looking at an image in the ordinary sense of that word. We may look at an actual icon of the ultimate mystery of the Church. Possibly the greatest of all icons is Rublev's icon of the holy Trinity, painted in 1425 and some fifty years later declared by the Council of the Hundred Chapters to be the model for all iconography and for all representations of the Trinity. The icon moves simultaneously on three planes. First, there is the visit of the three angels to Abraham at midday by the oaks of Mamre, those three angels whom the whole patristic and liturgical tradition has seen as a manifestation of the Trinity. Second comes the plane of the economy of our redemption. The three angels make up the divine council to form the plan of salvation: between them on the table lies the eucharistic cup enclosing the Lamb of the redemptive sacrifice. The third and final plane is merely suggested: it is transcendent and inaccessible, the mystery which remains always and ultimately a mystery, yet into which we can enter by faith, by contemplation, by activity. In being baptised we find ourselves already within this icon. The icon does not possess the kind of Renaissance perspective in which lines converge outside the picture. It is closer to Cubism where the onlooker looks from within at what is there to be seen. The three angels are in repose, in the supreme peace of What is in Itself. Yet they also go out of one another in such a way that the icon has a circular movement which takes off from the central angel and finally returns to him. Each angel might be taken for the other: their difference lies simply in the personal attitude of each to the others. As this might have been expressed in Western theology (for instance by St Thomas), the persons of the Trinity *are* their relationships. It is in being the relationships they are that they are other than the other persons. The world, represented by the rectangle of the table, is included in this circle of love that comes forth from the central figure and returns to him. This central angel is the Father, and his posture is one of pure activity wholly accomplished. But the inclination of the neck and head, and the outward-going folds of his cloak, express the dynamism that takes him to the Son. In this synthesis of movement and immobility lies the ineffable mystery of the Godhead. Ineffable – and yet expressed, spoken, revealed in the convex curving lines which the Son answers by the receptivity of his own concave lines, and the obedience, attention and abnegation these imply. The Father is in him, and what the Father has is his. The angel on the right, the Holy Spirit, occupies the region between the Father and the Son through the inclination and tendency of his whole being. He realises the communion between them, he is their *koinōnia*. The Son is the revelation of the Father, as the artist's colours make clear. The Spirit is the Spirit who fills and renews the earth and makes it green again. In this circular movement of the icon all nature is taken up: the rocks to the right, and a building to the left, the rocks of nature and the building of Christ's Church. But at the back of it all, the source of the movement and the colour is the Father, inaccessible in the density of his colours, in the darkness of his light, yet revealed in a gentler and more accessible form in the brightness of the Son and the Holy Spirit. The hand of the Father blesses the cup which contains the Lamb slain before the foundation of the world, the eucharistic chalice with its promise what we will one day drink the fruit of the vine anew in the kingdom of the Father.

The Russian Orthodox lay theologian Paul Evdokimov wrote:

> From this icon comes a powerful appeal: Be one as I and the Father are one. Man is made to the image of the trinitarian God; the church-communion is written into his nature as its ultimate truth. All men are called to unite themselves again around the one same Cup, to lift themselves up to the level of the heart of God and to take part in the messianic banquet, to become one single Temple, one single Lamb. 'By life eternal (the Spirit) they will know you, the one true God, and Jesus Christ whom you have sent' (Jn 17.3). The vision ends on this eschatological note: it is in anticipation of the kingdom of heaven bathed in a light which is not of this world, bathed in a pure, disinterested, divine joy, just because the Trinity exists and we are loved and all is grace. The soul is filled with wonder and falls quiet. Mystics never speak about the heights: only silence finds them.[5]

---

[5] P. Evdokimov, *L'art de l'icône: Théologie de la beauté* (Paris 1970), p. 216. Cf. the meditation on the Holy Trinity in *Hallowing the Time*, pp. 155–158.

Index of Names

Index of References

Index of Subjects